BEHIND THE CRIMSON CAPE

THE CINEMA OF GEORGE REEVES

BEHIND THE CRIMSON CAPE
THE CINEMA OF GEORGE REEVES

JAN ALAN HENDERSON
STEVE RANDISI

MICHAEL BIFULCO
GRAND RAPIDS, MICHIGAN

Published by Michael Bifulco

Cover art created by Larry Byrd

Library of Congress Cataloging-in-Publication Data

Henderson, Jan Alan.
    Behind the crimson cape ; the cinema of George Reeves / Jan Alan
  Henderson, Steve Randisi.
       p. cm.
    Includes bibliographical references and index.
    ISBN 0-9619596-6-5
     1. Reeves, George, 1914-1959.   I. Randisi, Steve, 1953-   II. Title.

PN2287.R293H45 2005
791.4302'8'092—dc22

                                                         2005041116

Manufactured in the United States of America

FIRST EDITION

10 9 8 7 6 5 4 3 2 1

To Jack Larson and Noel Neill,
and to the everlasting memory of
George Reeves

CONTENTS

ACKNOWLEDGMENTS

Jack Larson; Noel Neill; Fred Crane; Larry Thomas Ward; Lou Koza; Jim Nolt; Michael H. Price, for wisdom and guidance; Larry Byrd; Jerry Mezerow; Chuck McCleary; Mike Hawks; Lorraine Wagner; Art Harvey; Jack Roth; Cole Johnson; Harry Felker; Judi Gillan; Eddie, Heidi, Donovan, and Claire Brandt, whose tireless searching of the Brandt archive helped make this volume a reality; Jeff Falasca; the Margaret Herrick Library; John Antosiewicz; Glenn Damato; John Field; and Dave Siegel for his unbounded enthusiasm.

Special acknowledgment to Mary Lue Henderson for her typing skills and unlimited patience; and Carol Bifulco for her tireless efforts reading page proofs into the wee hours of the morning.

PREFACE

We Know a Man, and His Name Is George

It's amazing that George Reeves, forty-six years after his death, elicits so much interest. Mention his name, and people have varying reactions: "Wasn't he the guy who jumped out the window?" or "the guy who played Hercules in the late 50s?" Others confuse him with Christopher Reeve.

Over the years, a mountain of print has been fed to the public, some credible, some not so credible. One thing is certain: George Reeves kept his private life private. In the glare of his television stardom, Reeves could have taken full advantage of his celebrity; yet he opted for modesty. Instead of basking in the limelight, every time he turned that light on, he used it for the benefit of others, not himself. There were no tabloid headlines reporting George's wild weekends with a bevy of booze and babes.

To the audience of the 1950s, George Reeves was Superman. To the kids of the 50s, there was a Superman, and possibly a Santa Claus. There seemed to be a new Superman episode every week, as a generation lived out its endless summer before the waves of reality smashed down on the beach of youthful optimism. June of 1959 brought the big snap, when we found out that heroes don't last forever.

A generation that once believed, couldn't any more. It wasn't possible for Superman to die, but it happened. A preview of how a nation would feel some four years later, when a United States president was shot down in front of a crowd in Texas. The nation's youth got the same shock treatment when George Reeves opened the doors of eternity which presidents, paupers, and kings have passed through, into the great unknown. With Superman alive, there was a true hero to shed light on the blackness of the unknown; a hero who consistently made things right! But now there was a void. Suddenly, the unknown was all around, and there was no escape. Childhood's end.

One has to wonder what effect all this adoration had on George Reeves. How does one live a life with that pressure? The assumption could be that one becomes a millionaire, and can isolate one's self. Not true with Reeves or the other cast members. The Adventures of Superman cast missed the television bonanza by mere years, and all of them went on to different things, in and out of show business. The life of show people is never secure, never stable; yet some do quite well in the real world, and others go off the rails. Some have trouble with drugs, alcohol, and the law. Some avoid the pitfalls that consume others; others use the press to air their grievances, real or imagined.

One thing is certain, George Reeves never bellyached about whatever fate befell him. He never moaned, complained, or bitched about his work, his stardom, or his fellow players. He never found himself being awakened by the police in a strange bed, in an innocent stranger's house. No, George was a gentleman to the tragic end.

How would George like to be remembered? Probably not as Superman; although had he lived, he may have warmed up to it as he grew older, but most likely not. George would have wanted to have been remembered as an actor, and that is what this book is about.

This book is about life and art, not death and suspicion. This book is about the part of George Reeves' life that we hope he would have wanted his fans to know about, not about scandal and death.

In this volume, we try to bring attention to the career Reeves had prior to, during, and unfortunately not after, Superman—a career which formed every nuance and characteristic of Krypton's mighty Man of Steel.

Some of these films are classic, some are not. Some are from major studios, others are not. Some star George, and some merely provide him a supporting role. Sometimes George is window dressing in these productions (an extra), and in some he's almost invisible.

So settle back, put some popcorn in the microwave, and maybe for a third and final time, we may learn a little more about George Reeves.

BEHIND THE CRIMSON CAPE

The Cinema of George Reeves

George is about to meet his demise in *RIDE, COWBOY, RIDE.*

RIDE, COWBOY, RIDE

Bandito Reeves

The short subject is all but extinct in American cinema in the new millennium. Shorts, serials, and cartoons have been replaced by special effects-laden trailers, newspaper pitches and even car commercials.

Musicals and westerns have fared no better in the twenty-first century, which makes this George Reeves curio especially interesting if the viewer can allow a flight of fantasy. The concept of invisible musical accompaniment, orchestras, choral voices, etc., oftentimes is too much for contemporary audiences to swallow.

This two-reeler, shot in glorious Technicolor, opens with Denny (Dennis Morgan) happily singing "The Prairie is My Home" as he rides across the plains with his cohorts. All is peaceful until a gang of bandits, led by Pancho Dominguez (George Reeves), holds up a stagecoach expecting to seize a large Wells Fargo bankroll. Angered because the money has already been deposited, the bandits shoot the driver of the coach. Pancho, taking full advantage of the situation, snuggles next to Laura Ramsey, (Maris Wrixon), the demure passenger of the coach. The outlaw tries his best to captivate her with his gleaming smile and Spanish accent. He doesn't succeed. Realizing that the whole affair has been fruitless, Pancho rides off with the other desperadoes.

Denny notices the runaway stagecoach, and rescues it with the help of his partner (Cliff Edwards). The singing cowboy is immediately taken with Laura,

Behind the scenes (George–center) shooting *RIDE, COWBOY, RIDE.*

who reveals that she is en route to Armadillo County for a reunion with her mother. Since she has spent most of her life in the east, Laura experiences a measure of culture shock when she discovers that her mother is "Cactus Kate" (Esther Howard), a tough-as-nails saloon keeper. A grand homecoming party is staged at the saloon, which gives Denny an opportunity to belt out another tune, 'Whistle While You're Waltzing,' which is followed by the equally insipid 'Grab Your Partner,' sung by the other members of the cast.

The merriment does not last long. When Pancho and his gang break into the Armadillo County Bank (where the Wells Fargo loot has been deposited) their gunfire arouses the attention of the saloon patrons. A gun-fight quickly erupts, and the Ramsey women join forces with the townsfolk who take aim at the outlaws. Kate gets wounded in the arm, but isn't the slightest bit deterred from thwarting the robbery.

Amid all the ruckus, Denny and Pancho get into a fist fight after Denny jumps Pancho from the barn's hayloft. Seconds later, one of the approach-

George eyes the heroine's daughter (Maris Wrixon) in *RIDE, COWBOY, RIDE*.

ing good guys shoots Pancho as he is about to gun down Denny. Pancho is taken to Kate's place for treatment, where Kate demonstrates that she has a heart of gold underneath her gritty exterior. Pancho apologizes for all the trouble he has caused her. "That's all right," she says. "You've been pretty bad all your life, but maybe it wasn't your fault." A cigarette is placed in Pancho's limp mouth and he utters, "Thank you, amigo," just before he dies. Denny and Laura embrace, then take to the plains as the music on the soundtrack rises for the fadeout.

This was the second of George's dialect roles filmed (although the first released), and his talent is showcased throughout this tuneful short.

CAST: Dennis Morgan, Maris Wrixon, Cliff Edwards, George Reeves, Frank Wilcox, and Esther Howard.

A WARNER BROTHERS PICTURE; Directed by George Amy; Original Screenplay by Crane Wilbur; Art Director: Hugh Reticker; Film Editor: Frank Dewar; Sound by Stanley Jones; Costumes by Leah Rhodes; Make-up artist: Perc Westmore; Music and Lyrics by M. K. Jerome and Jack Scholl. Original theatrical release: September 9, 1939. Running time: 20 minutes.

ESPIONAGE AGENT
Another Day's Work in the Picture Biz

There are certain aspects of *Espionage Agent* that are still painfully relevant more than six decades after its release. It's a film about international spies, the sabotage of American properties, and the political ramifications in relation to these issues. The story begins in 1915, with a myriad of scenes depicting the malicious destruction of U.S. factories, plants, and private businesses. Then, after a period of equanimity, the nation is once again faced with the same problems as the 1930s draw to a close.

Barry Corvall (Joel McCrea), a young diplomat, is shocked when his new wife tells him that she is indebted to enemy agents. Even though Brenda (Brenda Marshall) was pressured into her involvement with the spies, Corvall must relinquish his position with the State Department. Nevertheless, he decides to take on the enemy forces (which are operating from abroad) and employs the help of his old colleague, Lowell Warrington (Jeffrey Lynn). At one point in the film, Brenda calls on her husband while he is in conference with Warrington. Just outside Warrington's private office is the desk of his impeccably dressed secretary (George Reeves), who utters a brief greeting to the visitor. This is the only glimpse of George in the entire movie.

Eventually, Corvall not only succeeds in thwarting the efforts of the enemy, he is instrumental in re-establishing legislation that will help keep a tighter lid on espionage.

Espionage Agent features an eclectic cast. Star Joel McCrea enjoyed fame with starring roles in *Dead End* (1937), *Sullivan's Travels* (1941), and a host of Western classics. In 1959 he starred in the television series *Wichita Town* with his son Jody, who was later featured in AIP's Beach Party series. McCrea died in 1990.

Co-star Stanley Ridges has the distinction of stealing a movie from Karloff and Lugosi, *Black Friday* (1940). Ridges entered films in 1923, and is a featured player in such productions as *Confessions of a Nazi Spy* (1939), *Each Dawn I Die* (1939), *Nick Carter, Master Detective* (1939), *Sergeant York* (1941), *They Died With Their Boots On* (1942), *To Be Or Not To Be* with Jack Benny (1942), *Mr. District Attorney* (1941), and *Eyes in the Night* starring Edward Arnold (1942). He died in 1951 in Westbrook, Connecticut.

Martin Kosleck is well known to horror film connoisseurs. He appeared in Universal's "B" productions *The Frozen Ghost* (1945), the Sherlock Holmes entry *Pursuit to Algiers* (1945), *House of Horrors* (1946), *The Mummy's Curse* (1944), *She Wolf of London* (1946), and the 1964 cheapie *The Flesh Eaters*.

With this unusual cast and strong script, Reeves is merely wallpaper. Too bad he wasn't give a better role. We feel certain he would have added a quality performance to this production. Another day, another dollar, and another waste of George's talent in a first rate production.

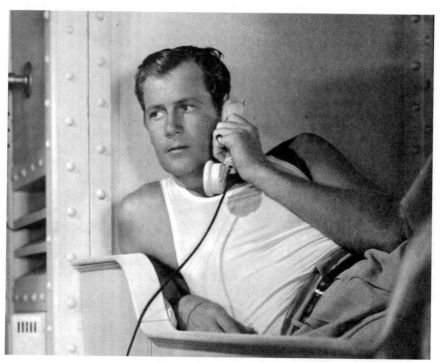

Whether a starring role or a brief walk-on, George always worked in good company. Joel McCrea in a scene from *Espionage Agent*.

The character players (without Joel or George) in *ESPIONAGE AGENT* listening to a pivotal radio message. George Bancroft is standing on the left.

CAST: Joel McCrea, Brenda Marshall, Jeffrey Lynn, George Bancroft, Stanley Ridges, James Stephenson, Howard Hickman, Martin Kosleck, Nana Bryant, Robert O. Davis, Hans Von Twardoowsky, Lucien Prival, Addison Richards, Edwin Stanley, Granville Bates, Grace Hayle, Egon Brecher, Emmet Vogan, and George Reeves (unbilled).

A WARNER BROTHERS—FIRST NATIONAL PICTURE; Jack L. Warner, in charge of production; Executive Producer: Hal B. Wallis; Directed by Lloyd Bacon; Associate Producer: Louis F. Edelman; Screenplay by Warren Duff, Michael Fessier, Frank Donoghue; From an original story by Robert Henry Buckner; Dialogue Director: Jo Graham; Director of Photography: Charles Rosher, A.S.C.; Art Director: Carl Jules Weyl; Film Editor: Ralph Dawson; Wardrobe: Milo Anderson; Sound by Francis J. Scheid; Make-Up Artist: Westmore; Music by Adolph Deutsch; Musical Director: Leo F. Forbstein; Original theatrical release: September 30, 1939. Running time: 74 minutes.

THE MONROE DOCTRINE
Romancing American History

Filmed in Technicolor, *The Monroe Doctrine* unfolds with a documentary style tempo that chronicles the many oppressions that burdened America's founding fathers. The opening scenes, set in 1775, vividly depict rebellion over such issues as "taxation without representation" and "the cruel and

Left to right, James Stephenson, Nanette Fabres, and George, in a scene from *THE MONROE DOCTRINE*. COURTESY OF THE ACADEMY OF MOTION PICTURE ARTS AND SCIENCES.

unusual punishments" that were routinely doled out for minor infractions. The narrator then expounds on the American Revolution, and its subsequent impact on the Latin American countries that renounced Spanish rule.

The action shifts to 1823, with the cabinet of President James Monroe addressing Spain's attempt to reclaim certain Latin American territories. John Quincy Adams (Grant Mitchell), the Secretary of State, refers to the problem as "the first great test of American democracy." President Monroe (Charles Waldron) joins the meeting and is informed that several foreign ministers are anxiously awaiting word of America's position. The president says that they'll have to wait until he delivers his message to Congress. As the American leaders debate this "latest menace to freedom," the representatives of several European monarchies convene in Madrid to pledge support for Spain.

Back in Washington, the Speaker of the House, Henry Clay (Frank Wilcox), delivers a riveting speech before Congress. "Let us become real Americans," he shouts, "and with our sister nations of the South, build an American system that nothing shall ever destroy!" The consensus is that the United States will not bow to the "whim" of European politicians.

Elsewhere in Washington, another meeting is taking place at the residence of Señor Dellatorre (James Stephenson), the deposed governor of a South American province. Dellatorre entertains several of the foreign min-

isters, all of whom recognize the possibility of U.S. involvement in the growing dispute. Much of their discussion is about Henry Clay, who is regarded
as a major threat to Spain's objective. Dellatorre amazes the leaders with his
familiarity of Clay, and is asked how such a vast amount of information was
obtained. Dellatorre attributes his extensive knowledge to his daughter, who
is romantically linked to Clay's secretary, John Sturgis (George Reeves).
Dellatorre does not approve of Sturgis. Nevertheless, he has encouraged his
daughter's involvement with the young patriot simply to use him as "a con-
venient information bureau." Moments later, Sturgis proudly escorts
Dellatorre's daughter Rosita (Nanette Fabres) into the meeting room.

In one of the most lavish scenes in the film, a grand ball is held to wel-
come the foreign ministers. Sturgis, who jokingly refers to Rosita as his own
"Latin American problem," politely approaches the girl's father. Señor
Dellatorre bluntly asks Sturgis if he is in love with his daughter; a pained
expression crosses his face when he hears the answer. Dellatorre tells Sturgis
that his intentions are an insult, calling him a "nothing" and a "nobody" to
his face. The startled young man tries to utter a defense, but his efforts are
eclipsed by the governor's persistent ranting. When he is referred to as "the
starving secretary of a cheap American politician," Sturgis finally reaches his
limit. He shouts, "Be quiet, Sir!" After regaining his composure, Sturgis
apologizes and says that he cannot permit his wife's father to make a fool of
himself. "For the past ten minutes," he explains, "I've been trying to tell you
that Rosita and I have just been married." Dellatorre nearly faints.

That night at the White House, President Monroe reads the document
that will define U.S. policy, essentially that the American continents "are
not to be considered as subjects for future colonization by any European
power." The message, which will be delivered before Congress on
December 3, 1823, also warns that any actions to the contrary will be considered a threat to the United States. Secretary of State Adams concurs
with the president. He asserts that, "Europe must not be allowed to spread
its political doctrines in the Americas. We don't need them and we don't
want them." Mr. Adams also predicts that the president's response will
never be forgotten. "Down through the years, " he says, "it will be known
as the Monroe Doctrine."

And indeed it would. The last few minutes of the film summarize events
that would cause the Monroe Doctrine to be invoked. The final scene
depicts President Theodore Roosevelt (Sidney Blackmer) delivering his
most famous speech, the one that included the unforgettable phrase, "Speak
softly and carry a big stick."

When shown on cable networks today (usually as a time filler), this two-
reel gem holds up surprisingly well, owing to its colorful production values
and top-notch cast.

Sidney Blackmer's Teddy Roosevelt is priceless, short as it is. Blackmer
began his film career in 1914 with *Perils of Pauline*, an early serial, and
returned to the cinema in 1927 for another serial entry entitled *Million
Dollar Mystery*. Highlights of his career include *The Deluge* (1933), *The
Count of Monte Cristo* (1934), *The President Vanishes* (1934), *The House of*

Secrets (1937), *Charlie Chan in Monte Carlo* (1937), *Thank You Mr. Moto* (1937), and *Ellery Queen and the Perfect Murder Case* (1941), *The High And The Mighty* (1954), *High Society* (1956), with his last screen role in Roman Polanski's *Rosemary's Baby* (1969).

In 1963, Blackmer turned in a stunning performance as an enemy agent who is transformed into a lookalike of a presidential candidate in the now legendary Outer Limits episode "A Hundred Days of the Dragon." Blackmer also spelled his name with a "y" and was born in Salisbury, North Carolina on July 13, 1896. He left this planet on October 5, 1973 in New York City after a battle with cancer.

CAST: Grant Mitchell, James Stephenson, Sidney Blackmer, Charles Waldron, George Reeves, Nanette Fabres, and Frank Wilcox.

A WARNER BROTHERS PICTURE; in Technicolor; Directed by Crane Wilbur; Original Screenplay by Charles L. Tedford; Director of Photography: Wilfred M. Cline, A.S.C.; Technicolor director: Natalie Kalmus; Art Director: Hugh Reticker; Film Editor: Everett Dodd; Sound by Dolph Thomas; Costumes: Leah Rhodes; Made-Up Artist: Perc Westmore; Original theatrical release: October 14, 1939. Running time: 16 minutes.

SMASHING THE MONEY RING

Now you see him, Now you don't?

Pictures like this in Reeves' cinematic repertoire make one wonder what kind, if any, career guidance he had. Although the studio system dictated what films an actor participated in, good management, working with the studio bosses, could have led to better choices (if any were offered).

The plot of this movie is simple, yet incredible. A gang of prisoners routinely churn out counterfeit money—right under the noses of the unsuspecting officials! Outside distribution is achieved by concealing the bills between copies of a newspaper, which is also a product of the prison print shop.

The leader of the operation, Dice Matthews (Joe Downing) devises a plan to circulate the fake currency on the S.S. Kismit, a popular gambling vessel. This proposition, however, is sternly rejected by Kismit's proprietor, Steve Parker (Charles D. Brown), a white-haired ex-con. Parker and his daughter (Margot Stevenson) begin to fear for their lives. When the case triggers the attention of the federal authorities, it falls on the shoulders of Lt. "Brass" Bancroft (Ronald Reagan) and his assistant, Gabby (Eddie Foy, Jr.).

Parker, who has long since reformed, decides that the safest place to be is a prison cell. That's just where he lands after deliberately slugging a cop. Amid much publicity, Parker appears in court for sentencing. Seated behind Parker is a well-tailored young man (George Reeves) who laughs

A rare publicity still of the 40th president from *SMASHING THE MONEY RING*.

heartily, along with the other spectators, as the defendant recalls his "irresistible urge" to sock someone! The judge, however, doesn't appreciate this levity and sentences Parker to one year behind bars, instead of the anticipated thirty days.

Bancroft detects a connection between Parker and the counterfeiters. Realizing that Parker's ship might be targeted as the "clearing house" for the phoney money, Bancroft gets himself incarcerated with the cooperation of Warden Denby (William B. Davidson).

In a ploy to unmask the leader of the ring (and to locate the printing plates) Bancroft soon gains Matthews' confidence. The prison sequences are realistically grim, especially the one in which Parker is found murdered in his cell, just as he is about to be pardoned.

After acquiring a gun that has been smuggled into the compound, Matthews leads Bancroft "over the wall" using the night captain (John Hamilton) as a decoy. After their escape, a burly guard named Davis learns that Bancroft is a secret agent. It is Davis who is actually the mastermind of the racket. In one of the film's most chilling moments, Davis shoots both Matthews and Bancroft on a dark and desolate road. Bancroft sustains a shoulder injury; Matthews is mortally wounded. Before dying, Matthews

George (left), Charles D. Brown (third from left), William Hopper (far right), and John Harron (second from right) in an ultra rare photograph of a deleted scene from *Smashing the Money Ring*. Photo courtesy of the John Field Collection.

Scene from *Smashing the Money Ring*, one of Ronald Reagan's first films. Joe Downing and Don Douglas standing in the center.

discloses that the plates are hidden in Davis' roadster. Bancroft manages to seize the plates and transport them to the warden's office for inspection. In a desperate attempt to retrieve the plates, Davis bursts into the warden's office and holds everyone at gunpoint. When Davis tries to escape through the prison yard, he is shot down by one of the guards stationed in a tower. In the end, Bancroft is lauded as a hero for smashing the counterfeit ring.

While viewers interested in Reagan cinema will find this highly entertaining, this is a case of bad choices for thespian Reeves. His shot in the background of the court room is so soft and out of focus it's next to impossible to be 100% sure it's George. Now you see him, now you don't!

CAST: Ronald Reagan, Margot Stevenson, Eddie Foy, Jr., Joe Downing, Charles D. Brown, Joe King, William Davidson, Charles Wilson, Elliott Sullivan, John Hamilton, Sidney Bracy, Jack Wise, Jack Mower, Don Turner, and George Reeves (unbilled).

A WARNER BROTHERS—FIRST NATIONAL PICTURE; Directed by Terry Morse; Original Screenplay by Anthony Coldway and Raymond Shrock; From an Idea by Jonathan Finn; Dialogue Director: Arthur Ripley; Director of Photography: James Van Trees, A.S.C.; Film Editor: Frank Magee; Art Director: Charles Novi; Sound by Dolph Thomas; Gowns by Milo Anderson; Technical Advisor: Charles Perry. Original theatrical release: October 21, 1939. Running time: 61 minutes.

ON DRESS PARADE
The Un-Dead End Kids Meet George—Well, Sort Of!

It is World War I, on the Western Front. Colonel William Duncan (Don Douglas) has an unshakable hunch that Captain Riker (John Litel) is in desperate need of help. He is correct. In the trenches, "Dunc" (as he is called) issues a command: "Have your men cover me as far as possible, Sergeant. I'm going out after Captain Riker!" The Sergeant turns to the man standing next to him and says, "A buck and a half he don't come back." With a Southern accent, the young soldier (George Reeves) replies, "I figure you're tryin' to give me a sucker bet, Sergeant." This is the only footage of Reeves to be found in *On Dress Parade*, the seventh film in Warner Brothers' highly successful "Dead End Kids" series.

On the dark battlefield, Dunc injures himself on some barbed wire, but manages to shoot the enemy who's taking aim at Riker. Nevertheless, the captain has been seriously wounded. After handing over some vital reports, Riker insists on remaining where he is. Dunc won't hear of it, and carries Riker back to safety.

The war is over and the film reflects subsequent events: prohibition; the first women voters; Lindbergh's transatlantic flight; the stock market crash; the great depression; and the Roosevelt years. The last shot brings us up to

Leo Gorcey stares down an officer (John Litel) in *On Dress Parade*.

1939. At Washington Military Academy, Colonel Riker (whose hair has whitened a bit over the years) receives a telegram informing him that Bill Duncan is dying. Riker pays a last visit to the man who once saved his life. Dunc explains that his wife left him years ago and, as a result, has never met his own son. Riker promises to look after the boy. However, when Riker meets Shirley "Slip" Duncan (Leo Gorcey), he finds him to be a rebellious youth bearing no similarities to his father; a pool hall ruffian. Worse yet, Riker can't interest him in military service. "Doesn't the idea of service mean anything to you?" Riker asks. "Yeah," says Slip. "I like people waitin' on me!", in typical hoodlum vernacular.

Slip eventually joins the Academy, but only as an alternative to reform school, thanks to some duplicity on Riker's part. When Cadet Duncan learns that he's been tricked, he quits on the spot. The other cadets try to stop Slip by tossing his satchel around like a football. While trying to retrieve his bag, Slip accidentally pushes Cadet Rollins (Billy Halop) out of a second-story window. Although Rollins survives, and is totally forgiving, the other cadets give Slip the cold shoulder treatment.

This incident makes a new man out of Slip, and he begins to excel academically. His full redemption occurs when he risks his own life to rescue Cadet Warren (Gabriel Dell) from a fire. Warren and Slip are seriously burned, but they both recover. Slip is finally accepted as one of the guys. In the end, a tearful Slip is saluted when Colonel Riker presents him with the Distinguished Service Cross that had belonged to his father.

This film has all the elements that a Dead End Kids show shouldn't have. The formula is reversed and only the Leo Gorcey character, Slip (ironically, he would adopt the name for the highly successful "Bowery Boys" series), bears any resemblance to the Dead End Kids, who started out in the play *Dead End*. None of the kids show any signs of street smarts, and soon the Slip character is crying, studying, and acting the part of a true hero, by saving the Gabriel Dell character's life in a near fatal fire.

While their characters changed throughout the Eastside Kids and Bowery Boys films, this was gradual. The six other films firmly establish the street-hardened kids, and this reworking is simply not believable. Leo's acting isnt' bad, but the other kids pale in comparison to their former selves. Being assigned to this picture shows Warner Brothers' lack of interest in the Dead-End Kids. The weakest entry in the series, a day's work for George, and not much else.

CAST: Billy Halop, Bobby Jordan, Huntz Hall, Gabriel Dell, Leo Gorcey, Bernard Punsley, John Litel, Frankie Thomas, Cissie Loftus, Selmer Jackson, Aldrich Bowker, Douglas Meins, William Gould, Don Douglas, and George Reeves (unbilled).

A WARNER BROTHERS PICTURE; Directed by William Clemens; Original Screenplay by Tom Reed; Dialogue Director: Frank Beckwith; Director of Photography: Arthur L. Todd, A.S.C.; Art Director: Esdras Hartley; Film Editor: Doug Gould; Sound by Stanley Jones; Technical Advisor: John Murphy; Original theatrical release: November 18, 1939. Running time: 62 minutes.

GONE WITH THE WIND
Tomorrow's Another Day—or is it?

The 1930s are unquestionably the renaissance of American cinema. With the advent of sound, all genres flourished. An audience weaned on silent films finally got to hear some of their silent stars' voices. Other players fell by the wayside with the introduction of sound. Everything from westerns to primitive science fiction, classic horror, as well as the sound serial, brought in big bucks at the box office. The romantic genre was no exception; films such as *Jezebel*, *Imitation of Life*, and the obscure *Scent of Nora Moran* (Majestic Pictures, 1933) starring Zita Johann fresh from her success in Karl Freund's Universal 1932 production of *The Mummy*, starring Karloff the uncanny.

Cut from the same swath, with the American Civil War as its backdrop, *Gone With The Wind* is essentially a romantic yarn about the stormy relationship between a headstrong Southern belle, and a blockade runner who hopes to profit from the war. The epic unfolds with an establishing shot of Tara, the O'Hara plantation in Georgia. On the veranda, Scarlett O'Hara (Vivien Leigh) entertains two red-haired, exuberant young men who have recently been expelled from college. Stuart Tarleton (George Reeves) and his twin brother Brent (Fred Crane) are both brimming with enthusiasm

GONE WITH THE WIND one-sheet with Fred Crane's autograph.

over the impending war. Miss Scarlett, however, is bored by talk of war. So another topic is broached: the much anticipated barbecue to take place at a neighboring plantation called Twelve Oaks.

Stuart tells Scarlett that he and his brother intend to dance every waltz with her at the barbecue. They will alternate repeatedly, "First Brent, then me, then Brent again, and so on," he promises. (George Reeves plays Stuart Tarleton in the film. However, the opening titles erroneously credit George with the role of Brent Tarleton.) Stuart also discloses some rather startling news: Melanie Hamilton (Olivia deHavilland) will soon marry her cousin Ashley Wilkes (Leslie Howard). Scarlett, who is secretly in love with Ashley herself, is upset by this news and runs off, leaving the Tarletons unattended. Mammy (Hattie McDaniel), the faithful O'Hara servant, scolds Scarlett for being rude to the nice gentlemen and for "not invitin' them to dinner."

At the barbecue, Scarlett continues her flirtation with Stuart and Brent. Teasing them, she confesses that she can't make up her mind which of them is more handsome. In fact, she "stayed up all night trying to figure it out!" Swallowing the empty compliment quite readily, the brothers beam from ear to ear. A short time later, Scarlett's attention is focused in the direction of an imposing figure: Captain Rhett Butler (Clark Gable), a visitor from Charleston, who arrives on the scene. He and the other gentlemen, including the Tarletons, engage in a provocative discussion about the war.

Like a big-screen soap opera, the war and its aftermath are intertwined with many patterns of human behavior—love, lust, hatred, greed—and the

A Tarleton Face-Off. *GONE WITH THE WIND*. Fred Crane and George.

On the plantation with the Tarleton twins, *GONE WITH THE WIND*, Fred Crane (left) and George (right) with an unidentified character actor.

Publicity photo from *GONE WITH THE WIND*.

never ending cycle of life and death. Although a few of these interludes are derisively humorous, most of them clearly reflect the consequences of war— the grim, makeshift hospitals; countless soldiers sprawled helplessly across the vast land; the burning of Twelve Oaks; and the loss of young lives. Not all of these events are conveyed visually. The death of the Tarletons, for instance, is revealed through Scarlett's expression of remorse when she learns that the brothers have become casualties of the Battle of Gettysburg.

Scarlett is the film's quintessential survivor; she overcomes such crushing blows as widowhood, the death of her parents, and financial ruin. The scene in which she vows never to go hungry again is inspiring, if not moving. Her inborn astuteness remains very much intact after she and Rhett marry, settle in Atlanta, and have a daughter named Bonnie Blue. At one point, when the Butlers get into an argument, the ever-resourceful Scarlett effectuates her most potent weapon: the announcement that she is pregnant again. Less than elated by this revelation, Rhett smugly suggests that an accident might occur, and indeed one does. Scarlett tumbles down a mammoth staircase and loses the baby.

More tragedies occur. Bonnie is killed when she is thrown from a horse, and Melanie is diagnosed with a fatal illness. In her last moments, Melanie implores Scarlett to look after Ashley and her son. While commiserating over the loss of Melanie, Scarlett and Ashley embrace innocently. They are spotted by Rhett, whose anger is instantly aroused. Realizing that his wife is still harboring feelings for Ashley, Rhett decides to head back to Charleston.

Scarlett desperately tries to convince Rhett that he is the only man in her heart, but it is too late. Rhett remains unmoved, and without a scintilla of sympathy, begins to pack his belongings. Scarlett runs after him, demanding to know where she should go and what she should do. Rhett responds with those now immortal words, "Frankly, my dear, I don't give a damn!" With Rhett gone, a weeping Scarlett sits on that magnificent staircase, contemplating the future. She will return to her beloved Tara. Drawing strength from her indomitable spirit, she speaks the words that close the film, "I'll think of some way to get him back. After all, tomorrow is another day."

Tomorrow certainly was another day, because in some respects, *Gone With The Wind* could be termed as a meeting of future heroes (although none had scenes together). Tom (Captain Marvel) Tyler has a brief scene in a church which was being used as a triage area for wounded soldiers. His alter ego, Frank (Billy Batson) Coghlan, Jr. is glimpsed as a fallen soldier on a road to nowhere. Victor Jory, who the next year would essay the classic pulp movies and radio hero known by some as Lamont Cranston, but known to everyone as "The Shadow" in Columbia's serial offering from 1940, played Jonas Wilkerson. Rand Brooks, who played Charles Hamilton, had a distinguished career, rode horses with Bill Boyd in the Hopalong Cassidy series as did George, but ended up as a space station radio man on the semi-hit television series *Rocky Jones, Space Ranger*. A couple other examples of this sci-fi summit are Jackie Moran, who played Buddy Wade to Buster Crabbe's serial essay of Buck Rogers in 1939; and William Bakewell who would travel into space with George Wallace in Republic's *Radar Men to the Moon*. Also

Fred Crane, Vivien Leigh, and George in publicity photos from the opening scene of
GONE WITH THE WIND.

Fred Crane and George in a publicity photo of the Tarleton Twins.

included from the Republic's stable of actors, stunt men, and directors, was Yakima Canutt. All of these contributions added to the authenticity of a film which is beyond a classic, sometimes ridiculously so.

CAST: Clark Gable, Vivien Leigh, Leslie Howard, Olivia deHavilland, Thomas Mitchell, Barbara O'Neill, Evelyn Keyes, Ann Rutherford, George Reeves, Fred Crane, Hattie McDaniel, Oscar Polk, Butterfly McQueen, Victory Jory, Everett Brown, Howard Hickman, Alicia Rhett, Rand Brooks, Carroll Nye, Laura Hope Crews, Eddie Anderson, Harry Davenport, Leona Roberts, Jane Darwell, Ona Munson, Paul Hurst, Isabell Jewell, Cammie King, Eric Linden, J.M. Kerrigan, Ward Bond, Jackie Moran, Cliff Edwards, L. Kemmple-Cooper, Yakima Canutt, Marcella Martin, Louis Jean Heydt, Mickey Kuhn, Olin Howard, Irving Bacon, Robert Elliott, William Bakewell, Mary Anderson, Frank Coghlan, Jr. as an exhausted soldier, Tom Tyler as a dying soldier..

A SELZNICK INTERNATIONAL PICTURE, in association with Metro-Goldwyn-Mayer, in Technicolor, based on Margaret Mitchell's story of the old south. Produced by David O'Selznick; Directed by Victor Fleming; Screenplay by Sidney Howard; Music Score: Max Steiner; Production Designer: William Cameron Menzies; Special Photographic Effects by Jack Cosgrove; Photographed by Ernest Haller, A.S.C.; Technicolor Associates: Ray Reinahan, A.S.C. and Wilfred M. Cline; Art Director: Lyle Wheeler; Interiors: Joseph B. Blatt; Interior

Decorations: Edward G. Boyle; Costumes by Walter Plunkett; Supervising Film
Editor: Hal C. Kern; Associate Film Editor: James E. Newcom; Scenario Assistant:
Barbara Keon; Production Manager: Raymond A. Klune; Assistant Director: Eric
G. Stacey; Recorder: Frank Maher; Technicolor Co. Supervisor: Natalie Kalmus;
Assistant Musical Director: Lou Forbes; Historian: Wilbur G. Kurtz; Technicolor
Advisors: Susan Myrick and Will Price. Released by Loews Incorporated
December 31, 1939. Original running time: 220 minutes plus intermission.
Theatrical re-releases: 1947, 1953, 1961, 1968, 1974, & 1998.

FRED CRANE

An autographed photo of Fred Crane as he appeared in the 1990s. He worked as a
disc jockey for one of the leading classical radio stations in Los Angeles.

FOUR WIVES

Ensemble Silliness

This is another of those films where George is featured in one scene, and has only one line. *Four Wives* was the much anticipated sequel to 1938's *Four Daughters*. Like its predecessor, this is a heart-warming saga of the Lamp women: Ann (Priscilla Lane), Kay (Rosemary Lane), Thea (Lola Lane), and Emma (Gale Page). While the previous film focused on the Lemps as single women, this one deals with the trials and tribulations following their marriages. The major theme is who's having a baby, and who's not. The dreaded word "pregnant," of course, is never uttered throughout the picture.

HERE COME THE BRIDES!

JUST MARRIED!

SOMETHING OLD!
The lovable cast of 'Four Daughters'

SOMETHING NEW!
New laughs, new thrills, new joys!

SOMETHING BORROWED!
The same gay charm of their last hit!

SOMETHING BLUE!
A tear... even while you're laughing!

PRISCILLA LANE
ROSEMARY LANE
LOLA LANE
GALE PAGE

The 'Four Daughters' are now the

"FOUR WIVES"

(It's a Four Belle Picture)

with CLAUDE RAINS
Jeffrey Lynn · Eddie Albert
MAY ROBSON · FRANK McHUGH
DICK FORAN · HENRY O'NEILL
Screen Play by Julius J. and Philip G. Epstein and Maurice Hanline · Suggested by the Book, "Sister Act," by Fannie Hurst
Music by Max Steiner · A Warner Bros.-First National Picture
Directed by
MICHAEL CURTIZ

The Character of 'Mickey Borden' as He Appeared in 'Four Daughters,' is Portrayed by
JOHN GARFIELD

Produced by
WARNER BROS.
And Now Showing

40

Ann's husband, Mickey (portrayed by John Garfield in the previous film), is now deceased, having died in an accident. After Ann gives birth to his baby, a complication arises which requires the infant to receive a transfusion. The current love in Ann's life, Felix Dietz (Jeffrey Lynn), offers to donate his blood in order to save the newborn girl. As always, it is necessary to determine whether or not the blood is the right type. In the hospital laboratory, tests are conducted by a young technician (George Reeves), who peers pensively into a microscope. He informs the father-son doctor team (Henry O'Neill and Eddie Albert) that the sample is indeed the right type.

Hardly a big moment for George. Once again, had George been given more sides he could have shone among this distinguished cast, featuring Universal horror veterans Claude Rains and Dick Foran. This film will not appeal to all of Reeves' fans, and is dated.

CAST: Priscilla Lane, Rosemary Lane, Lola Lane, Gale Page, Claude Rains, Jeffrey Lynn, Eddie Albert, May Robson, Frank McHugh, Dick Foran, Henry O'Neill, Vera Lewis, John Qualen, and George Reeves (unbilled). The character of "Mickey Borden" as he appears in Four Daughters is portrayed by John Garfield.

A WARNER BROTHERS FIRST NATIONAL PICTURE; Jack L. Warner in charge of Production; Executive Producer: Hal B. Wallis; Directed by Michael Curtiz; Associate Producer: Henry Blanke; Screenplay by Julius J. And Philip G. Epstein and Maurice Hanline; Suggested by the book "Sister Act" by Fannie Hurst; Music by Max Steiner; Dialogue Director: Jo Graham; Director of Photography: Sol Polito, A.S.C.; Film Editor: Ralph Dawson; Art Director: John Hughes; Sound by Oliver S. Garretson; Gowns by Howard Shoup; Makeup Artist: Perc Westmore; Mickey Borden's Theme by Max Rabinowitsh; Orchestral Arrangements: Hugo Friedhofer, Ray Heindorf; Musical Direction: Leo F. Forbstein. Original Theatrical release: January 3, 1940. Running time: 110 minutes.

THE FIGHTING 69TH

Lessons Learned from War?
(Private Bessolo Marches Again)

By 1940, the United States looked as if it was on a collision course with World War II. The carnage, terror, and repulsion of the war in Europe were blasted into the American psyche via radio, newspapers, and cinematic newsreels. So it's no wonder the Hollywood moguls would bankroll war pictures to keep their film catalogues contemporary, and Jack Warner and Warner Brothers Studios were no exception.

Instead of essaying the current situation in Europe, Producer Hal B. Wallace chose World War I as a backdrop for this morality play about cowardice and redemption.

THE FIGHTING 69TH, Pat O'Brien (left), George, James Cagney, and Alan Hale.

It is 1917, and the onset of war brings a shipment of inductees to the famous 69th Regiment (the 165th Infantry, A.E.F., as the opening title explains) at Camp Mills, New York. Among the recruits is Jerry Plunkett (James Cagney), a tough Irishman from Brooklyn who instantly makes waves with nearly everyone. The only one who seems to understand the recalcitrant private is Father Francis Duffy (Pat O'Brien), who is revered by all. Father Duffy takes an interest in the personal lives of the men, as evidenced by his encounter with a young private named Jack O'Keefe (George Reeves). Father Duffy inquires about Mrs. O'Keefe, and the gum-chewing soldier proudly announces that she is "expecting again." George delivers his lines with a convincing Irish accent.

The Alabama 4th National Guard march into the picture, and its men begin to brag about how the South "shot the pants off the Fighting 69th during the Civil War." This boasting results in a grand scale melee. Plunkett, mindful of Father Duffy's safety, approaches him after the fracas, but is chastised for doing so. George stands next to Cagney throughout this scene, still enjoying his chewing gum!

While in action, Plunkett's cowardice causes a number of his comrades to be killed. Sentenced to die at sunrise, Plunkett begs Father Duffy to help him formulate a plan of escape. When a bomb destroys a portion of the structure where the condemned soldier is incarcerated, Father Duffy discloses the existence of two possible roads. One may lead to freedom, the other to the location where his comrades are fighting for their lives. Revealing his true spirit, Plunkett opts to assist in the battle against the Germans. Seriously wounded, Plunkett dies a hero, with a mournful but proud Father Duffy at his side.

An interesting footnote is that Frank Coghlan, Jr., who played Billy Batson in *The Adventures of Captain Marvel* (Republic 1941) has another screen role in a George Reeves flick. As Coghlan recalled in his autobiography "They Still Call Me Junior" (McFarland & Company 1993) in Chapter 42 "I Play a Ghost," he described his supernatural awakening making *The Fighting 69th*.

> "In the beginning I had scenes at the home parish where it was established that I was an altar boy, a good parishioner, and a friend of our pastor, Father Duffy, who was played by Pat O'Brien.
>
> "Later there was a sequence where I was a young soldier in the same training camp where Father Duffy was the Catholic chaplain. He meets me on the company street and tells me he has received a letter from my mother and she is worried about me because I have not been writing. He gives me a good fatherly counseling and extracts a promise from me that I will write to my mother on a regular basis.
>
> "In the trenches in France I am seen as a member of a company about to go over the top as part of an infantry charge. There is a huge explosion from an enemy shell and I am seen trapped under dirt and heavy timbers. Then I had a big close-up where the camera dollied in until my face filled the screen and I say the entire Act of Contrition and then die.
>
> "The final sequence of the picture shows the statue of Father Duffy as it stands in Times Square in New York City. All the principal players who died in the film (George was shot) are shown superimposed as images as they march by the statue and wave to Father Duffy."

The ethereal image of George Reeves is also featured in this montage of the dead. For war film enthusiasts this show is a classic, but for George Reeves fans it could disappoint, because Reeves is relegated to a less than supporting role, and could be considered window dressing in the trenches of World War I. At least he fares better than in his 15 seconds of pain in the last Dead End Kids entry at Warner Brothers, *On Dress Parade*.

CAST: James Cagney, Pat O'Brien, George Brent, Jeffrey Lynn, Alan Hale, Frank McHugh, Dennis Morgan, Dick Foran, William Lundigan, Guinn "Big Boy" Williams, Henry O'Neill, John Litel, Sammy Cohen, Harvey Stevens, and George Reees (unbilled)

A WARNER BROTHERS – FIRST NATIONAL PICTURE; Executive Producer: Hal B. Wallace; Directed by William Keighley; Associate Producer: Louis F. Edelman; Original Screenplay by Norman Reilly Raine, Fred Niblo, Jr., and Dean

Franklin; Director of Photography: Tony Gaudio, A.S.C.; Film Editor: Owen Marks; Art Director: Ted Smith; Sound by Charles Lang; Special Effects by Byron Haskin, A.S.C. and Rex Wimpy, A.S.C.; Technical Advisors: Captain John T. Prout and Mark White; Make-up: Perc Westmore; Music by Aldolph Deutsch; Orchestral Arrangements: Hugo Friedhofer; Musical Director: Leo F. Forbstein. Original theatrical release: January 27, 1940. Running time: 89 minutes.

CALLING PHILO VANCE
A Day Player, A Sandwich, and a Cup of Coffee

This entry in the Philo Vance series is a remake of an earlier film titled *The Kennel Murder Case* (1933), which starred William Powell as the aristocratic detective created by S.S. Van Dine. With James Stephenson portraying the title character, *Calling Philo Vance* was updated by setting the story amid a wartime atmosphere. Although George has a speaking role in the film, he is only on screen for six seconds and his name does not appear in the credits.

Philo Vance is assigned to uncover information concerning Archer Coe (Richard Kipling), a veteran aircraft designer who is suspected of selling secret plans to enemy agents. Vance begins his mission in Vienna, but makes the mistake of getting caught and is promptly deported. Back in the States, the master sleuth attempts to pick up where he left off. But by the time he arrives at the Coe estate, the old man is already dead. With the body slumped in an armchair, and a gun firmly clenched in the victim's hand, the police label the case a suicide. Vance, however, doesn't buy this theory. With the help of a flustered coroner, Vance is able to convince Inspector Markham (Henry O'Neill) that a murder has been committed. Practically everyone becomes a suspect. Even the descedent's brother Bisbane (Wedgewood Nowell) is placed under a cloud of suspicion—until his corpse is found in the hall closet! A few characters manage to avoid the wrath of the law, including Coe's lovely niece Hilda (Margot Stevenson) and a chap named Philip Wrede (Donald Douglas).

Eventually, Vance discovers dog hairs on a fireplace poker, which had been used as a weapon, and concludes that "the murderer of Archer Coe left his signature when he struck that dog." This piece of evidence leads Vance and Markham to the home of Doris Delafield (Sheila Bromley), a next-door neighbor who owns a police dog. Delafield arouses suspicion, especially with her packed suitcases and discernable fidgeting, which make her seem like a woman planning to skip town. Her interrogation, however, is interrupted by a ringing telephone. Markham picks up the receiver, and the scene switches to the other end of the line, which happens to be a steamship office. Attired in a good-looking business suit, the clerk (George Reeves) tells Markham that Miss Delafield's reservation for "A deck" is unavailable. Would she be "interested in making a reservation for B deck?" Delafield doesn't get a chance to respond on her own behalf. Markham emphatically informs the

Studio portrait of George from *Calling Philo Vance*.

clerk that "Miss Delafield won't be sailing on either deck!" As a result of this meeting, Delafield and her Italian amour, Edwardo Grassi (Edward Raquello) are soon fingerprinted.

As in most respectable who-done-its, the person who is the least suspected turns out to be the slippery criminal. When the Delafield canine is retrieved from the vet, it quickly attacks Philip Wrede during an altercation, exposing him as the true killer. The closing scene explains how Wrede was motivated by intense greed and envy.

An engaging remake of a 1930s murder mystery, but again a waste of George's talent. The curse of the contract player is evident in this show for George. After strong exposure in such shows as *Gone With The Wind* and the Warner shorts, Reeves could have expected better roles if Warner Brothers would have taken his development as an actor in a serious light. Unfortunately this was the credo of George's professional life. Nothing has changed in Hollywood.

CAST: James Stephenson, Margot Stevenson, Henry O'Neill, Edward Brophy, Sheila Bromley, Ralph Forbes, Donald Douglas, Martin Kosleck, Jimmy Conlon, Edward Raquello, Creighton Hale, Harry Strang, Richard Kipling, Wedgewood Nowell, Bo Ling, and George Reeves (unbilled).

A WARNER BROTHERS—FIRST NATIONAL PICTURE; Directed by William Clemens; Screenplay by Tom Reed, from "The Kennel Murder Case" by S.S. Van Dine; Dialogue Director: Jo Graham; Director of Photography: L. Wm. O'Connell, A.S.C.; Film Editors: Benjamin Liss, Louis Lindsay; Art Director: Ted Smith; Sound by Charles Lang; Gowns by Howard Shoup. Original theatrical release: February 3, 1940. Running time: 63 minutes.

'TIL WE MEET AGAIN
Broken Glasses, Broken Hearts

'Til We Meet Again is a film about two people who are incapable of letting go. It begins in Hong Kong, when the highly refined Joan Ames (Merle Oberon) meets the suave Dan Hardesty (George Brent) at a bar. The two of them get acquainted over a "paradise cocktail." When his glass is empty, Dan smashes it against the bar. After Joan cracks her glass, Dan places the two stems together, neatly and symbolically. They go their separate ways, only to be reunited a short time later on an ocean luxury liner. This marks the beginning of an ill-fated romance, for Dan and Joan are both living on borrowed time.

Joan suffers from a chronic heart ailment (angina pectoris) and frequently passes out. With the clock ticking loudly in her ears, Joan is traveling around the world, determined to make every moment count. Dan, on the other hand, has been convicted of murder and is being escorted to San

Pat O'Brien and George Brent in a scene from '*Til We Meet Again*.

Quentin where he is to be executed. In the custody of a sympathetic detective named Steve Burke (Pat O'Brien), the prisoner is permitted to move about freely, even though he has made more than one attempt at escape. As Dan and Joan grow closer and closer, they never delve into each other's roots. Throughout most of the film, he doesn't know anything about her health, and she knows nothing about his past.

With his appeals entirely exhausted, Dan's only hope is to make a run for it when the ship docks in Honolulu. He has the help of two loyal allies. They are Rockingham T. Rockingham (Frank McHugh), a hard drinking con man, and Comtesse de Bresac (Binnie Barnes), a former lover who plays up to Steve in order to subvert his custodial duties. Also aboard are Jimmy Coburn (George Reeves), and his young wife Bonny (Geraldine Fitzgerald), who becomes a confidant to Joan during the long cruise. While Fitzgerald's character develops a close connection to the leads, George's does not. His dialogue is very sparse, with the bulk of his lines occurring when his screen wife invites the couple to an island luau.

In Honolulu, Dan manages to elude Steve, but postpones his getaway in order to spend time alone with Joan. After a brief interlude on the beach, Dan's final opportunity slips away as he tries to explain his impending departure to Joan. Unable to disclose the truth, he attributes his actions to important business. Fearing that she may never see Dan again, Joan begins to panic and suffers another fainting spell. Dan carries the girl back to her cabin, where her doctor reveals that it is now only a matter of months, if not weeks. The journey ends in San Francisco, where it is finally time to say good-bye. The lovers have another paradise cocktail, then repeat their glass breaking ritual. Once again, Dan informs Joan that he is on the move, this time to Mexico. The couple vow to meet at the Palace Bar in Mexico City on New Year's Eve. However, Joan's feeling of hopefulness is shattered when an overzealous reporter tells her that the man she loves is destined to meet the hangman. As the police take Dan into custody, he looks back at a tearful Joan, who is left behind on the larger-than-life ship. They now know each other's secret, but remain committed to meet one more time.

The closing scene takes place in the Palace Bar, where a New Year's Eve party is in progress. The bartender comments that he can't wait until the night is over. Amid the music and laughter, we hear the sound of glass cracking. Then we see two broken glass stems resting on the bar, side by side, with no one standing over them. A rendezvous has indeed occurred. As the New Year rings in, Bonny and Jimmy Coburn raise their glasses in celebration.

This film might be a tad mushy for contemporary audiences. This is a solid Warner Brothers romantic programmer, with lots of Kleenex power.

CAST: Merle Oberon, George Brent, Pat O'Brien, Geraldine Fitzgerald, Binnie Barnes, Frank McHugh, Eric Blore, Henry O'Neill, George Reeves, Frank Wilcox, Doris Lloyd, Marjorie Gateson, Regis Toomey, William Halligan, Victor Kilian, Wade Boteler.

A WARNER BROTHERS—FIRST NATIONAL PICTURE; Jack L. Warner in charge of production; Executive Producer: Hal B. Wallis; Associate Producer: David Lewis; Directed by Edmund Goulding; Screenplay by Warren Duff; From an Original Story by Robert Lord; Director of Photography: Tony Gaudio, A.S.C.; Film Editor: Ralph Dawson; Art Director: Robert Haas; Special Effects by Byron Haskin, A.S.C.; Gowns by Orry-Kelly; Sound by E.A. Brown; Make-Up Artist: Perc Westmore; Orchestral Arrangements: Ray Heindorf; Musical Director: Leo F. Forbstein. Original theatrical release: April 20, 1940. Running time: 99 minutes.

TEAR GAS SQUAD

Irish Eyes, In A Tuneful, Tear Gas Fog

After pulling a robbery, two thugs slip into a neighborhood drug store while the police sirens are still blaring in the night. One of the criminals, Mitch (Steven Durrell), has sustained a gunshot wound and is bleeding from the arm. (The other crook, Sully, is played by future Superman villain Ben Welden.) Joe McCabe (George Reeves), the good-natured pharmacist on duty, recommends a visit to the emergency room. But the thugs cannot take such a risk and demand on-the-spot treatment. While gathering the gauze

John Payne (left) is climbing out of the car as Dennis Morgan (right) looks on in a scene from *TEAR GAS SQUAD*.

and bandages, Joe pulls a fast one and whips out a revolver. "Stick 'em up," he says calmly. It was the sirens that tipped him off. The police are summoned, and Joe is lauded as the hero who captured two members of the notorious Rocks Dawson mob. Amid much publicity, Joe receives a sizable reward for his quick thinking.

Eager to share the good news, Joe calls on his big brother, Tommy (Dennis Morgan), who performs nightly at an upscale nightclub. Tommy's act consists of singing Irish songs while outfitted in a policeman's uniform. (In the 1930s and early '40s, the Irish cop was a familiar cinematic stereotype.) After the show, Tommy flirts innocently with an attractive blonde nicknamed Jerry (Gloria Dickson). Jerry, however, misinterprets Tommy's humor as brashness and takes an instant dislike to him. In an effort to discourage any romantic intentions, Jerry invites the singer to her house where she lives with her parents and two hulking cousins.

On the way over to Jerry's place, Tommy receives a speeding ticket from a smug cop, Sgt. Bill Morrisey (John Payne). When he arrives at the Sullivan home, an irritated Tommy starts making cracks about policemen, implying that most of them are incapable of doing any other kind of work. What Tommy doesn't realize is that Jerry's father and cousins, all of whom are cops, are in the next room listening to every unflattering word. Nevertheless,

Tommy manages to win over the Sullivans with his rendition of "When Irish Eyes are Smiling." Jerry's father, Lt. Sullivan (Harry Shannon), is particularly taken with the lad, as is Mama Sullivan (Mary Gordon). All goes smoothly until Morrisey walks through the door. He's the lucky chap who is dating Jerry! Naturally, the two men are soon at each other's throats.

Determined to win Jerry over, Tommy decides to become a "real" cop. He joins the police academy and immediately locks horns with Morrisey, who goes out of his way to make things as difficult as possible for the young cadet. When Morrisey and another officer are nearly killed during a training accident, Tommy comes to their rescue and saves their lives. He receives high praise from the Chief of Police (John Hamilton), and ultimately graduates with flying colors. But when the positions are assigned, Tommy is disappointed to learn he's been relegated to the policemen's chorus. As the city's crime situation grows worse each day, Tommy tries to convince the chief to transfer him to the force. The chief isn't sure Tommy is ready for such a promotion, and asks Morrisey for an evaluation of the rookie's performance. Morrisey blatantly says that Tommy is "not fit." Tommy loses his temper and belts Morrisey in the jaw, an action that results in his dismissal from the department.

Tommy goes back to singing at the club. One night, Tommy receives a backstage visit from Jerry, who has warmed up considerably towards him. Overjoyed by the conquest he's made, Tommy drops in on Joe, now firmly

Dennis Morgan and George in a scene from *TEAR GAS SQUAD*.
PHOTO COURTESY OF LOU KOZA.

George, Steven Durrell, and Ben Welden in a scene from *TEAR GAS SQUAD*.

Lobby card from *TEAR GAS SQUAD*.

Lobby card with Steven Durrell, Ben Welden, and George from *Tear Gas Squad*.

established in the new drug store he's purchased with his reward money. While the brothers catch up on the new developments in each other's lives, a rough looking character walks into the store. He identifies himself as a "friend" of Rocks Dawson, pulls out a hand gun, and shoots Joe in cold blood. Tommy looks on in horror as the assailant speeds away in a waiting limousine. Tommy demands that the police department beef up the investigation of his brother's murder. He also asks to be rehired, but is rejected. It isn't until the mobsters shoot two patrolmen that the department finally goes all out.

Lt. Sullivan, who had always been fond of Tommy, throws him a lead when the gangsters take cover in an abandoned building. Determined to capture his brother's killer, Tommy climbs a drainpipe, dangles from an electrical wire, and crashes through a skylight to close in on the gangsters who are now holding Morrisey hostage. United in a common cause, the two lawmen make a formidable team as they take on the mobsters. Ultimately, the police draw everyone out of the building with tear gas, hence the title of the picture. Tommy and Morrisey emerge unscathed and shake hands. A newspaper headline says it all: "Rookie Cop Avenges Killing of Brother; Leads Capture of Bandit Trio Who Slew Druggist." Not only does Tommy get his job back, he also wins Jerry's love.

There is plenty of singing, shooting, and slugging in this Warner Brothers programmer. Dennis Morgan is in fine form as he spends a lot of the show crooning favorite Irish ditties, and romancing Gloria Dickson.

While this is a good showcase for George's talents, one wishes he had more sides. His work is confined to two scenes in a drugstore, and one in a night-club. Despite this small role (George is fourth billed), he shines in true movie star fashion. John Hamilton's role is larger (as the police chief), and it's easy to see why he was Warner Bothers' resident cop, judge, and D.A.

An interesting entry, splitting the musical, gangster, and romance genres. Frank Wilcox is on board again, in one of his five screen appearances with George in 1940.

CAST: Dennis Morgan, John Payne, Gloria Dickson, George Reeves, Frank Wilcox, Herbert Anderson, Julie Stevens, Harry Shannon, Mary Gordon, William Gould, John Hamilton, Edgar Buchanan, Dick Rich, DeWolfe Hopper, Steven Durrell and Ben Welden (unbilled).

A WARNER BROTHERS-FIRST NATIONAL PICTURE; Directed by Terry Morse; Original Screenplay by Charles Belden, Don Ryan, and Kenneth Garnet; Dialogue Director: John Langan; Director of Photography: Sid Hickox, A.S.C.; Art Director: Charles Novi; Film Editor: Louis Hesse; Gowns by Milo Anderson; Sound by Stanley Nes; Musical Lyrics by M.K. Jerome and Jack Scholl. Original theatrical release: May 4, 1940. Running time: 55 minutes.

VIRGINIA CITY

Don't Blink!

Set during the Civil War, this grand scale epic stars Errol Flynn as a Union officer who saves Virginia City's gold from the hands of a relentless Southerner, portrayed by Randolph Scott. Miriam Hopkins is cast as a woman torn between her love for both men. George appears in the last third of the film, as a Yankee telegraph dispatcher.

Captain Kerry Bradford (Flynn) escaped from a Confederate prison which is under the command of Captain Vance Irby (Scott). Some time later, Bradford confronts Irby in Virginia City, a territory safeguarding millions of dollars worth of gold, a good portion of which belongs to Southern depositors. Irby and a band of rebels conspire to abscond with the gold in order to support the Confederate war effort. To ensure a successful heist, Irby engages John Murrell (Humphrey Bogart), a Mexican bandit with a sizable brigade, and pays him ten thousand dollars. Irby's most effective weapon, however, is his girlfriend Julia (Hopkins), a diffident saloon singer who is deeply attracted to Captain Bradford. With Julia's participation, the rebels not only manage to flee with the gold, they also take Bradford prisoner

At one point during the long and arduous journey, the wagon train reaches a Union observation post. When the guard on duty conducts a cursory inspection of the wagons, he notices that the wheels are sinking into the

sand, anchored by some tremendous weight. When further scrutiny is ordered, a blaze of gunfire erupts. Bradford manages to escape during the fracas, and makes his way to an isolated cabin equipped with a telegraph set. Bradford transmits a message which is intercepted by a young soldier (George Reeves), who reads it aloud: "Gold . . . train . . . pass through here after killing guard . . . send force immediately . . . equipped for long." Suddenly there's an interruption in the signal. Bradford, on the other end, is startled by the arrival of his two comrades (Alan Hale and Guinn "Big Boy" Williams). He pauses for a few moments to greet them warmly, then continues the communication: ". . . will . . . wait . . . here . . . for . . . you!"

Studio portrait of George from the 1940s.

The dispatcher writes the message in longhand, and the Cavalry is soon on its way. (George is on camera for approximately thirty seconds.)

The plot culminates with the ambush of the wagons, initiated by Murrell and his mob, following an unsuccessful attempt at extortion. Irby becomes a casualty of the attack. Bradford tells the dying Irby that they might have been friends under different circumstances. This change of heart inspires Bradford to do the unthinkable: he conceals the gold in a location where the Confederate Army will be able to recover it. Bradford is Court-martialed for his actions, and is sentenced to be executed. Julia intercedes on his behalf, making a tearful appeal to President Lincoln (Victor Kilian), who is seen only in silhouette. Mr. Lincoln assures her that Bradford won't be executed, as the war has finally come to an end. The closing shot depicts a beaming Captain Bradford, reunited with Julia, hand in hand.

George has a grand total of fourteen words in the western. It's a pity that Director Michael Curtiz didn't give George more to do, as his presence would have added another dimension to this highly revered classic.

CAST: Errol Flynn, Miriam Hopkins, Randolph Scott, Humphrey Bogart, Frank McHugh, Alan Hale, Guinn "Big Boy" Williams, John Litel, Douglas Dumbrille, Moroni Olsen, Russell Hicks, Dickie Jones, Frank Wilcox, Russell Simpson, Victor Kilian, Charles Middleton, and George Reeves (unbilled).

A WARNER BROTHERS PICTURE; Executive Producer: Hal B. Wallace; Directed by Michael Curtiz; Associate Producer: Robert Fellows; Original Screenplay by Robert Buckner; Dialogue Director: Jo Graham; Music by Max Steiner; Director of Photography: Sol Polito, A.S.C.; Film Editor: George Amy; Art Director: Ted Smith; Sound by Oliver S. Garretson and Francis J. Scheid; Special Effects by H. F. Koenkamp, A.S.C.; Make-Up Artist: Perc Westmore; Orchestral Arrangements by Hugh F. Friedhofer; Musical Director: Leo F. Forbstein. Original theatrical release: May 23, 1940. Running time: 121 minutes.

TORRID ZONE

Bandito Reeves Numero Dos

This is the second picture in which Reeves portrays a character of Hispanic descent (*Ride, Cowboy, Ride* being the first). A first-rate Cagney–O'Brien show, it offers little, if any, character development for George's character, Sancho. While he and partner Victor Kilian are merely set dressing, their characterizations add authenticity, in spite of their brief screen time. George will fare better in *Calling All Husbands* opposite George Tobias, who plays Rosario in this film.

Steve Case (Pat O'Brien) is the fast-talking proprietor of a Central American fruit plantation that is experiencing major setbacks. One evening, Case meets a sultry nightclub singer, Lee Donley (Ann Sheridan), and

A television ad for *Torrid Zone* from the 1960s. George Tobias, James Cagney, Ann Sheridan, and Pat O'Brien.

eventually has her arrested for cheating at cards. Even in jail, Lee is unbeatable with a deck of cards, and wins a few hands with a notorious bandit named Rosario (George Tobias). Rosario has been terrorizing the plantation, claiming to be the rightful owner of the land. Much smarter than he appears, Rosario outwits the chief of police just as he's about to be shot by a firing squad.

While embarking for the States, Lee meets Nick Butler (James Cagney), the former manager of the once prosperous plantation. Although Butler is headed for his new job in Chicago, Case persuades him to stick around long enough to pump life into the company's banana crop (the current manager isn't working out too well). Butler, who is very much attracted to Lee, conceals her from the authorities. All goes well between them—until Butler surmises that he's been cheated out of a small fortune during a game of cards. Lee sneaks aboard the train that transports Butler to Plantation 7, the much troubled banana crop. While attempting to restore productivity there, Butler finds himself torn between Lee and Gloria Anderson (Helen Vinson), the wife of the current manager. (The script reveals that Butler had also indulged in an earlier fling with Case's wife!)

When Rosario becomes a threat to the plantation once again, Butler decides to take the matter into his own hands. He hires two of the laborers, Sancho (George Reeves) and Carlos (Victor Kilian), to track down the desperado, and agrees to pay them $50 apiece. What Butler doesn't realize, however, is that the two amigos are actually members of Rosario's gang. At a campfire feast consisting of roasted potatoes (with bananas on the side) Rosario is alerted, and he encourages the duo to play along with the ruse. He also advises them to get paid before disclosing any information. But when the men return to the plantation, Butler refuses to pay up until Rosario is actually found. Sancho protests: "No, Señor, if we don't see money, we don't see Rosario!" Not one to be intimidated, Butler roughs him up a bit.

The hunt for Rosario is on. When the two informants try to misdirect the search party, Butler realizes he's been had. Without hesitation, he pushes Sancho and Carlos over a hill. This is followed by the inevitable gunfire and, ultimately, Rosario's capture. Once again Rosario finds himself in custody, making flirtatious gestures at the unobtainable Lee. And once again Rosario outsmarts his captors, and he escapes.

Seeking revenge, Rosario holds a gun aimed at Butler, Case, Lee, and the Andersons. Lee tells him that this is not the way to win back his land. Butler socks Rosario square in the face, but allows him to flee. Lee pretends to be shot during the brief fracas. Case, visibly concerned, sets out to obtain medical assistance. Butler, however, walks over to the "victim" and tosses her off the mattress. "There was only one bullet fired—and I caught it," he says while smugly displaying his injured wrist. Nevertheless, it is Lee who wins Butler's affections in the end. The film's closing line makes reference to Sheridan, who would be remembered in years to come as "the oomph girl." As Butler embraces Lee, he snaps, "You and your fourteen-carat oomph!"

An all-star cast with Cagney and O'Brien playing off leading lady Ann Sheridan. No stranger to the Warner Brothers roster, Sheridan starred in such Warner Brothers favorites as *The Black Legion* (1937), *San Quentin* (1937), *Mystery House* (1938), *Angels With Dirty Faces* (1938), *They Made Me A Criminal* (1938), *Dodge City* (1938), *Naughty But Nice, Angels Wash Their Faces* (1938), *They Drive By Night* (1940), *City of Conquest* (1940), and *Treasure of the Sierra Madre* (1948).

Born Clara Lou Sheridan in Denton, Texas on February 21, 1915, she performed on stage, radio, and found work on the screen in 1927, and also worked on television. Sheridan died on January 21, 1967, after a battle with cancer.

CAST: James Cagney, Ann Sheridan, Pat O'Brien, Andy Devine, Helen Vinson, Jerome Cowan, George Tobias, George Reeves, Victor Kilian, Frank Puglia, John Ridgely, Grady Sutton, Paul Porcasi, Frank Yaconnelli, Dick Boteler, Frank Mayo, Jack Mower, Paul Hurst, George Regas, Elvira Sanchez.

A WARNER BROTHERS—FIRST NATIONAL PICTURE; Jack L. Warner, in charge of production; Executive Producer: Hal B. Wallis; Directed by William Keighley; Associate Producer: Mark Hellinger; Original Screenplay by Richard Macaulay and Jerry Wald; Director of Photography: James Wong Howe, A.S.C.; Film Editor: Jack Killifer; Sound by Oliver S. Garretson; Technical Advisor: John Mari; Art Director: Ted Smith; Gowns by Howard Shoup; Special Effects: Byron

Haskin, A.S.C. and H. F. Koenekamp, A.S.C.; Make-Up Artist: Perc Westmore; Music by Adolph Deutsch; Song "Mi Caballero" by M.K. Jerome and Jack Scholl; Musical Director: Leo F. Forbstein. Original theatrical release: May 24, 1940. Running time: 87 minutes.

GAMBLING ON THE HIGH SEAS
Gambling With A Young Actor's Career

Although George receives billing in both the opening and closing credits, he isn't seen until the last third of the movie. And even then, he's only on screen very briefly, but he does have some significant dialogue. In fact, George's delivery in one scene basically outlines the whole plot of the film.

Gambling on the High Seas is one of those fast-paced programmers that blends a gratuitous amount of romance (mushy stuff would be a more accurate description) with the action. The film centers around ace reporter Jim Carter (Wayne Morris) and his efforts to help the government win a conviction against the notorious gangster, Greg Morella (Gilbert Roland). Of special note is a blonde Jane Wyman in the role of Morella's encumbered secretary. She also provides the love interest for Carter.

Jane Wyman (Mrs. Ronald Reagan) and Wayne Morris in a scene from *GAMBLING ON THE HIGH SEAS*.

George and Wayne Morris at play on the beach with some friends. *Could this sweet lady in the foreground be George's mom, Helen?*

After the authorities tighten the net around the cutthroat gambling racket, Morella is finally brought before the grand jury. When he is indicted, the members of the press beat a path to the courthouse telephone booths. Among them is a young reporter (George Reeves) who can barely contain his excitement as he phones his editor with the scoop. "Hold it for an extra, chief!" he shouts. "The Federal Government just indicted Greg Morella. They've charged him with operating crooked gambling machines on the high seas. Piracy! Call him Captain Kidd, what do I care?" Despite its brevity, this scene is memorable, not only because of George's youthful exuberance, but because we're seeing him as a fedora-wearing newspaper reporter (á la Clark Kent) early in his screen career.

During the Morella trial, Reeves is seated alongside Wayne Morris in the courtroom. The young reporter and the more-seasoned Carter take copious notes as the photographic exhibits are introduced into evidence. At one point during the proceedings, everyone in the courtroom is shocked when the judge dismisses the case due to lack of evidence. That "evidence" is the government's key witness, Laurie Ogden (Jane Wyman), who has suddenly taken ill. All of the reporters (including Reeves) do not believe this, and with good reason. It isn't true. Ogden has actually been kidnapped. In order to prevent his secretary from testifying against him, Morella has the young woman brought aboard his boat, supposedly for her own good. Carter manages to rescue his lady love in an action-packed, yet somehow lackluster climax. This is followed by close-ups of newspaper headlines, one of which declares: "MORELLA GUILTY!" After Morella is sent to prison, the romantic couple celebrate their honeymoon aboard a luxury liner.

A better showing of George's acting abilities, but still a disappointment for hard-core Reeves fans. Maybe it was George who didn't put in a more aggressive contribution to his career, that led to this string of minor roles; or was it the studio system's indifference that dictated George's fate?

CAST: Wayne Morris, Jane Wyman, Gilbert Roland, John Litel, Roger Pryor, Frank Wilcox, Robert Strange, John Gallaudet, Frank Ferguson, Harry Shannon, George Reeves, George Meader, William Pawley, Murray Alper.

A WARNER BROTHERS—FIRST NATIONAL PICTURE; Directed by George May; Screenplay by Robert E. Kent, from an idea by Martin Mooney; Dialogue Director: Harry Seymour; Director of Photography: L. Wm. O'Connell, A.S.C.; Film Editor: Frederick Richards; Art Director: Hugh Reticker; Sound by Francis J. Scheid; Gowns by Milo Anderson. Original theatrical release: June 22, 1940. Running time: 56 minutes.

THE MAN WHO TALKED TOO MUCH
The Invisible George, on Cutting Room Floor?

Steve Forbes (George Brent) is a hard nosed prosecutor delivering his closing argument in a much publicized murder trial. The defendant, Gerald Wilson (David Wilson), is convicted solely on circumstantial evidence. Even so, Steve asks for the death penalty. In open court, Wilson loudly professes his innocence, and calls the prosecutor a murderer for sending him to the electric chair. Later on, the true killer confesses to the crime. At the very last minute, District Attorney Nelson (Ed Stanley) tries to halt the execution. Just as he is about to reach the warden via telephone, the prison lights start blinking, indicating that the sentence has been carried out. Horrified and guilt-ridden over the error he's made, Steve relinquishes his job and goes into private practice with his younger brother Johnny (William Lundigan).

As a defence attorney, Steve wins a series of acquittals for some underworld bigwigs, causing some people to regard him as a "gangster's mouthpiece." Ironically, Johnny gets falsely accused of murder and is placed on death row. In desperation, Steve and his cohorts confront the real murderer and try to wring a confession out of him. All efforts are unsuccessful—until Steve's secretary (Virginia Bruce) resorts to trickery with a fake newspaper headline. Steve manages to get the governor (John Hamilton) on the phone in the nick of time, thus sparing his brother from the chair.

George Reeves is reported to have had a bit role in this film as a hotel clerk. All footage of him, however, seems to have been eliminated from extant

Lobby card from *The Man Who Talked Too Much* featuring George Brent (left) who was once married to Warner's leading lady Ann Sheridan.

prints. It could have been a bit part that ended up on the cutting room floor, or someone with indigestion of the imagination. Because there is a record of George's participation, it is included for completeness and clarity.

A nice cast, with or without George. George Brent is highly effective, and future star of the *Mad Ghoul* (Universal 1943) David Bruce, and TV's Perry White (in an unbilled role) round out this courtroom drama.

CAST: George Brent, Virginia Bruce, Brenda Marshall, Richard Barthelmess, William Lundigan, George Tobias, John Litel, Henry Armetta, Alan Baxter, David Bruce, Clarence Kolb, Louis Jean Heydt, Marc Lawrence, Ed Stanley, Kay Sutton, Elliott Sullivan, Dick Rich, Phyllis Hamilton, John Ridgely, William Forrest, Maris Wrixon, Dana Dale, John Hamilton (unbilled).

A WARNER BROTHERS—FIRST NATIONAL PICTURE; Jack L. Warner in charge of production; Associate Producer: Edmund Granger; Directed by Vincent Sherman; Screenplay by Walter DeLeon and Earl Baldwin; From a Play by Frank J. Collins; Director of Photography: Sid Hickox, A.S.C.; Film Editor: Thomas Pratt; Sound by Dolph Thomas; Art Director: Hugh Reticker; Technical Advisor: Charles Perry; Gowns by Howard Shoup; Make-Up Artist: Perc Westmore; Music by H. Roemheld; Orchestral Arrangements: Ray Heindorf; Musical Director: Leo F. Forbstein. Original theatrical release: July 6, 1940. Running time: 76 minutes.

PONY EXPRESS DAYS

Wild Bill George?

Like the other Warner Brothers shorts that were derived from the pages of history, *Pony Express Days* was photographed in lavish 3-strip Technicolor (unfortunately, prints that are available today on cheaper film stocks are so faded that they look like 2-strip Technicolor) and boasts a rousing musical score. The narrator opens the film by recalling the California gold rush, circa 1849, a time when interstate transportation required endless weeks on the barren trail, usually in the face of life-threatening obstacles. By 1860, with the dawn of the Civil War, it became necessary to devise a system whereby mail could be delivered, without interference, between two major stations: St. Joseph, Missouri and Sacramento, California. To fulfill this need, the firm of Russell, Majors & Waddell establishes the Pony Express system, a concept hailed as "one of the greater ventures in the annals of American enterprise."

An earnest chap, Bill Cody (George Reeves), shows up at the Pony Express headquarters seeking a riding job. Bill describes himself as "young and wirey" and offers assurance that he can "ride with the best of 'em." He also conforms to the company's strict moral code in that he doesn't swear, drink, or chew tobacco. In fact, the only drawback to this squeaky-clean applicant is his weight, which is twenty-five pounds over the limit. Bill's

J. Farrell MacDonald, George, and Frank Wilcox in a scene from *PONY EXPRESS DAYS*.

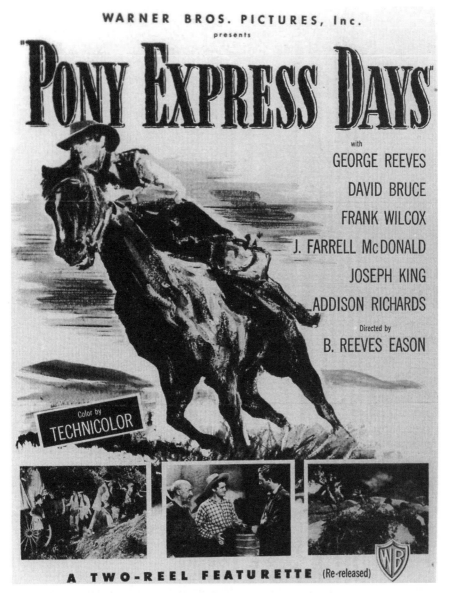

A re-issue one-sheet from *PONY EXPRESS DAYS*.

enthusiasm compensates for this one liability, and he is hired as a stock tender for the company's Northern Nevada station. Bill is grateful for the position, even though it is a non-riding one, and looks forward to the day when he might actually get the chance to ride. As Bill walks out of the office, one of the hiring partners says, "The kid's got spunk!"

On April 3, 1860, amid much fanfare, Bolivar Roberts (Frank Wilcox, who was George's best man at his 1940 wedding) saddles up for California, anticipating the seven stops he'll have to make in order to change horses. In

J. Farrell MacDonald (who meets George again in *SUPERMAN AND THE MOLE MEN*), with George in a scene from *PONY EXPRESS DAYS*.

Sacramento, at the other end of the line, the east bound rider is beginning his journey as well. Among the cheering spectators are two rather conspicuous dissenters: Colonel Joseph Randall (Joe King) and his"assistant"Tipton Waldron (Addison Richards), both of whom initiate an argument over the possibility of California's secession from the Union. The two men pretend to be Southern gentlemen when, in fact, they are merely con men exploiting the political climate in order to profit from slavery. Meanwhile, at the Nevada station, Bill is kept busy by tending the horses for his boss, "Nevadie" (played by future *Superman and the Mole Men* supporting player J. Farrell MacDonald). The old man regales Bill with tales about the number of buffalo he's slaughtered over the years. Bill listens politely, but keeps track of how that number steadily increases with each retelling!

One afternoon, a rider, Johnny Frey (David Bruce) arrives with the latest news from the east. David Bruce three years later would star as the *Mad Ghoul* for Universal. Bruce's film debut was *The Man Who Talked Too Much* (with an invisible George Reeves). He was in such classics as *The Sea Hawk* (1940), *Santa Fe Trail* (1940), *Sergeant York* (1941), *Flying Tigers* (1942), the Inner Sanctum favorite *Calling Dr. Death* (1943). He survived two Jungle Jim adventures, *Pygmy Island* (1950) and *Cannibal Attack*, and played Alan Duncan in Sam Katzman's waterlogged serial *The Great Adventures of Captain Kidd* (1953). Born Andrew McBroom on January 6, 1914 (a day after George's birthday), he disappeared from the screen for twenty-two years, returning to acting in 1976 for the film *Moving Violation*. He passed away on May 3 of that same year, of a heart attack.

It seems that some "fellow" named Lincoln has entered the presidential race. After Johnny rides away, Bill and Nevadie discuss the growing concern that the South might pull out of the Union. Such a loss would include the State of California and its vast gold resources. Nevadie believes that even Lincoln, whose administration would assure California's alliance, will not be able to avert such a problem.

News about the Republican candidate eventually reaches Sacramento, where Randall and Waldron quickly assess the situation. Since they want the South to secede from the Union, they decide to agitate as many Southern sympathizers as possible. Their main problem, however, is the fact that the election, set for November 8, will precede the State Legislature's vote on the

George and Frank Wilcox in *PONY EXPRESS DAYS*.

George is escorted away by two soldiers in *PONY EXPRESS DAYS*.

secession issue. Thus, the two men conspire to halt the delivery of the crucial election results—at least until mid-November.

Back in St. Joseph, Missouri, the Pony Express executives are faced with the realization that their enterprise is a financial failure; the company is in desperate need of subsidizing in order to remain in operation. The partners believe that the government might extend a contract, but only if the election results can be delivered to the Fort Churchill telegraph office within eight days. If the Pony Express system is to survive, it must set a new record for speed—weather and Indians permitting. To sabotage the Pony Express, the Southern sympathizers bribe the Indians with guns to block any white riders from passing through the territory. On the night of November 8, the St. Joseph telegraph office receives confirmation that Lincoln has been elected president.

Back at Nevadie's place, Roberts asks Bill to pick up the mailbag that Johnny had been carrying. While being treated for his injury, Johnny discloses that he was only 187 miles away from the Ft. Churchill telegraph station. Without saying a word to anyone, Bill prepares to deliver the election results on his own. When the Indians start firing, Roberts and Nevadie put up a good fight in defending the station. Both of them catch a glimpse of Bill riding off with the mailbag, and they wish him good luck. It is now up to Bill to complete the 187 mile route, alone, and at record speed.

In Sacramento, Randall and his cronies are already drinking to victory. In the meantime, Bill is fiercely carrying out his mission, without the benefit of any "relief" riders as anticipated. At Castle Rock, the last stop before his final destination, Bill discovers that two of his comrades have become casualties of another Indian rampage. This setback makes him even more determined to reach Ft. Churchill on time. After two agonizing days of firing and dodging bullets, a very weary Bill Cody finds himself at the threshold of the Ft. Churchill station. Barely able to stand up after his long ordeal, Bill is assisted by two Union soldiers. Amazingly, the election news is telegraphed on schedule.

The dispatch of Lincoln's victory is trumpeted all over Sacramento. Randall, not quite believing his ears, says he can't understand how the message could have gotten through so fast. "Here it is," says the elated telegraph officer. "The Pony Express brought it to Ft. Churchill in seven days and seventeen hours!" The crowd cheers in the revelation that California will remain in the Union.

The narrator explains that while the Pony Express had a great impact on our nation's destiny, the system quickly became obsolete due to the Civil War, which necessitated an even swifter means of communication. The camera depicts the workmen lining up strands of copper wires and connecting them to telegraph poles. In October of 1862, at the offices of Russell, Majors & Waddell, the old "Pony Express" sign is replaced with a new banner advertising the "Transcontinental Telegraph."

J. Farrell MacDonald, George, and Frank Wilcox in *PONY EXPRESS DAYS*.

In the closing scene, Johnny, Bill, and Nevadie contemplate the future. Johnny says there's nothing left to do except join the army. Nevadie says he'll go back to hunting buffalo, a profession "where a man can use his brains," he contends. "And my young friend Buffalo Bill Cody is coming along with me!" Bill smiles and says wistfully, "Buffalo Bill Cody! It's got kind of a nice sound, doesn't it Johnny?" The three men walk away smiling.

A wonderfully paced short, showcasing Reeves' mastery of dialect. Effectively directed by action director B. (Breezy) Reeves Eason. Eason directed the Gene Autry sci-fi, western, serial classic *The Phantom Empire* (Mascot 1935) and would go on to direct the King Features favorite *The Phantom* (Columbia 1943).

The writing is tight, and the cast serve up satisfying performances.

CAST: George Reeves, David Bruce, Frank Wilcox, J. Farrell MacDonald, Joseph King, and Addison Richards.

A WARNER BROTHERS PICTURE; Directed by B. Reeves Eason; Original Screenplay by Charles L. Tedford; Director of Photography: Charles P. Boyle, A.S.C.; Art Director: Charles Novi; Technicolor Color Director: Natalie Kalmus; Film Editor: Frank Dewar; Sound by Robert B. Lee; Made Up Artist: Perc Westmore. Original theatrical release: July 13, 1940. Running time: 19 minutes.

LADIES MUST LIVE

Pighead, Fogface, Broadway Shapes Hooters, and Wiseacres

Corey Lake (Wayne Morris) loves nothing more than working on his spacious farm under the sunny skies of South Falls, somewhere in Middle America. Young, strong, and good-looking, his life is the picture of contentment until he meets Pat Halliday (Rosemary Lane), a young actress whose car gets stuck in a mud hole. Ever the gentleman, Corey extricates Pat's vehicle from the mud. Pat is so grateful that she invites Corey to look her up the next time he's in New York. He decides to do just that. At the Manhattan nightclub where she is performing, Pat is happy to reacquaint herself with Corey. But she's also a bit dismissive, thinking he is merely a farmhand. Her attitude changes when Corey explains that his parents are deceased, and that he is the sole owner of his father's large company.

Easily taken by Pat's vivaciousness, Corey wants to know if she is already spoken for. As it turns out, the only guy in Pat's life is Joe Barton (William Hopper), a football player who has wanted to marry her since they were six years old. With no serious contenders in the picture, Corey begins to date Pat. She introduces him to her parents and her charismatic brother George (George Reeves), an up-and-coming whiz on Wall Street. Corey takes an instant like to George and gives him a cushy position with Lake and Company at $15,000 per year (an incredible salary in 1940). Corey also

Left to right: Roscoe Karns, Lee Patrick, Wayne Morris, Rosemary Lane, and George in a scene from *LADIES MUST LIVE*.

helps Dad Halliday (Ferris Taylor) by financing the new can opener he has developed. With everything going so smoothly, Corey pops the question to Pat. She accepts.

With the wedding not far away, Corey sends for his buddy Pete "Pighead" Larrabee (Roscoe Karns), who will serve as best man. Pete and his wife Mary (Lee Patrick) move into Corey's luxurious penthouse. The Larrabees are a strange couple. In addition to being a boozer, Pete is narrow minded and stubborn. Mary, his cynical but level-headed mate, has a full time job saving her husband from himself. They marvel at all the perks of high society, including Corey's butler, Chief Thunderbird (Cliff Saum). A totally imposing figure, Chief's only response to any question or statement is a resounding, "Ughh!"

The meeting between the Larrabees and the Hallidays takes place at Pat's nightclub. During the course of the evening, George recounts all the wonderful things Corey has done for the Hallidays. He acknowledges his generous salary, the summer home made available to the elder Hallidays, and the financing of Dad's can opener. Unfortunately, Pete misinterprets George's enthusiasm and concludes that the Hallidays are a bunch of moochers. Pete later expresses his concerns to Corey. Though entirely sincere, Pete's words take on a disparaging tone as he suggests that his friend is being taken for "a sucker." Corey listens intently to Pete's tirade, but grows increasingly angry and winds up smacking his "best man" in the jaw.

The Hallidays, of course, have no idea that Corey and Pete have had a falling out. Thus, they are totally shocked when Pete verbally assaults them

George (right) watches as Rosemary Lane receives an urgent telephone call in a scene from *LADIES MUST LIVE*.

at Corey's apartment (during his absence, of course). He cuts into the entire family, calling them "sharpshooters" and "gold-diggers." Understandably, the Hallidays storm out of the place in complete anger. When Corey finds out what Pete has done, he calmly reads his pal the riot act. He explains that George is a "steal" at fifteen-grand, as he is worth much more than that. He also explains that Pat had unselfishly relinquished a role in a Broadway show in order to marry him. And that Dad Halliday had earned his own comfortable retirement years earlier; his can opener invention was merely a side venture, and a very lucrative one for Lake and Company. Having digested all these facts. Pete feels like the "hick" that he is.

Corey overhears a phone conversation between Pat and Joe Barton, who has been seriously injured on the football field. Overcome with emotion, she calls him "darling." Corey tries to conceal his jealousy, as he's trying to patch things up after Pete's outrageous conduct. Pat, however, wants nothing to do with Pete and insists that Corey select another best man. When Corey refuses to comply, they get into a big squabble. Pat returns the engagement ring and the wedding is off.

To take their minds off their troubles, Corey takes the Larrabees out on the town. Shortly after their arrival home, they receive a late night visit from George, who has come to return a $40,000 necklace that Corey had given to Pat. George also turns in his resignation. "You had your choice—the Hallidays or the Larrabees," he says sternly. At this point, Pete makes the

William Hopper (left), Wayne Morris (right), and George (middle) in another scene from *Ladies Must Live*.

George with the cast of *Ladies Must Live*.

mistake of trying to apologize to George. But George, having had quite enough, gives Pete a third-degree verbal thrashing with great eleoquence (Reeves' best moment in the film). Following this, Corey makes an effort to square things with Pat, but she refuses to listen.

Realizing that his suspicious nature is the cause of everyone's troubles, Pete attempts to bring about a reconciliation. He shows Corey the necklace case which is now empty. Corey simply can't bring himself to phone Pat. So Pete places a call to George, asking about the missing necklace. Believing he's been accused of thievery, George races back to Corey's place in order to defend himself and his family.

Back at the Lake penthouse, George accuses the Larrabees of stealing the necklace. But before another feud can erupt, Pete whips out the "stolen" object. "It was the only way I had of rounding up all you Mavericks," he explains. Peter takes advantage of this second chance, and makes a complete and sincere apology to George. Then, in a rare display of affability, Pete places the necklace on Pat's shoulders. With everyone now forgiven, Corey and Pat are soon smooching again. The champagne is brought out, and Pete turns on the radio for some music.

As he swings into a rhumba with Mary, Pete asks, "How am I doing, Chief?" For the first and only time, Chief delivers a clear concise sentence: "On the reservation, sir, we consider that on the corny side!" But when asked to pitch in and serve some lemonade, Chief immediately reverts to his old response: Ughh!"

Ladies Must Live showcases George as he should have been in all his films. His performance rivals his exceptional performance in *So Proudly We Hail* (1943) or any other show one would care to recall. Here in this delightful screwball comedy, George proves beyond a shadow of a doubt that he is a bonafide movie star. His acting is seamless and totally believable, as are the rest of this brilliant ensemble cast. Roscoe Karns turns in a stellar performance, and almost steals the show.

This is Reeves' second film with pal Wayne Morris, who died a few months after George in 1959 (September 14). He succumbed to a heart attack on an aircraft carrier.

All Reeves fans should catch this flick.

CAST: Wayne Morris, Rosemary Lane, Lee Patrick, Roscoe Karns, George Reeves, Ferris Taylor, Lottie Williams, DeWolf Hopper, Cliff Saum, Billy Dawson, Mildred Gover, Dana Dale, Mildred Coles.

A WARNER BROTHERS—FIRST NATIONAL PICTURE; Directed by Noel Smith; Screenplay by Robert E. Kent; From a play by George M. Cohan; Associate Producer: William Jacobs; Director of Photography: Ten McCord, A.S.C.; Dialogue Director: Harry Seymour; Art Director: Esdras Hartley; Film Editor: Everett Dodd; Gowns by Milo Anderson; Sound by Francis J. Scheid; Make-Up Artist: Perc Westmore; Original theatrical release: July 27, 1940. Running time: 59 minutes.

CALLING ALL HUSBANDS

You Can't Tell Love What To Do!

George is in top form as the romantic hero of this ensemble "B" comedy. The story centers around the good-natured, but enormously henpecked, Homer Trippe (Ernest Truex). As an assistant manager in a small town department store, Homer hasn't exactly conquered the world, but has managed to be a good provider to his family for some thirty years. This means very little to his wife Emmie (Florence Bates), a self-centered and unappreciative woman who berates Homer at every given opportunity. Emmie's icy sarcasm stems from her conviction that Homer doesn't measure up to Oscar Armstrong, her girlhood beau. In her mind, Oscar is still the smartest, handsomest, and most cultured man in the world, even though she hasn't seen or heard from him in decades. Homer's only domestic ally is his 21 year-old daughter Bette (Lucille Fairbanks), who continually deflects her mother's harsh criticisms. Bette is in love with Dan Williams (George Reeves), the delivery clerk who works with Homer in the "used furniture department." Though Dan is hardworking and ambitious, Emmie holds him in disdain, believing he will never amount to anything.

On a cold and blustery evening, Emmie and Aunt Mabel (Virginia Sale) attend the local picture show while Homer stays home to wash the dishes. When Dan drops by to pick up Bette, he presents Homer with a jug of potent cider. The lovers then head for the railroad station, the only place in town where they can find some privacy. After sampling the cider, a rather tipsy Homer opens the door to a hobo and invites him in for a bowl of homemade stew. To his astonishment, Homer learns that the bum seated in his kitchen is actually Oscar Armstrong (George Tobias). A short time later, Dan and Bette return home with Judge Todd (Clem Bevans) who agrees to marry them in the living room. Homer offers Oscar five dollars to come to dinner the following evening, hoping that the appalling sight of him will shock some sense into Emmie. When Emmie and Mabel return home, they are kept in the dark about the wedding ceremony that has just taken place.

The next day, Oscar visits Homer during work in order to break the dinner date, stating that he must tend to a friend who has just arrived in town. Homer remedies the problem by forking over some cash for a cheap hotel room. Homer's boss, Mr. Weaver (Charles Halton), takes notice of this little conference and is about to reprimand his employee for socializing on company time. Oscar prevents this by identifying himself as Mr. Leffington, a West Coast businessman interested in establishing a chain of stores patterned after Weaver's. When questioned about his tattered clothing, Oscar explains that his appearance is merely a subterfuge which allows him to spy on competitors without arousing suspicion. Back at his hotel, Oscar and his "friend" Chunky (Elliott Sullivan) conspire to rob the safe at Weaver's Department Store. Despite his innocuous demeanor, Oscar is really a con man who has spent most of his life in jail. Later that evening, after closing time, the two crooks break into the store safe. Before fleeing into the night,

Lucille Fairbanks and George in *CALLING ALL HUSBANDS*.

Oscar steals the garments off a mannequin and foolishly leaves his own rags behind. His discarded clothing serves as the clue that leads the sheriff to Homer's door.

When dinner is about to be served, a nervous Homer begins to worry that Oscar might not materialize. Dan goes over to the hotel to investigate. Dan doesn't find Oscar, but quickly notices the pile of company bonds being concealed by Chunky. Dan and Chunky get into a fistfight (as usual, George's boxing prowess is very much in evidence).

Back at the Trippe residence, Oscar shows up looking like a million dollars in his spiffy new suit. Homer is stunned by this transformation, and realizes that his plan has backfired. At the dinner table, Emmie is totally captivated by every word uttered by Oscar. Her swooning comes to an abrupt end when Mr. Weaver and the sheriff (John Alexander) come to arrest Homer and "Mr. Leffington." Homer has no knowledge of the robbery, of course, and declares his innocence. Emmie's indignation is remarkable as she vigorously defends Oscar, while pointing an accusatory finger at her own husband! Just then, Dan shows up with Chunky and the stolen bonds. After Chunky sets the record straight, he is carted off to jail along with Oscar. Mr. Weaver apologizes to Homer and promotes him from assistant manager to manager, with a meager two dollar raise. Dan is rewarded with a much more substantial promotion and a paid vacation. Having disclosed the fact that they are now married, Dan and Bette happily embark on their honeymoon. In the closing scene, an apologetic Emmie finally acknowledges the silliness

From the right, George Tobias, Lucille Fairbanks, Reeves, and Ernest Truax in a scene from *CALLING ALL HUSBANDS*.

Left to right: George, Lucille Fairbanks, Florence Bates, Ernest Truax, & George Tobias.

of her past behavior. Homer, basking in his new role as head of the house, forgives his wife and agrees to take her on a second honeymoon.

People get born, married, and die, is a good part of the message of this film. One of the other components of this great Warner Brothers screwball comedy is the unexpected caper element three quarters of the way through the picture. Reeves goes from underdog newlywed to hero in the last reel.

Calling All Husbands is a terrific showcase of George's ability to handle all types of acting in one film. Furthermore, this is an example of 30s and 40s cinema that, despite the adversities, rose to leaving the audience with a happy ending, no matter how appalling world conditions were!

CAST: George Tobias, Lucille Fairbanks, Ernest Truex, George Reeves, Florence Bates, Charles Halton, Virginia Sale, John Alexander, Clem Bevans, Sam McDaniel, and Elliott Sullivan.

A WARNER BROTHERS—FIRST NATIONAL PICTURE; Directed by Noel Smith; Screenplay by Robert E. Kent, from a play by Martin Flavin; Associate Producer: William Jacobs; Director of Photography: Ted McCord, A.S.C.; Dialogue Director: Harry Seymour; Art Director: Charles Novi; Film Editor: Frank Magee; Gowns by Milo Anderson; Sound by Francis J. Scheid; Make-Up Artist: Perc Westmore. Original theatrical release: September 7, 1940.
Running time: 64 minutes.

ARGENTINE NIGHTS

Pseudo Hispanic, with Three Brothers Who Weren't Stooges

Unless you're a devotee of the Ritz Brothers, the Andrews Sisters, or George Reeves, *Argentine Nights* will be a disappointment. And even if you're a die-hard fan, be prepared for a succession of tired gags and stale one-liners spread over a very thin screenplay that doesn't play to contemporary audiences. Nevertheless, George's performance as a pseudo Spanish bandit is definitely worth seeing. It's his genuine enthusiasm, more than anything else, that diverts attention from the weak humor in this silly, disjointed farce. The best Ritz Brothers film is quite possibly *The Gorilla* (20th Century-Fox, 1939) with Bela Lugosi and Lionel Atwill.

The hilarity begins at the annual stockholders meeting of Colossal Ideas, Inc., a company that is virtually insolvent. The board of directors, comprised of Al, Harry, and Jimmy Ritz, are unable to appease the angry investors who demand to know where their money went. In their usual out-landish manner, the Ritz Brothers reveal that large expenditures were made to procure costumes and instruments for the girls in the Colossal band. With bankruptcy looming over their heads, the "directors" announce that the all-

George and Constance Moore in ARGENTINE NIGHTS.

girl band will recoup the money by taking on Argentina. According to the Ritzes, the proposed show will be "the biggest thing to hit Latin America since the Monroe Doctrine" (the actual event, not the film George made at Warner Brothers).

As their ship is about to depart, the girls notice a suave passenger named Eduardo (George Reeves), who speaks with a beguiling Spanish accent. He makes it a point to "accidentally" lock lips with several of the female passengers, including Bonnie Brooks (Constance Moore), the star of the show. In Buenos Aries, Eduardo tries his best to woo Bonita, as he calls her, but she rejects him because of his brashness and the stolen kiss. When Eduardo is arrested during his exchange with Bonnie, her expression of annoyance quickly turns to one of disbelief. The arrest, as it turns out, is as fake as Eduardo's accent. This Latin lover is actually a good-natured American playboy. And while he has been brought before the police officials, it is only for the purpose of being named the new leader of the singing gaucho riders.

George with Constance Moore on a lobby card for *ARGENTINE NIGHTS*.

The Colossal troupe learns that they've been booked into an isolated dump called the Hotel Manana. The owners of the establishment are an elderly couple who are the victims of swindlers. The husband (Paul Porcasi) is something of a prankster; he delights in telling the girls wild stories about bandits. Thus, when the girls hear ominous sounds in the night, they automatically assume that some outlaws are lurking about. Realizing that they need plenty of cash, the girls decide to capture the so-called bandits, with the intention of procuring a substantial reward. What they don't realize is that the men they've apprehended are actually the singing gauchos, under the guidance of Eduardo.

Eduardo decides to play along with Bonnie's false impressions, and confesses to being a notorious figure known as "El Tigre." After each of the girls takes custody of a bandit, Al, Harry, and Jimmy go out to summon the authorities. However, in the midst of all the shenanigans, Bonnie has a change of heart and allows Eduardo to escape. The other girls do the same thing, and the gauchos waste no time in getting away. When the Ritz Brothers finally locate a hapless policeman, Eduardo and his amigos listen secretly. The gang decides to carry the ruse even further, and before long, the hotel is swarming with ruffians. They arrive with goods and supplies for the show, thanks to Eduardo, who promises to flood the place with paying customers. Bonnie, however, refuses to accept help from a rogue, and forbids the girls to go on. Eventually, an elaborate show is presented, with musical numbers by the Andrews Sisters, and some tried-and-true slapstick from the Ritz Brothers. Afterward, Eduardo tells Bonnie the truth about his alter ego. When Eduardo persists in trying to patch things up, Bonnie becomes angry and snatches a pistol from his cummerbund. She is surprised to learn that the weapon is as phony as its owner's accent. Eduardo laughingly assures her that "only real bandits carry real guns." But even this isn't enough proof that "El Tigre" is a put-on. With a beseeching smile, Eduardo says, "You're going to force me to become this big, bad bandit again!" (He makes no such attempt, of course.) When Bonnie finally acknowledges Eduardo as a good guy, she has no qualms about kissing him.

With the show over, the brothers take to the road (something they should have done much earlier) and begin their trek back to Brooklyn— only 4,939 miles away! Having ignored several danger signs, they casually stroll off an uncompleted wooden bridge. After doing so, they miraculously stand in mid-air for a few seconds before plummeting into the waters below, a gag used much more effectively in the animated adventures of Bugs Bunny.

Argentine Nights was the first film the Ritz Brothers made at Universal Pictures, their new "home" after leaving 20th Century-Fox. More significantly, the film has the distinction of marking the screen debut of the legendary Andrews Sisters—Patty, Maxene, and Laverne. The sisters, who went on to make more movies and sell millions of records, were among the most beloved entertainers during World War II. In fact, two of their recordings, "Boogie Woogie Bugle Boy" and "Don't Sit Under the Apple Tree," have remained indelible imprints of that bygone era. The three sisters continued to perform together until Laverne's death in 1966.

Peggy Moran was the female star of Universal's classic *The Mummy's Hand* (1942), along with Dick Foran and Wallace Ford; and Anne Nagel co-starred with Boris Karloff and Bela Lugosi in another Universal Sci-Fi/Crime drama hit, *Black Friday* (1940). Both of these luscious ladies had varied acting careers.

CAST: The Ritz Brothers, Patty Andrews, Maxene Andrews, Laverne Andrews, Constance Moore, George Reeves, Peggy Moran, Anne Nagel, Kathryn Adams, Ferike Boros, and Paul Porcasi.

A UNIVERSAL PICTURE; Directed by Albert S. Rogell; Associate Producer: Ken Goldsmith; Screenplay by Arthur T. Harmon, Ray Golden, Sid Kuller; Original Story by J. Robert Breu, Gladys Atwater; Musical Director: Charles Previn; Director of Photography: Elwood Bredell, A.S.C.; Art Director: Jack Otterson; Associate: Ralph M. DeLacey; Film Editor: Frank Gross; Set Decorations: R.A. Gousman; Sound Supervisor: Bernard A. Brown; Technician: Jess Moulin; Gowns by Vera West; Assistant Director: Joseph A. McDonough; Songs: "Oh! He Loves Me," "Amigo, We Go Riding Tonight," and "Once Upon a Dream" by Sammy Cahn and Saul Chaplin; "Spirit of 77B," "Brooklynonga," and "Hall of the Mountain Queen" by Kuller, Golden, and Borne; "Rhumboogie" and "Hit the Road" by Raye, Prince, and Schoen; Orchestrations by Frank Skinner and Vic Schoen. Original theatrical release: September 10, 1940. Running time: 72 minutes.

KNUTE ROCKNE, ALL AMERICAN

Rah! Rah! Rah! Siss, Boom Reeves!

This is the film that solidified Pat O'Brien's place in film history, and provided a pivotal role for up-and-coming Warner contract player Ronald Reagan. It's the life story of Knute "Rock" Rockne, regarded by many as the greatest college football coach of all time. George has a small speaking role in one scene, and can be spotted on the football field if you look closely enough. O'Brien plays the adult Rockne. Early in the film, young Knute is played by Johnny Sheffield, best known for his role as "Boy" in the Tarzan films. Johnny Sheffield was later to star in Monogram's teenage Tarzan programers, the Bomba series. His father, Reginald Sheffield, was a stage, screen, and television actor, whose credits include *David Copperfield* (1923), *House of Rothschild* (1934), *Adventures of Robin Hood* (1938), and the origi-

George listens intently to Pat O'Brien in *KNUTE ROCKNE, ALL AMERICAN*.

Studio portrait from the 1940s with that Knute Rockne feel.

nal and the remake of *The Buccaneer* (1938 and 1958). He was a featured character player in the juvenile 1950s favorite *Rocky Jones, Space Ranger.*

Born in Voss, Norway in 1888, Knute migrates to the Unites States at age seven with his parents and sisters. While growing up, Rock learns the basics of football from the other kids in the neighborhood. Years later, he saves his wages from a job at the Post Office, working his way into the halls of Notre Dame. In 1918, after establishing himself as an amiable over-achiever, Rock takes on the task of coaching the Fighting Irish, leading the team to unparalleled victories. Among his contributions are the innovation of the forward pass, which "revolutionized" the game, and the discovery of George "The Gipper" Gipp (Reagan). The most memorable line in the film, and in O'Brien's entire career, is: "Win one for the Gipper!" (A line that politico Reagan used as PR!)

About an hour into the film, there is a locker room scene in which one of the Fighting Irish strongly defends his performance on the field. The distraught young man is played by George Reeves. "You can't expect me to do everything," he says with a voice full of rancor. "I'm only one man. I can't play all the positions." He apologizes to Rockne for causing the team to lose the first half. Rock says an apology isn't necessary, making a slightly snide comment to the effect that this guy collects (and presumably believes) his own press clippings! The coach then delivers one of his famous pep talks, thereby spurring the team to victory in the second half.

As the years roll by, Rockne helps foster the acceptance of sports as a rewarding and respectable aspect of college life. Then one day in 1931, Rockne receives a telegram which causes him to embark for Los Angeles. His wife Bonnie (Gale Page) urges him not to fly. But Rock is in a hurry to get the trip over with, mainly so he can get back to his wife and kids. Tragically, the tiny plane carrying the beloved football coach crashes over a Kansas farm, leaving no survivors. An untimely end to a colorful figure who will be revered by football enthusiasts and historians for decades to come.

A tear-jerker in the mold of *Pride of the Yankees, Knute Rockne, All American* is regarded by most as classic sports cinema.

CAST: Pat O'Brien, Gale Page, Ronald Reagan, Donald Crisp, Albert Basserman, John Litel, Owen Davis, Jr., Nick Lukats, Kane Richmond, William Marshall, William Byrne, The Moreau Choir of Notre Dame, Henry O'Neill, John Qualen, Dorothy Tree, John Sheffield, Howard Jones, Glenn "Popp" Warner, Alonzo Stagg, William "Bill" Spaulding, and George Reeves (unbilled).

A WARNER BROTHERS—FIRST NATIONAL PICTURE; Jack L. Warner, in charge of Production; Executive Producer: Hal B. Wallis; Directed by Lloyd Bacon; Associate Producer: Robert Fellows; Original Screenplay by Robert Buckner; Based upon the private papers of Mrs. Rockne, and reports of Rockne's intimate associates and friends; Director of Photography: Tony Gaudio, A.S.C.; Film Editor: Robert Haas; Sound by Charles Lang; Gowns by Milo Anderson; Special Effects by Byron Haskin, A.S.C., Rex Wimpy, A.S.C.; Makeup Artist: Perc Westmore; Technical Advisors: Nick Lukats, J.A. Haley; Musical Director: Leo F. Forbstein; Orchestral Arrangements by Ray Heindorf. Original theatrical release: October 5, 1940. Running time: 97 minutes.

FATHER IS A PRINCE
The Vacuum In George's Life

John Bower (Grant Mitchell) is a self-made man who lives in a spacious abode with his wife and three kids. Despite his success in the business world (he owns a factory that produces carpet sweepers) John is downright miserable—and cheap. He's the type of man who storms around the house shut-

Jan Clayton, Grant Mitchell, and George in *Father Is A Prince*.

Title lobby card from *Father Is A Prince*.

Billy Dawson, Jan Clayton, Nana Bryant, and George in *Father Is A Prince*.

Grant Mitchell, Jan Clayton, and George.

ting off lights in order to keep the electric bill down. His long suffering wife is Susan (Nana Bryant) and by contrast, she is an enormously pleasant soul who takes everything in stride. Their eldest child is lovely young Connie (Jan Clayton), who is away on vacation. Eagerly awaiting her return are the two Bower sons (Billy Dawson and Richard Clayton), neither of whom will be going to college, as the high cost of tuition is out of the question. When Bower is informed that he owes $8,000 in back taxes, he becomes even more penurious and totally unbearable—a totally agitated Scrooge.

Connie returns from her trip, accompanied by Aunt Tess (Lee Patrick) and a charming man named Gary Lee (George Reeves). Gary, who has a promising career as a lawyer, is madly in love with Connie and has presented her with an engagement ring. Gary is far from being a starving young professional; his father is the manufacturer of an electric vacuum cleaner, which is a superior rival to the Bower carpet sweeper. The main problem facing Connie and her mom is how to break the "good news" to the old man, who openly despises college men, lawyers, and vacuum cleaners!

A dinner party is held at the Bower home so the two families can meet and get acquainted. Gary, in black tie, proudly introduces his parents (played by Mary Currier and future Superman serial and television series character actor Pierre Watkin) both of whom are also impeccably dressed. The Lees are delighted with Susan, and all goes well until the man of the house shows up. Initially, the guests are taken aback by John's disheveled appearance; then they become utterly appalled by his rude conduct. When John notices a shiny new vacuum cleaner in the hall closet (which Gary had presented as a gift) he goes ballistic. Susan tries to apologize for her husband, who continues to rant and rave about everything that's bugging him. Gary, clearly more outspoken than his parents, calls Bower a "selfish, egotistical, opinionated old miser." Bower orders the young lawyer out of the house, and tells him not to come back. Before following his parents out the door, Gary promises Connie that he will call her. Connie, of course, is inconsolable.

Susan confronts her husband in private and tells him she is fed up with his disgraceful behavior and chronic stinginess. The argument culminates with Susan asking for a divorce. Before John can react to this bombshell, Susan, who has been quietly suffering from fainting spells, collapses under the emotional strain. The family physician, Dr. Stone (John Litel), is summoned and he rushes Susan into emergency surgery. Though the precise nature of her illness isn't disclosed, it is quite apparent that Susan is undergoing some sort of life-threatening procedure.

In the hospital waiting room, the Bower sons, and especially Aunt Tess, help John to realize how his selfishness and neglect have contributed to the crisis at hand. Worried that his wife might die and consumed by guilt, John finally acknowledges that family is more important than finances. He vows to provide Susan with any luxury she might desire, including the full-time domestic help which he can readily afford. Miraculously, Susan survives the delicate operation. One of the disappointing aspects of the screenplay is its failure to resolve the conflict between Bower and his future son-in-law. Since

Jan Clayton, George, and Grant Mitchell in a publicity photo from *FATHER IS A PRINCE*.

the romantic angle is also left unfinished, we can only assume that Gary does become a member of this now-harmonious family. The film wraps itself up with Susan in recuperation, with a caring and lovable husband in attendance.

Female lead Jan Clayton is best remembered for being Lassie's first television Mom. John Litel is most readily identified as Henry Aldrich's father in the Paramount series, and Pierre Watkin also guest starred in "Beware the Wrecker" (1953) and "The Last Knight" (1957) on the *Adventures of Superman* television series. He was the first live-action Perry White in the two Kirk Alyn serials at Columbia. He made his first film in 1935 and his last film in 1959. He passed away on February 3, 1960.

Father Is A Prince is an uneven entry in George's film career.

CAST: Grant Mitchell, Nana Bryant, John Litel, George Reeves, Jan Clayton, Lee Patrick, Billy Dawson, Richard Clayton, John Ridgely, Frank Wilcox, Vera Lewis, Frank Ferguson, Pierre Watkin, Mary Currier, Frank Orth.

A WARNER BROTHERS—FIRST NATIONAL PICTURE; Directed by Noel Smith; Associate Producer: William Jacobs; Screenplay by Robert E. Kent; Director of Photography: Ted McCord, A.S.C.; Dialogue Director: Gene Lewis; Art Director: Charles Novi; Film Editor: Frank Magee; Gowns by Howard Shoup; Make-Up Artist: Perc Westmore; Sound by E.A. Brown. Original theatrical release: October 12, 1940. Running time: 58 minutes.

ALWAYS A BRIDE

His Honor, Mayor Reeves

Anyone who thinks George's talents were limited to playing Superman will be delighted with *Always A Bride*. Despite Rosemary Lane's top billing, the film belongs to George, whose natural charisma livens up this little romantic farce. Similar to the character he played in *Calling All Husbands*, Reeves is the good guy who is pegged as a loser. He's actually a winner but doesn't realize it until the end of the picture.

Alice Bond (Lane) lives with her parents in a modest little home with a white picket fence. In this seemingly blissful setting, Marshall Winkler (played by future Superman villain John Eldredge) waits impatiently for Alice to come downstairs. Marshall is a successful, but very stuffy, businessman who considers himself the best catch in town. Despite her engagement to Marshall, Alice is on the phone with Michael Stevens (George Reeves), the man she truly loves. Alice's mother, Lucy Bond (Virginia Brissac), disapproves of Mike and regards him as a "shiftless no-account bunch of laziness." Alice's dad (Francis Peirlot) also thinks Mike is a bum, and encourages his daughter to stick with the unbearable Marshall. In truth, Mike is a good-natured underachiever who has the ability to turn on the charm, usually with spectacular expressions of flattery. Mike also has a wealthy and influential relative, Uncle Dan (Oscar O'Shea), who has offered him the position of county tax appraiser. But even Uncle Dan can't motivate his perpetually unemployed nephew, who has repeatedly rejected the job.

Knowing that Mike is on his way over to propose, Lucy tactfully gets Marshall out of the house. When Mike arrives, he presents Alice with an engagement ring. But when he attempts to slip it on Alice's finger, he notices that she is already wearing a ring—the one she accepted from Marshall earlier that day. Mike, who is madly in love with Alice, feigns gladness that a fine man like Marshall has won her over. Later, when Marshall returns to the house, Mike really lays it on thick. "Here's mud in your eye," he says as he bids the couple good-bye. "And money in your purse, happiness in your hearts, and a few kind words on your lips. Good luck and bless you my children!" While Alice is stunned by Mike's acquiescence, Marshall is more than happy to see his rival go out the door. A few weeks later, however, the threesome is reunited at a political party in honor of Mayor Paul Loomis (Ferris Taylor). Mike succeeds in making Alice extremely jealous by dancing boldly with his new girlfriend. Adding to Alice's frustration is Marshall's domineering personality, which seems to be getting worse by the minute. Having

John Eldredge, George, and Rosemary Lane in *ALWAYS A BRIDE*.

reached the point where she can no longer tolerate Marshall's criticisms, Alice abruptly heads for home.

The funniest scene in the film occurs at the Bond residence, after the party, when Mike engages in some clever dialogue with Marshall about the "joys" of matrimony. Mike devilishly reminds the prospective groom about such things as marital spats, nagging, and headaches stemming from taxes and bill payments. "No marriage for me," says a self-assured Mike. "I'm going duck shooting. Ducks can't talk back!" This bit of chicanery nearly backfires, as Alice has heard every word from the next room. Later, Mike reassures Alice that his comments were intended to trick Marshall into calling off the wedding. Mike is thrilled when he finally wins Alice's hand (over the protestations of her father), and remains upbeat when he encounters some of the very problems he had spouted earlier. For instance, Uncle Dan threatens to have Mike put in jail if he doesn't start paying his own debts. And there's nagging aplenty from Mama and Papa Bond, who insist that Alice must divorce Mike if he doesn't get a job.

Mayor Loomis is up for re-election. A shifty politician in every possible way, Loomis aids the opposing party in nominating a stooge, thereby assuring himself of another term in office. While the big shots are searching for a suitable "candidate," Mike shows up to apply for the tax appraiser job. After informing Mike that the position has been filled, Loomis pitches another opportunity. Actually, it's more of a deal. The mayor will take care of Mike's unpaid bills, thus keeping him out of the slammer. In return, Mike must become the Progressive mayoral candidate and deliberately conduct an unsuccessful campaign. In other words, he must become a "stooge." Since the Bonds are steering their daughter in the direction of the divorce court, Mike agrees to run against Mayor Loomis. To everyone's astonishment, Mike's campaign posters urge the public not to vote for him. Because he's deliberately running a bad campaign, the whole town thinks Mike has taken leave of his senses. Even the seasoned crooks, who are familiar with all the known ploys, are puzzled by Mike's actions. One of them asks, "Why can't he be a plain, everyday chiseler like us instead of using tricks we can't figure out?"

During his campaign speech, Mike warns everyone that if he's elected, the town won't get the new city hall Loomis had promised to build. That's because the old one is "good enough for another fifty years." Candidate Stevens also says the incumbent mayor, who owns a large construction firm, stands to profit quite handsomely from such an unnecessary building project. The message is clear: if voters like the idea of wasting their tax dollars, then they should not vote for Mike Stevens. Mike is so honest he'll even withdraw from the race, thereby saving the city $50,000 in elections costs, if that's what the people really want. The crowd starts roaring, "We want Mike for Mayor!"

On election night, Mike and Alice listen to the election returns with Uncle Dan and the Bonds. The race is too close to call, and as the final ballots are being counted, both parties nervously await the results. After teetering back and forth, the radio announcer declares Mike as the winner—by one vote. Uncle Dan takes credit for Mike's victory, claiming that it was his

Lobby card from *ALWAYS A BRIDE*.

vote that won the elections. Beaming with joy, Mike realizes that he's not only won the race, but also the respect of Alice's mom and dad. From Mike's perspective, the happiest aspect of being an elected official is the fact that he'll "never have to work again!"

This is the first on screen battle between Reeves and his future Superman co-star John Eldredge, who played Mr. Big in "Crime Wave" (1951), and Mr. X in "Superman's Wife" (1957). Eldredge's 27-year film career included such cinematic treasures as *Charlie Chan at the Olympics*, (1937), *King of the Underworld* (1939), *Dr. Kildare's Strangest Case* (1940), *Life Begins for Andy Hardy* (1941), *The Black Cat* (1941), *High Sierra* (1941), *Horror Island* (1941), *The Mad Doctor of Market Street* (1942), *Lost City of the Jungle* (1946), *Angels Alley* (1948), *The Sky Dragon* with Noel Neill (1949), *Meet Me In Las Vegas* (1956), and *I Married a Monster From Outer Space* (1958). He was born in San Francisco on August 30, 1904, and passed away on September 23, 1961.

The verbal encounters bristle, and their dialogue about matrimony is simply hilarious in an ironic, well-written scene midway through the film. Paced like a speeding locomotive at 58 minutes, George displays a charm that even in contemporary times is irresistible. His range and characterization make one forget he's acting.

CAST: Rosemary Lane, George Reeves, John Eldredge, Virginia Brissac, Francis Pierlot, Oscar O'Shea, Ferris Taylor, Joseph King, Phyllis Ruth, Lucia Carroll, Jack Mowler, and Tom Wilson.

A WARNER BROTHERS—FIRST NATIONAL PICTURE; Directed by Noel M. Smith; Associate Producer: William Jacobs; Screenplay by Robert E. Kent, from a play by Barry Conners; Director of Photography: Charles Schoenbourn, A.S.C.; Dialogue Director: Hugh MacMullan; Film Editor: Frank Magee; Art Director: Ted Smith; Gowns by Milo Anderson; Sound by Stanley Jones; Make Up Artist: Perc Westmore. Original theatrical release: November 2, 1940. Running time: 58 minutes.

MEET THE FLEET
Carl Denham, Clark Kent, and Uncle Sam in Technicolor!

This 20-minute "Technicolor" special was produced by the shorts department at Warner Brothers, with the cooperation of the United States Navy. What makes this film particularly "special" is the fact that much of it was shot in and around the San Diego Naval Base. The light storyline (and the fact that it was distributed theatrically) distinguishes it from the "documen-

George, William T. Orr, and Herbert Anderson in a scene from MEET THE FLEET.
PHOTO COURTESY OF THE ACADEMY OF MOTION PICTURE ARTS AND SCIENCES.

tary" or "military training" films that George was to make during World War II. (You know, the ones that would deal with such subjects as venereal disease, and would be seen only by servicemen!)

George appears in this one as Benson, one of three young recruits subjected to rigorous training in such courses as seamanship, signaling battle maneuvers, and the use of wireless equipment. Benson and the other men also tackle "specialized subjects" in order to ensure their proficiency as sailors. The courses, which are fully illustrated, are intended to serve as an inspiration to young men "in the first line of our national defense."

Besides George, the most familiar face in *Meet The Fleet* is probably that of Herbert Anderson, best remembered as the perplexed dad in the sitcom *Dennis the Menace* (1959-63). Also of note are Robert Armstrong and William T. Orr. In the late 1950s, Orr made quite a name for himself in television as the executive producer of numerous Warner Brothers' action shows (*77 Sunset Strip, Hawaiian Eye*) and countless westerns (*Maverick, Cheyenne, Sugarfoot*).

Robert Armstrong is no stranger to genre enthusiasts. His portrayal of super-showman Carl Denham in the original *King Kong* ensured him a place in cinema heaven, along with such actors as Colin Clive, Peter Lorre, and Basil Rathbone—monster makers and monster wranglers. His hyperactive performance as film director/pitchman Denham is classic cinema. His other films include *The Most Dangerous Game* (1932), *Adventures of the Flying Cadets* (1943), *The Kansan* (with George, 1943), *The Mad Ghoul* (1943), *Blood On The Sun* (1945), *The Falcon in San Francisco* (1945), and his final

George (third from the left), Anderson, and Orr in a scene from *Meet the Fleet*.
Photo courtesy of the Academy of Motion Picture Arts and Sciences.

film *For Those Who Think Young* (1964). Armstrong passed away on August 20, 1973, in Santa Monica, California. He was 77 years old.

Cast: Robert Armstrong, William T. Orr, George Reeves, Mary Cheffey, and Herbert Anderson.

A WARNER BROTHERS PICTURE; Directed by B. Reeves Eason; Original screenplay by Owen Crump; Director of Photography: Charles P. Boyle; Film Editor: Louis Lindsay; Technicolor consultant: Natalie Kalmus. Original theatrical release: December 21, 1940. Running time: 20 minutes.

THE LADY AND THE LUG
Slapsie, Maxi, and George

This Warner Brothers short is something of a tribute to the great slapstick two-reelers of the previous decade. Like so many classic comedies of the 1930s, this one features some jazzy background music, and allows the main stars to use their real names within the story. Elsa Maxwell, who receives top billing, was already a renowned columnist and party-giver when this film was released. Maxwell was to gain even greater fame in the late 1950s through her controversial appearances on Jack Paar's late night talk show. For more on Elsa, see the following review of *Throwing A Party*.

"Slapsie" Maxie Rosenbloom, the "lug" referred to in the title, was a former boxer who had established a second career by specializing in gangster and roughneck roles in motion pictures. A formidable foil for many screen comics, Rosenbloom remained active in films through the 1960s.

Highlights of Rosenbloom's film career include *Nothing Sacred* (1937), *Mr. Moto's Gamble* (1938), *The Amazing Dr. Clitterhouse* (1938), *Each Dawn I Die* (1939), *Follow the Boys* (1944), *Ghost Crazy* (1944), *Skipalong Rosenbloom* (1951), *Guys And Dolls* (1955), *Abbott & Costello Meet the Keystone Cops* (1955), *Hollywood or Bust* (1956), *I Married a Monster From Outer Space* (1958), with his last film being *My Side of the Mountain* in 1969. He passed away in Pasadena, California on March 6, 1976.

The short opens with the clang of a bell at a boxing ring, followed by Elsa's introductory remarks to the camera. This is a story "about what happens when a lady sticks her chin out," she informs us. After Elsa bumps into her butler (who happens to be carrying a tray, of course), she gets busy on the telephone chatting with one of her society chums. Suddenly, a dapper young man with a pencil-thin mustache bursts into the room. He is Elsa's nephew, Doug Abbott (George Reeves). Doug explains that he's now working as a reporter, and has won money in a poker game from Ace Thomas,

Slapsie "Maxie" Rosenbloom (in the robe on the right) in *Lady and the Lug*.

Elsa Maxwell proves she is the fireball of fisticuffs as she KOs Slapsie Maxie Rosenbloom and friend in a scene from *LADY AND THE LUG*.

one of the guys in the newsroom. The only problem is that Thomas could not afford to pay the debt in cash (even though it was only $4.80) and has assigned Doug the contract for one of his fighters. Doug tries to sell his aunt on the idea of sponsoring the fighter, but she isn't interested. However, Else changes her mind upon realizing that the fighter can be exploited as "entertainment" for the Milk Fund Bazaar, an event that she is organizing. (Milk fund charities were quite common during the 1930s and early 1940s.)

Enter Slapsie Rosenbloom, a dull-witted veteran of the ring who greets Elsa with a chipper, "Hi 'ya, toots!" The boxer isn't exactly thrilled when he learns that Elsa wants to sponsor him, and he refuses to go along with the idea. Even after some heavy duty coaxing, Slapsie remains unconvinced— until Elsa demonstrates what she's made of, and roughs him up a bit. After that, Slapsie reluctantly submits to Elsa's management.

The film incorporates several slapstick vignettes that are throwbacks to the late silent and early talkie comedies. For example, when Slapsie gets into an altercation with the butler, Elsa finds herself without a servant just as she's about to give a swanky dinner party. Guess who pinch-hits for the butler and makes a shambles of the evening? The knockabout stuff is kept to a minimum until Elsa gets stuck under the dinner table, and Slapsie has to extricate her in front of all the bemused guests. Gags used in this sequence, and in others throughout the film, were certainly well-worn by 1940, but they were still undeniably funny.

It's time for Slapsie's workout. Elsa, decked out in a sweat suit, joins her protégé for some road work. Despite her girth, the hostess is actually more energetic than the sluggish fighter. As they're jogging along, their small talk informs us that they've also indulged in some "shadow boxing." When it comes time to take a breather, the runners perch themselves on a torn-down tree. But their respite is short lived, thanks to a large beehive that starts buzzing right behind them. With the angry bees in pursuit, the joggers quickly take to the road. And this time, Slapsie has no difficulty whatsoever in keeping up with Elsa.

That night, Doug returns to the Maxwell mansion and gleefully announces himself, "Here's your favorite nephew back again!" Doug asks his aunt for a progress report. Elsa, lying on a sofa with a headache and sore backside, says, "Terrible. I've done twice as much training as Slapsie!" Upbeat as ever, Doug gives his aunt a pep talk and reveals that he's secured One Punch McGurk for the impending exhibition. Slapsie enters the room, complaining that he can't fall asleep because he has "amnesia." Elsa suggests he read a book, and hands him a copy of Romeo and Juliet. That night, Slapsie dreams that he is Romeo, and Elsa is his Juliet. In a spoof of the famous balcony scene, "Romeo" woos his lady love (in Brooklynese) and begins to climb up the ladder. Unfortunately, the balcony isn't as sturdy as the lovers, and they both plummet to the ground with a resounding thud! Doug brings the dream to an end when he rushes into the fighter's room and awakens him. It is the day of the big event.

The Milk Fund Bazaar is well attended. Just before the bout, Doug informs Elsa that their man has suddenly "turned into a prima donna" and will not fight. Having learned that the exhibition is being staged for a milk charity, Slapsie refuses to participate in what he believes will be a 'tea party.' He snaps, "What would 'da boys in 'da pool room say?" Elsa remedies the problem with some sweet talk, equating Slapsie's prowess to that of a gladiator. The flattery routine works, and the fight is on.

Slapsie is shocked to learn that McGurk is to be his opponent. Doug tries to convince him that there's nothing to worry about. "He can't hurt us," says Doug reassuringly. Slapsie groans, "To think I'd give my life for a bottle of milk!" Doug is in Slapsie's corner as the tough-looking McGurk enters the ring. To everyone's astonishment, Slapsie holds his own during the first round. But Doug is soon appalled when he notices McGurk resorting to a foul tactic. Elsa cries, "What's that palooka doing to my boy?" Doug explains that McGurk is "using his famous thumb punch. Now Slapsie hasn't got a chance!"

Elsa cannot allow her boy to get creamed, so she dives into the ring to help him. When the referee tries to restrain Elsa, he accidentally tears off her dress. But even this doesn't deter the unflappable hostess, who proceeds to slug everyone within her range—Slapsie, McGurk, and even the referee! The spectacle is punctuated by the bizarre sight of Elsa, in her underwear, taking a few bows before the cheering crowd.

To wrap up the film, Elsa addresses the camera once again, this time to impart the moral of the story, "If you can't be happy, be slap happy!" With the jazzy theme music rising on the soundtrack, Elsa says, "I'll be seeing you" at the fade-out.

CAST: Elsa Maxwell, Maxie Rosenbloom, George Reeves, Georgia Caine.

A WARNER BROTHERS PICTURE; Directed by William McGann; Screenplay by Charles Marion and Arthur V. Jones, from an original story by Owen Crump and Jack Henley; Director of Photography: L. Wm. O'Connell, A.S.C.; Dialogue Director: Owen Crump; Film Editor: Louis Hesse; Art Director: Charles Novi; Sound by Charles Lang; Gowns by Orry Kelly; Make-Up Artist: Perc Westmore. Original theatrical release: December 23, 1940. Running time: 20 minutes.

THROWING A PARTY
Hangovers and Honeymoons

This Elsa Maxwell two-reel comedy is a companion piece to 1940s *The Lady and the Lug*. This time, however, George is not cast as Elsa's nephew, but merely an acquaintance.

Elsa, the quintessential party-giver, brags that she can take any unknown girl and turn her into front-page news practically overnight. A dynamic young reporter, Larry Scoffield (George Reeves), doubts that the old gal has the power to do it. So Elsa makes a bet with Larry, promising to accomplish the feat in just two weeks.

Photo of Elsa Maxwell (center) at a real Hollywood party for *THROWING A PARTY*.

Another photo of Elsa Maxwell (second from the left) for *THROWING A PARTY.*

In order to win the bet, Elsa resorts to what she does best—throwing a party. She gets one of her actor cronies, Horace (Leonid Kinskey), to impersonate an explorer who had recently returned from a remote area of the world. Dr. Boris Ivanovitch (alias Horace) makes a splashy appearance at a party given in his honor at the Maxwell residence. He brings along an attractive native girl, Princess Reeka (Lynn Merrick), as his date. Although the "princess" is just as much a fake as the "doctor," they blend into the proceedings rather swimmingly (or drowningly, if you prefer). Elsa tells all the gathered socialites that she will take the princess under her wing as a protege. Despite this newsworthy announcement, nothing turns up in the papers the next day. That's because Larry's reporter buddies have been tipped off and are thus wise to Elsa's chicanery.

With the clock ticking away, Elsa tries a few outlandish tricks to get her protege's picture in the newspaper. For instance, she and the princess dress up in leopard skins and stroll through the park in the company of a large ape. When this fails to attract attention, a worried Elsa sets up a tent on the front lawn of the City Hall. But even this stunt proves useless. However, during all the slapstick shenanigans, Larry has taken a fancy to the pseudo-princess. And when he learns that she is merely a waitress, he marries her. This event does make the headlines, and with photos of the happy couple plastered all over the newspapers, Elsa wins the bet after all.

Maxwell was the prototype of today's celebrity groupie, with a solid showbiz background. In the 1920s, Maxwell toured with a Shakespeare company, but it was a high society party for Arthur Balfour (the British Secretary of Foreign Affairs) at the Ritz Hotel in Paris that established her as a world-famous hostess with the mostess. She was an accomplished pianist and composer, as well as an author ("Elsa Maxwell's Own Story," and "How To Do It"). She had her own radio program, and described herself as "a short, fat, homely piano player from Keokuk Iowa, with no background or money [who] decided to become a legend and did just that!" A regular guest on the old Tonight show (hosted by Jack Paar), Maxwell died in late 1963.

This was her second and last film with George Reeves. A portrait of Maxwell by Vogue artist Ren Bouch hangs in the Smithsonian Museum, giving credit to her legend.

Also in the cast is William Hopper, son of Hedda and deWolf Hopper. William worked in many films with George Reeves in 1940, including *'Til We Meet Again, Calling Philo Vance, Virginia City, Knute Rockne, All American, The Fighting 69th*, and *Tear Gas Squad*. Like George, Hopper found fame on television as private investigator Paul Drake on the long running Perry Mason show with Raymond Burr.

CAST: Elsa Maxwell, George Reeves, Marilyn Merrick, Leonid Kinskey, Robert Homans, John Ridgely, and William Hopper.

A WARNER BROTHERS PICTURE; Directed by Ray Enright; Screenplay by Owen Crump and Richard Weil; From an original story by Richard Weil; Director of Photography: Arthur L. Todd; Film Editor: Louis Hesse; Production Designer: Charles Novi; Dialogue Director: Harry Seymour; Costumes by Orry Kelly; Sound by Charles Lang. Original theatrical release: December 23, 1940. Running time: 20 minutes.

THE STRAWBERRY BLONDE

Tangled Up in the Ivy League

While the studio system of the 1930s and 1940s produced many one hit wonder actors and actresses, dream factories like Warner Brothers stuck with some of their talent and allowed them to develop. James Cagney was truly a movie star in training! His breakout role in Warner's 1931 *Public Enemy* as the unrepentant Tom Powers is only equaled by Edward G. Robinson's performance the year before in *Little Caesar*. Cagney, Bogart, Robinson, to name a few, had this carte blanche at Warner's. George Reeves did not.

In Reeves' third pairing with James Cagney, Reeves fares slightly better than in the previous outings. On a Sunday afternoon during the gaslight era, the neighborhood dentist, Biff Grimes (James Cagney), finds himself enjoying a game of horseshoes with Nick, the local barber (George Tobias). In an adjacent backyard, a group of college kids are led in song by a guitar-strumming Yale man named Harold (George Reeves). Resplendent with his slicked-down hair and dapper mustache, Harold is actually an antagonist. When Biff accidentally tosses a horseshoe over the brick wall that divides the two properties, Harold picks a fight with him.

Harold and the young ladies he is entertaining are impressed with 'And the Band Played On,' the song that is being played by a traveling street band. Harold tips the bandleader and asks him to keep playing the popular melody. This doesn't sit too well with Biff, who dislikes the song because its lyrics remind him of a certain strawberry blonde. When Biff orders the band to stop playing, Harold threatens to knock out his teeth. An altercation is avoided, thanks to the brick wall which Biff can't quite overcome, and Harold's quick-thinking girlfriend (Lucille Fairbanks) who restrains the combative college chap.

Biff learns that his former boyhood friend, Hugo Barnstead (Jack Carson) is in need of dental treatment and will soon be calling on him. Seething with anger, Biff reveals to Nick the reasons why he loathes Hugo and the song that could have cost him his teeth.

Via flashback, Biff relives the day that he and Hugo first met Virginia Brush (Rita Hayworth), who was known adoringly in their community as "the strawberry blonde." Biff has eyes for Virginia, but Hugo, the consummate con artist, marries her instead. On the rebound, Biff marries Virginia's best friend, Amy Linn (Olivia deHavilland), a sweet girl who is "bold" enough to work as a nurse.

Some time later, Virginia suggests that her husband, now an enormously successful contractor, can advance Biff's career by offering him a position with Hugo's thriving firm. Biff accepts the job, but isn't the least bit suspicious when he isn't given anything to do except sign a myriad of legal documents, the contents of which he can't even begin to understand. When a wall collapses due to defective materials, a number of people are killed, including Biff's father (Alan Hale). Hugo, who has always exploited the good-natured Biff, tells the authorities that he knows nothing about the use

George (upper left) with Lucille Fairbanks, and George Tobias, and James Cagney in a rare photo from *Strawberry Blonde*.

of inferior materials. Since Biff is the corporate officer who signed all the contracts, it is Biff who must bear all the blame. He spends the next five years behind bars, during which time he earns his dental diploma.

With the flashback over, Biff prepares to "treat" Hugo's toothache. He decides to administer a lethal overdose of gas, then claim medical error. But the dentist has a change of heart after the Barnsteads arrive at his office. Biff tells Hugo that he doesn't hold a grudge against him, while simultaneously yanking the troublesome tooth without the benefit of any gas at all! Virginia finds this painful spectacle amusing, her remorseless laughter an indication of the cruel streak she has acquired from her insufferable husband.

Realizing that he is a happy man while his erstwhile friend is deservedly miserable, Biff no longer hates the Barnsteads or 'And the Band Played On.' In fact, he would like to hear the song one more time. Biff yells over the wall, demanding to know why the band has stopped playing it. Up pops Harold, who indignantly asserts that he and his chums have grown weary of the tune, and that it won't be played. The two men prepare to tear each other up. This time, however, Harold is accompanied by several strapping buddies who leap over the wall, ready to launch an assault on the dentist. Despite his smaller stature, Biff takes on the gang single-handedly. Within seconds, all of the roughnecks, including Harold, are lying on the ground unconscious.

Amy, who disapproves of violence, scolds her husband for acquiring the latest in a succession of black eyes he had endured throughout the film. She whispers something in Biff's ear, and his reaction conveys that a blessed event will soon take place in the Grimes household. The couple stroll down the street to the happy strains of "And the Band Played On" as the picture fades out.

But let's not forget the end credits. Here we have a rollicking reprise of "And The Band Played On," complete with a 'follow the bouncing ball' on the crawl title!

Good Reeves curio, but for special tastes otherwise.

CAST: James Cagney, Olivia deHavilland, Rita Hayworth, Alan Hale, Jack Carson, George Tobias, Una O'Connor, George Reeves, Lucille Fairbanks, Edward McNamara, Helen Lynd, and Herbert Heywood.

A WARNER BROTHERS-FIRST NATIONAL PICTURE; Executive Producer: Hal B. Wallace; Directed by Raoul Walsh; Associate Producer: William Cagney; Screenplay by Julius J. and Philip G. Epstein; From a play by James Hagen; Director of Photography: James Wong Howe, A.S.C.; Dialogue Director: Hugh Cummings; Art Director: Robert Haas; Film Editor: William Holmes; Sound by Robert B. Lee; Special Effects by Willard Van Enger, A.S.C.; Make-up by Perc Westmore; Gowns by Orry-Kelly; Music by H. Roemheld; Orchestral Arrangements: Ray Heindorf; Musical Director: Leo F. Forbstein. Original theatrical release: February 22, 1941. Running time: 98 minutes.

DEAD MEN TELL
Future Hero, Chinese Sage

Earl Derr Biggers' famous detective Charlie Chan was brought to life by Swedish actor Warner Oland in the 20th Century-Fox features. From 1930 to 1937 Oland starred in 16 films, and was scheduled to appear in more when he was taken ill and died in his native Sweden. In 1938, actor Sidney Toler stepped in, and portrayed the Chinese sleuth (both at 20th Century-Fox and at Monogram) until his death in 1947. The Fox Chans are superior to the Monograms, and *Dead Men Tell* is a stellar example, even if produced by the lot's B-unit.

This Charlie Chan programmer centers around an old pirate map unearthed by an elderly eccentric, Patience Nodbury (Ethel Griffies), who is sponsoring a much publicized treasure hunt. Nodbury arranges the expedition with the assistance of Steve Daniels (Robert Weldon), a smooth talking entrepreneur. But with a sixty million dollar jackpot at stake, someone

George (third from the left), Sidney Toler (center), and the cast confront the ghostly pirate in a scene from *Dead Men Tell*.

attempts to steal the map from Nodbury just before her ship embarks for Cocas Island. As a result, Nodbury postpones the hunt.

Lieutenant Charlie Chan (Sidney Toler) turns up on the dreary vessel, the Suva Star, which is docked in an equally dreary harbor. While searching for his "number two son," the detective comes face to face with Nodbury. She tells him about the attempted theft, and how the map has now been divided into four portions for precautionary measures. Nodbury has retained one piece, while the other three have been given to various members of her party for safekeeping. She intends to reassemble them once the ship eventually reaches its destination. Chan's attention is eventually drawn to the portraits on the wall, one of which depicts Matthew Nodbury, an ancestor known as Black Hook. There is a legend surrounding this notorious pirate, whose distinctive getup includes the traditional peg leg and sinister iron hook. Nodbury says whenever a member of her family is about to die, Black Hook's ghost materializes to guide the doomed soul into the "next world."

Later that evening, Daniels introduces Chan to a suspicious looking character, Bill Lydig (George Reeves), who has been lurking around the ship. While propped comfortably in his cabin bed, Lydig says he is a reporter from St. Louis, on board to cover the story of the treasure hunt. Chan finds this a bit strange, since the "Mr. Lydig" he knows to be a newspaper man died some time ago. Lydig says it was his brother Phil who passed on.

Though the cruise has been termporarily called off, the other members of the expedition begin to show up after being phoned by an anonymous caller. Suddenly, a blood-curdling scream is heard. Kate Ransome (Sheila Ryan), one of the passengers, recoils in terror when she detects movement inside a coffin-like crate. The unfortunate lad trapped inside the thing is Jimmy Chan (Sen Young), who is a stowaway. The elder Chan wonders why Miss Nodbury didn't respond to Kate's scream. Kate goes to check on Nodbury, only to find the old woman's body on the floor. One of the other passengers, Jed Thomasson (Don Douglas), suggests Nodbury was frightened to death, taking into accound her firm belief in ghosts. Not surprisingly, Nodbury's piece of the map is missing.

Chan believes Nodbury's death is attributable to Black Hook, and there's sufficient evidence to support his theory. First, there's the look of fear etched on the victim's face. Then, there are the imprints of a peg leg on the floor, along with the ominous scratches embedded on Nodbury's cabin door. In truth, this "ghost" has left behind traces of theatrical make-up and strands of a cheap wig. These findings place suspicion on another passenger, Charles Thursday (Paul McGrath), an actor traveling with his new bride (Kay Aldridge). From a respectable distance, Lydig listens to every word as everyone ponders how the murder could have been committed.

Chan orders his son to find a telephone and summon the police. As Jimmy walks across the dimly lit deck, he is approached by a startling figure. It is Lydig, who pretends to be gathering information for the feature story he's writing. While asking questions, Lydig quietly picks up a large wooden pin and attempts to strike Jimmy. But when Lydig realized he's being watched, he quickly drops the pin in the ocean. Young Chan hears the splashing sound, and asks what dropped in the water. Lydig says it must have been a flying fish. "I'd sure like to catch one," says Jimmy. "You almost did!" says Lydig.

At a sleazy waterfront saloon, Jimmy spots Captain Kane (Truman Bradley) and tells him about the murder. Jimmy also overhears the conversation of a strange couple, seated at a table sequestered from the other patrons. The woman, Dr. Anne Bonney (Lenita Lane), is conferring with her patient, a fey looking character named Gene La Farge (Milton Parsons). She advises him to go to the police and disclose "everything" about the murder. Believing he has stumbled upon a confession in the making, Jimmy overreacts and winds up falling in the ocean through a trap door. When this information is relayed to Chan, Dr. Bonney offers a plausible explanation. She says La Farge is suffering from an "anxiety neurosis," and is attempting to face unpleasant situations head on, as part of his therapy. La Farge, in turn, admits he saw Nodbury's body on the floor, but swears he had nothing to do with her death. La Farge also tells Chan he witnessed Lydig's attempt to clobber Jimmy. Lydig, who is present during this exchange, becomes incredulous. "What? He yells at Jimmy. "Did I try and hit you with a pin?" With all the innocence of a schoolboy, the younger Chan answers,

George, Paul McGrath, serial queen Kay Aldridge, and Sidney Toler in a thoughtful scene from *DEAD MEN TELL*. PHOTO COURTESY OF JOHN ANTOSIEWICZ.

"No. You said it was a fish!" With the guests now pointing fingers at each other, Chan attempts to gather all the map fragments in an effort to avert a second homicide. Even so, pieces of the coveted map begin to get bounced around like a basketball.

Chan and the others notice that Lydig, who had gone to summon the police, has been missing for some time. Kate is also missing. She is found unconscious, though in good condition, after having been stuffed in an iron museum piece. After coming to, Kate describes how Lydig put his hand over her mouth and shoved her into the contraption. Lydig did this because Kate was in possession of an incriminating magazine article, one which reveals him to be a criminal at large. All attention is now focused on the pseudo newspaper reporter. However, Lydig is eliminated as a suspect when his corpse is found tucked inside a bathysphere! Why was Lydig murdered? La Farge has a simple answer: "Dead men tell no tales."

Since no one has managed to summon the police, Chan decides to do it himself. En route to the nearest telephone booth, the veteran detective catches a glimpse of Captain Kane, who has been persistently aloof throughout the case. Kane tells Chan he knows who committed the murders, and recalls a time when he and the killer were partners on a Peruvian expedition. Kane says his former associate suddenly turned greedy and betrayed him, leaving him marooned to die. The scoundrel doesn't know Kane is still alive, hence the reason for the captain's refusal to be seen.

Kane also refuses to disclose the killer's identity, and promises to "handle" him in his own way.

Jimmy manages to convince everyone that Steve Daniels had sufficient motive to kill Nodbury and Lydig. In fact, his argument is so convincing that the police immediately take Daniels into custody. Thomasson, however, says he doesn't believe Steve is the murderer. Chan tells his son that an innocent man has been sent to prison. "Now is time to set trap for real murderer," he says. Chan knows the true killer possesses three pieces of the map, all of which are useless without the fourth fragment. With the missing portion secured in his pocket, Chan concocts a tantalizing trap.

As father and son walk across the harbor, Chan instructs Jimmy to listen for a whistling signal, then immediately summon help. Suddenly, La Farge emerges through the fog and approaches Chan, under the pretense of needing directions. While Chan and La Farge exchange remarks, the sound of a dragging peg leg is heard in the distance. Chan gives the whistling signal. Jimmy, however, is unable to respond; once again, he has plummeted into the water. Suddenly, a familiar hook slowly rises up near Chan's face. Undaunted, the detective rips the mask off the "ghost" of Black Hook, revealing a very lively Jed Thomasson hiding underneath. Armed with a pistol, Thomasson boasts how the fourth piece of the map will enable him to "cash in" on all the trouble he's been through. The killer is about to strike Chan, but his efforts are thwarted by an unforeseen attacker. It is Captain Kane, who has been waiting for just the right moment to fire a bullet into Thomasson, his former partner. Chan stops him, advising that it's better to let the law punish the guilty.

The sleuth now has only one more mystery to solve: the disappearance of his number two son. Chan finds Jimmy drying off in the saloon, which is now totally desolate. Jimmy cautions his pop about the trick doorway, and suggests they use another exit. To demonstrate his point, Jimmy walks through an alternate portal—only to fall right back into the murky sea. This time, Jimmy receives some navigational advice from his father. Chan calmly tells his offspring, "Honolulu directly west!"

This Chan offering has an ample amount of atmosphere, to please even the most diehard horror movie fans, and the ensemble cast plays off each other with maximum results. Reeves shows his best acting chops in his shifty portrayal of a newspaper reporter with ulterior motives. One of the best Toler Chans.

CAST: Sidney Toler, Sheila Ryan, Robert Weldon, Sen Young, Don Douglas, Katharine Aldridge, Paul McGrath, George Reeves, Truman Bradley, Ethel Griffies, Lenita Lane, Milton Parsons.

A TWENTIETH CENTURY FOX-PICTURE; Associate Producers: Walter Morosco, Ralph Dietrich; Directed by Harry Lachman; Original Screenplay by John Larkin; Based on the character Charlie Chan created by Earl Derr Biggers; Director of Photography: Charles Clarke, A.S.C.; Art Direction: Richard Day, Lewis Creber; Set Decorations: Thomas Little; Film Editor: Harry Reynolds;

Costumes: Herschel; Sound: Alfred Bruzlin, Harry M Leonard; Musical Direction: Emil Newman. Original theatrical release: March 28, 1941. Running Time: 61 minutes.

BLOOD AND SAND

Hayworth vs. Reeves—Bullfights Among Lovers

Here is a picture that showcases Reeves' acting talents almost as well as *Gone With The Wind*. A role that dreams could have been made of! Another start, a new beginning, better days, and of course some days are better than others. This Technicolor remake of the classic Valentino film was a sure bet to stir audience interest in the early 1940s. War paranoid theater goers yearned for a *Gone With The Wind* substitute, and this epic was a crowd pleaser. George has some great scenes with Rita Hayworth, who is one of the most photogenic ladies to grace the lens of a 1000-pound Technicolor camera.

Juan Gallardo (Tyrone Power) is the handsome but impoverished son of one of the greatest matadors Spain has ever known. Juan enters the ring and begins to win rave reviews in his own right, thereby restoring wealth and honor to the family name. Despite his immense talent, Juan cannot read or write. While returning home by train, he asks a fellow passenger (played by future Superman villain Maurice Cass) to read him the glowing notices he has garnered. All shortcomings aside, Juan is lovingly generous with Carmen (Linda Darnell), the former childhood sweetheart he has married, his sister (Lynn Barri), and his long-suffering mother (Nazimova). He also basks in the adulation he receives from a lingering entourage of former childhood friends.

Juan attracts the attention of the sultry Dona Sol (Rita Hayworth), the niece of a wealthy dignitary. Dona tosses a rose to him after a victory. He, in turn, tosses her his sombrero. Dona invites Juan to a party where he is feted and introduced to several illustrious guests, including the dashing Captain Pierre Lauren (George Reeves), who is the current object of Dona's desire. After a sumptuous dinner, Pierre and Dona assess their relationship. Having ended her affair with Pierre, Dona immediately sets out to snare the married matador. She succeeds. When Carmen learns of her husband's infidelity, she leaves him.

Juan takes to drinking and begins to lose his confidence. As Juan's career falters, one of his friends, Manolo dePalma (Anthony Quinn), begins to emerge as the new star matador. Dona, now totally bored with the declining Juan, becomes infatuated with the up-and-coming Manolo. When Juan and Manolo are scheduled to perform on the same day, all eyes are eagerly focused on them. Before the match, a nervous Juan slips into a chapel to say a prayer. He meets Carmen at the altar, who is there to pray for his safety. Carmen and Juan reaffirm their love for each other.

Behind-the-scenes photo featuring George and Rita Hayworth filming a scene for the Technicolor production of *BLOOD AND SAND*.

Once again, Juan is victorious in the ring. This time, however, he turns his back on the beast and is instantly gored. A grim silence permeates the arena as Juan is brought behind the scenes for treatment. He dies with a grieving Carmen at his side. Dona tosses a rose to Manolo. As the crowd cheers the new victor, the camera pans the ground of the arena, revealing a few scattered flowers near the blood of the slain idol.

This show could have been a breakthrough for Reeves, but sadly he returned to the same routine of character roles.

From *BLOOD AND SAND* with George at the far left end of the table, Tyrone Power at the far right end of the table, and Rita Hayworth at the head of the table.

CAST: Tyrone Power, Linda Darnell, Rita Hayworth, Nazimova, Anthony Quinn, J. Carrol Naish, Lynn Barri, John Carradine, Laird Cregar, William Montague, Vicente Gomez, George Reeves, Pedro deCordoba, Fortunio Bonanova, Victor Kilian, Michael Morris, Charles Stevens, Ann Todd, Cora Sue Collins, Russell Hickes, Maurice Cass, Rex Downing, John Wallace, Jacqueline Dalya, Cullen Johnson, Larry Harris, Ted Fry, and Schuyler Standish.

A 20th CENTURY-FOX PICTURE; Produced by Darryl F. Zanuck; Directed by Rouben Mamoulian; Based on the novel by Vincente Blasco Ibancz; Associate Producer: Robert T. Kane; Screenplay by Jo Swerling; Photographed in Technicolor; Directors of Photography: Ernest Palmer, A.S.C., and Ray Rennahan, A.S.C.; Technicolor Director: Natalie Kalmus; Associate: Morgan Padelford; Music by Alfred Newman; Guitarist: Vicente Gomez; Art Directors: Richard Day and Joseph C. Wright; Set Decoration: Thomas Little; Film Editor: Robert Bischoff; Costumes: Travis Banton; Jewels by Flatch; Sound by W. D. Flick and Roger Heman. Original theatrical release: May 30, 1941. Running time: 125 minutes.

LYDIA

Growing Old With George, in a Box Office Bomb

Lydia is a story of unrequited love, told through a series of flashbacks which span a period of some forty years. It's an episodic journey through time, owing much of its effectiveness to the Westmore make-up team, which transformed the youthful cast into white-haired oldsters. The film is visually rich, with dramatic photography, elaborate sets, and stunning costumes, all of which compensate for a somewhat sluggish screenplay. Most intriguing of all is an impression of what George might have looked like, if he had lived into his seventies. This alone makes *Lydia* a must-see for all devotees of Reeves.

Dr. Michael Fitzpatrick (Joseph Cotten) listens intently to a radio broadcast about Lydia Macmillan (Merle Oberon), a wealthy socialite who operates an institution for blind and crippled children. After returning from a dedication ceremony, Lydia receives a surprise visit from Michael, one of her former admirers. Michael notices how little she's changed since their last meeting many years earlier. "That's one reward for being a spinster," says Lydia. "You don't change. You disintegrate, but you don't change." Michael invites Lydia to his home, without telling her that he's also invited two of her other former beaus. Naturally, Lydia is taken aback when reunited with Bob Willard (George Reeves), a successful nightclub owner, and Frank Audrey (Hans Yaray), a blind pianist. On an elegant terrace overlooking Central Park, Lydia recalls her romances with the three men seated around her.

The time flips back to 1897, where a nubile Lydia shows off the gown she plans to wear at an upcoming ball. Michael, son of the Macmillan's butler, is a struggling young doctor who is very attracted to Lydia. She loves him, but only as a friend. Michael scores a much bigger hit with Granny

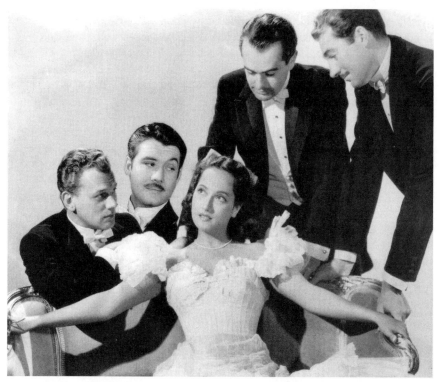

Joseph Cotten, George, Merle Oberon, Hans Yaray, and Allan Marshall in *LYDIA*.

Macmillan (Edna May Oliver), the widowed matriarch of the wealthy Boston family. A feisty hypochondriac, Granny is delighted with Michael's diagnosis of her liver disease (her favorite) and engages him as the new family physician. Granny is at her best when at odds with the vain and headstrong Lydia. Their most humorous clash revolves around Lydia's gown, with its "shameful" open shoulders. According to Granny, a woman who bares her shoulders in public is "parading around in the nude!"

It is at the ball that Lydia meets her "prince charming." Lydia falls for young Bob Willard almost instantly. The two of them waltz around the glittery ballroom, looking as though they're dancing on air. In addition to dancing, Bob excels in football and drinking. He's in no pain, so to speak, after winning the Yale-Harvard football game, which transpires just hours before his introduction to Granny. To ensure a good first impression, Bob is briefed on all the do's and don'ts. Lydia makes him promise to profess a disdain for tobacco, liquor, and President McKinley. When they finally meet, Granny puts the young man to the test, offering him a cigarette and a drink. "I hate cigarettes, strong drink, and McKinley! How's that?" says Bob, slurring his words ever so slightly. All goes well until he demonstrates how the game was won. In his enthusiasm, Bob inadvertently tackles a piece of furniture, a clear indication that he is soused. Granny not only throws Bob out, she forbids him to return. Nevertheless, Lydia plans to elope with him.

When Bob and Lydia are stood up by the Justice of the Peace, they decide to check into their honeymoon suite anyway—just to have dinner. With the kitchen closed for the evening, there will be no dinner. But there is plenty to drink. Bob gets drunk and becomes so obnoxious that his "bride" runs away in sheer anguish. As she darts into a parked carriage, Lydia startles the dapper looking gent who's exiting it. Although she has a hard time getting Bob out of her system, Lydia eventually manages to move on with her life. At the conclusion of this flashback, a very embarrassed Bob learns that he almost ended up being Lydia's "favorite memory."

Next, Lydia begins to relive the day Michael embarked for wartime military service. Moments after Michael departs, Lydia meets a blind boy, Johnny (Billy Ray), who is living in abject poverty. Lydia is so moved by his condition that she vows to offer assistance to all the handicapped children in the slum district. This resolution is the basis for the institution funded by the Macmillan money. It is through her work with the blind youngsters that Lydia meets Frank Audrey. Despite his blindness, Frank is an excellent pianist. One of his gifts is the ability to let music represent such visual wonders as the sun going down, the raging waves in the ocean, dancing clowns, and even the City of Boston! Frank finds Lydia very desirable. And like Michael and Bob before him, he finds her utterly unobtainable.

Merle Oberon and George in a scene from *LYDIA*.

George and Merle Oberon at the party.

Merle Oberon and George in a scene from *LYDIA*. Photo courtesy of John Antosiewicz.

There is a fourth man in Lydia's past. The man of her dreams turns out to be Richard Mason (Allan Marshall), the chap she'd bumped into after running out on Bob. Lydia describes him as "bad, wicked, and as marvelous as they come." They share a cozy retreat (chaperoned, of course) at Macmillan Port, the great house on the ocean where Lydia was born. Then, without warning, Richard goes off to sea. Lydia receives a letter from him, explaining a previous relationship which constitutes a problem. There's a ring enclosed with the letter, an encouraging sign of Richard's intentions.

Merle Oberon, George, Joseph Cotten and Edna May Oliver in a scene from LYDIA.

But when Richard doesn't return, Lydia drifts into melancholia. She lingers at Macmillan Port, hoping to capture any residual echoes of the happiness that occurred there. Finding nothing but ghosts, she goes home unfulfilled. But many moons later, Lydia receives another letter. This time, Richard promises that their wedding will indeed take place on New Year's Eve. Lydia waits at the altar as instructed, but her man never shows up.

Eventually, Lydia agrees to marry Michael, but Granny's untimely death prevents her from doing so. Michael does his best to convince Lydia that he can make her happy, but her heart still belongs to the elusive Richard. "It's too late," she tells Michael. "If I can't have all there is, I don't want less." And with that, Lydia closes the romance chapter of her life, preferring to dedicate her time to the orphanage.

In the present, Michael has one more nostalgic surprise up his sleeve. The door opens and in walks a distinguished, bearded gentleman. It is Captain Richard Mason, looking as "old and crusty" as Lydia and her contemporaries. "What's this reunion all about?" he asks. With hope in her eyes, and trepidation in her voice, Lydia greets the one man she wanted so desperately. But with the passing of so much time, Richard clearly doesn't recognize the elderly woman standing before him. Michael, however, says he would recognize Lydia even "a hundred years from now."

Hurt and embarrassed, Lydia escapes to the terrace where Michael offers some consolation. Reflecting on her bittersweet life, Lydia says she represented different things to different men, and that she's now paying a price for her foolishness. In one of the most poignant endings ever filmed, Lydia realizes that she wasted her love on a man who not only neglected her, but forgot she ever existed.

Lydia in today's world would have been classified as a player, that finally got played. This all star cast, with tremendous supporting actors, should have been a box office bonanza, but once again the public can be a fickle beast. This film is an example of how wrong the mass public can be in their judgment of true art.

Viewed today, this sentimental farce is highly satisfying for connoisseurs of romantic schmaltz, with a manipulative twist.

CAST: Merle Oberon, Edna May Oliver, Alan Marshall, Joseph Cotten, Hans Yaray, George Reeves, John Halliday, and Sara Allgood.

ALEXANDER KORDA FILMS, INC., RELEASED THROUGH UNITED ARTISTS; Produced by Alexander Korda; Directed by Julien Duvivier; Original Story by Julien Duvivier and L. Bush Fekete; Screenplay and Dialogue by Ben Hecht and Samuel Hoffenstein; Production Designed by Vincent Korda; Associate Producer and Director of Photography: Lee Garmes, A.S.C.; Production Manger: Walter Mayo; Art Director: Jack Okey; Make-Up: The House of Westmore; Costumes Designed by Marcel Vertes and Walter Plunkett; Interior Decoration: Julie Heron; Assistant Director: Horace Hough. Original theatrical release: September 12, 1941. Running time: 104 minutes.

MAN AT LARGE
Noir, Reeves

For George Reeves fans, *Man At Large* will come as a pleasant surprise, as it contains the actor's best work since *Always A Bride*. In this one, George is featured as an FBI agent who poses as a not-so-mild-mannered reporter. The most entertaining aspect of this suspenseful tale is George's cat-and-mouse banter with the female reporter (Marjorie Weaver), which clearly foreshadows Clark Kent's professional relationship with Lois Lane (bitchy, yet endearing).

At a Canadian military prison, the guards fire at an escaped Nazi Ace who has fled into the night. The next morning, the incident is splashed all over the front page of *The New York Guardian*. At the paper's editorial offices, Dallas Gilmartin (Marjorie Weaver), a perky receptionist, badgers her boss for a promotion to photographic journalist. At the same time, a dapper character named Bob Grayson (George Reeves) is cooling his heels, also seeking work as a reporter. Both candidates are rejected by Editor Grundy (Richard Lane). Moments later, the elderly Hans Brinker (Kurt Katch) enters the office, fearful that his life is in danger because he's no longer "needed." Sure enough, when Grayson turns his back to take a drink of water, someone zaps

Richard Derr, Marjorie Weaver, and George in a scene from *MAN AT LARGE*.

the old man with a silencer. Before Brinker dies, he warns Grayson about a secret organization known as 'The 21 Whistlers.' Dallas points an accusatory finger at Grayson, and believes he is the killer. In an effort to get her out of his hair, Grundy dispatches Dallas to the Canadian border, on the off-chance that she might locate the escapee, Colonel Max Von Rohn.

At a quiet location near the St. Lawrence River, Max (Richard Derr) confers with Grayson, who is passing himself off as a reporter. "Max" is actually a British Intelligence officer who is impersonating the escaped Colonel in order to infiltrate 'The 21 Whistlers.' In the night air, Max whistles an eerie melody, which is actually a signal used alternately as a means of communication and identification. One of the enemy agents, residing nearby, responds to the call and give Max the "contact" information he'll need for his mission in New York. Dallas catches a glimpse of Max through an open window, and notices the enemy uniform underneath his trench coat. Believing she's cornered the man-at-large, Dallas sneaks into Max's room and snaps a photo of him. Grayson tells his ally not to worry, as he'll catch up with him in New York. And in the meantime, he'll take care of both "the girl" and the incriminating picture. When Grayson snatches the camera away from Dallas, a comical commotion ensues. Because the sheriff (George Cleveland) doesn't know which reporter is the camera thief, he handcuffs the two of them to each other! Seated on the edge of a bed,

Grayson raises his eyebrows at Dallas and asks, "Do you snore?" This type of humor abounds throughout the movie, and balances nicely with the darker elements of the script. Curiously, there is no musical scoring in the film, even during the edgy scenes.

When Dallas returns to New York, she interviews Charles Botany (Steve Geray), an author of detective stories. Dallas is surprised to discover that he is blind. Believing that Botany is a harmless eccentric, Dallas discloses everything she knows about Grayson who, in her mind, is a Nazi sympathizer. In his soft German-accented voice, Botany encourages Dallas to pursue Grayson, a ploy that leads the tenacious reporter to a second-rate hotel. The desk clerk (Elisha Cook, Jr.) refuses to let Dallas visit Grayson in his room, as this is a "respectable joint." Nevertheless, she manages to sneak up to room 224, where Grayson and Max are deciphering clues in a radio commercial for Dr. Cataloni, a prominent throat specialist. Grayson finds Dallas lurking behind the door. In one of the film's most amusing bits, the two brawny heros are seen rolling over the bed in a tussle with the diminutive reporter, whose screams are drowned out by the radio. They leave her tied up with a note on her mouth: "Do not open till X-mas!"

Grayson and Max visit Dr. Cataloni's office. Max poses as the patient while Grayson sits out in the reception area. A sinister figure greets Max in

George and Marjorie Weaver find a corpse in *MAN AT LARGE*.

Publicity photo of dapper George from *MAN AT LARGE*.

the examination room. It is Botany. The phoney doc instructs him to swallow an elixir, supposedly a routine part of the exam. Max whistles the melody, and asks for assistance in getting back to Germany. Moments later, the "patient" passes out from the liquid he has just consumed. Just then, the real Dr. Cataloni enters through a back door. Even though the doctor is a card-carrying member of the organization, he is horrified to see his office being used for such tactics.

Out in the waiting room, a nervous Grayson has one more problem to deal with—Dallas. Once again she has appeared out of nowhere, this time to "warn" the doctor. Grayson vehemently tells Dallas that she must leave at once. She doesn't. When the two of them burst into the examination room, they find only one person, the real physician, lying on the floor. At this point, Grayson realizes the need to confide in Dallas, and divulges his true identity as an FBI agent. He also explains how Max, an officer with British Naval Intelligence, was purposely "detailed" in order to expose the enemy agents. Not believing one iota of this, Dallas manages to leave the G-man chained to an office typewriter. The next day, the headlines scream: "Typewriter Repair Man Sought for Murder of Dr. Cataloni!"

Marjorie Weaver and George find each other in *Man at Large*.

Dallas revisits Botany and tells him everything, including Grayson's alleged connection to the FBI. The two of them confer over the suspicious doctor, who had his watch repaired a dozen times within one month. With Botany's encouragement, Dallas decides to snoop around the watch repair shop owned by Otto Kisling. Botany orders his servant to take care of both Kisling and the girl.

That night, Dallas quietly slips into Kisling's shop. In the dark, a mysterious figure sneaks up behind Dallas and covers her mouth. It is Grayson, who orders her to leave at once. When a cuckoo clock sounds off, the startled Dallas jumps into Grayson's arms. The disturbance alerts Kisling (William Edmunds), who holds the duo at gunpoint. Grayson warns Kisling that the people he had been working for are now finished with him, and that his life is in danger. He also assures him that he'll receive police protection if he cooperates with the FBI. Kisling doesn't get a chance to think it over; he is shot on the spot by an unseen sniper. In his last moments, Kisling manages to whisper some vital clues. Following this, Grayson tells Dallas that he is really counting on her. If she cooperates with him, he'll guarantee her the exclusive story the moment it breaks.

The action shifts to a sleazy nightclub. The set is instantly recognizable to anyone familiar with Fox's B-movies of the period. Backstage, Grayson discreetly observes the management, a sinister looking elderly couple. When the old lady receives an envelope, she immediately telephones Botany, who warns her to be extremely careful tonight, as the FBI is lurking about. After he hangs up, Botany gleefully informs Max (who's strapped to a chair) that his organization has just received the complete details of the Navy convoy sailing. Meanwhile, Grayson and Dallas have become instant thespians and take to the stage. Their "act" will be the old mind-reading technique where the female assistant, stationed in the audience, holds up an object to be identified by the blindfolded psychic. By accident, Dallas intercepts the envelope containing the secret information acquired by the enemy. Following a mild ruckus, Dallas informs Grayson that she's been feeding information to Botany all along. Grayson immediately phones someone named Ruby to request assistance at the Botany residence. Dallas assumes that "Ruby" is Grayson's wife, much to her disappointment.

Grayson and Dallas sneak into the Botany house. Wearing a headset, Botany is busy in the transmission room, relaying the classified information to Berlin. When he discovers the intruders, Dallas identifies herself under the pretense of making a social call. Though Botany is blind, his other senses are razor sharp; he knows that Grayson is also in the room. The climactic showdown between Grayson and Botany is charged with tension. When Grayson blows a police whistle to summon help, Botany fires a few shots in his direction. Grayson is unarmed, thanks to Dallas, who removed the bullets from his gun. However, the resourceful G-man pulls the carpet out from under Botany, causing him to fall. After Grayson gets hold of the loaded weapon, he releases Max, still restrained in the adjoining chamber.

When FBI boss Walter Ruby arrives, Grayson keeps his word and credits Dallas with turning up the major lead in the case. Suddenly, a cuckoo clock announces the hour. Dallas, startled as usual, jumps right into Max's arms. "Here, here, here," shouts an irate Grayson. With a 'that's-my-girl' gesture, Grayson grabs Dallas and plants a big one right on her lips.

The late George E. Turner (creator of THE FORGOTTEN HORROR series, author of THE MAKING OF KING KONG and former editor of *American Cinematographer* magazine) once told us that in his learned opinion, *Man at Large* was the quintessential Reeves performance. There can be no doubt that this is another example of Reeves' superior acting chops. Like a confident musician on a solo, Reeves' acting is believable and assured, yet tender in places.

This film also boasts a roster of future Superman co-stars Steve Geray (The Deadly Rock), Lucien Littlefield (The Runaway Robot), and Elisha Cook, Jr. (Semi-Private Eye).

Richard Derr is an excellent antagonist for Reeves, and is the protagonist in George Pal's 1953 production of *When Worlds Collide*.

This show could have ensured George movie stardom, but once again so many things in life slip through our fingers.

CAST: Marjorie Weaver, George Reeves, Richard Derr, Steve Geray, Milton Parsons, Spencer Charters, Lucien Littlefield, Elisha Cook, Jr., Minerva Urecal, Bodil Ann Rosing, Richard Lane, Barbara Pepper, William Edmunds, George Cleveland, Kurt Katch.

A TWENTIETH CENTURY FOX-PICTURE; Produced by Ralph Dietrich; Directed by Eugene Forde; Original Screenplay by John Larkin; Director of Photography: Virgil Miller, A.S.C.; Art Direction: Richard Day and Lewis Creber; Set Decoration: Thomas Little; Film Editor: John Brady; Costumes: Herschel; Sound: Oscar Lagerstrom and Harry M. Leonard; Musical Direction: Emil Newman. Original theatrical release: September 26 or October 3, 1941. Running time: 69 minutes.

BLUE, WHITE AND PERFECT
To Excitement, Adventure, Romance, and Mystery!

Fast paced and decidedly amusing, *Blue, White and Perfect* is an entry in Fox's "Michael Shayne, Private Detective" series. Lloyd Nolan, one of the most recognizable character actors in motion pictures, is totally believable in the role of the wily sleuth created by Brett Halliday. Blue is especially interesting because it provides George with ample screen time, and an opportunity to demonstrate his linguistic skills. With remarkable fluency, he delivers a toast in Spanish at the beginning of an ocean voyage that promises to be full of "excitement, adventure, and romance," to which Shayne adds "mystery." George, in his third outing as an Hispanic character, is highly effective.

Lloyd Nolan and George are under ship's arrest in *BLUE, WHITE, AND PERFECT.*

Mike Shayne gets himself employed as a riveter in an aircraft company, hoping the job will appease Merle (Mary Beth Hughes) his temperamental girlfriend who tosses knick-knacks in his face. Minutes after he's hired, an alarm is sounded when some industrial diamonds are stolen from the plant. Mike's boss explains that industrial diamonds are regulated by the government, as they are essential in grinding various elements vital to the war effort. The detective soon learns how the stones are ingeniously smuggled out of the States by a gang of Nazis. Operating out of a Los Angeles dress shop, the spies conceal the diamonds inside buttons, which are then sewn onto each garment. Trunks full of these specially "decorated" dresses are shipped to Hawaii, then immediately transported to German factories. Shayne loses the first round in his battle against the enemy agents. However, after getting fired, money becomes his number one problem. So he resorts to larceny, swindling Merle out of $1,000 in a phoney real estate transaction. This sizable sum enables Shayne to board the Princess Nola, the vessel transporting the contraband to Honolulu.

Aboard ship, Shayne runs into an old acquaintance, Helen Shaw (Helene Reynolds), who is traveling under the name Connie Ross. She is in cahoots with one of the smugglers, Rudolf Hagerman (Henry Victor), who is also aboard. Connie's reunion with Shayne is interrupted by a suave stranger named Juan Arturo O'Hara (George Reeves), who introduces himself as "one of the nicest chaps you'll ever know." He explains that his dual ethnic name is attributable to his father, who "married a wonderful girl from Chile." All smiles and kidding aside, O'Hara is a no-nonsense FBI agent who is secretly trailing Connie and the diamonds. As the journey gets underway, Mike,

O'Hara, and Connie get acquainted over cocktails. While making small talk, O'Hara mentions that Nappy (Curt Bois), an innocuous looking steward, can discern much about a passenger simply by unpacking his or her luggage. In a display of ability, Nappy reckons that O'Hara is "a banker by profession." The G-man goes along with this incorrect assessment, knowing it will help snuff out any suspicions that might interfere with his work.

Soon after the party, Shayne begins to search for the diamonds by rummaging through a few of the trunks. He finds nothing. What the detective doesn't realize is that O'Hara is watching his every move, from a respectable distance, in the darkened storage area. This spectacle causes the agent to conclude that Shayne is a member of the smuggling ring. During the course of events, Hagerman fires a few shots at the sleuth, utilizing a silencer, but misses each time.

On the last night of the voyage, Shayne, Connie, and O'Hara gather for a round of farewell drinks. Suddenly, a messenger arrives with a note, inviting the threesome to a midnight scavenger hunt—for buttons! Connie immediately perceives this as a trap orchestrated by Hagerman; she wastes no time in dashing over to his cabin. Hagerman tells her what Shayne and O'Hara already know: There are no diamonds to be found in any buttons. With Shayne already wise to the button trick, the spies have devised a new smuggling technique. The stones are now disguised to resemble candy, packed in jars like a homemade confection. Hagerman gives Connie a "bon voyage basket" containing the inconspicuous jars, which she is ordered to deliver.

During the scavenger hunt, O'Hara closes in on Shayne and attempts to arrest him. The two men get into a scuffle in one of the lower compartment

George, Helene Reynolds, and Lloyd Nolan (seated) in *BLUE, WHITE, AND PERFECT*.

hatches. Although the detective manages to hold his own, he is no match for O'Hara and is quickly overpowered. Fortunately, Shayne manages to establish his true identity just as he is about to be handcuffed by the overzealous agent. O'Hara apologizes for his error, and says that they've both acted like a couple of "four star saps." In the meantime, Hagerman has quietly locked the two men in the hatch, and activated a valve which produces a flood. With the water rising higher and higher, O'Hara reveals that he initiated the scavenger hunt, hoping it would ultimately incriminate Shayne, Connie, and "the guy with the silencer." While retaining her anonymity, Connie notifies the captain about the flooding. Captain McCordy (Arthur Loft) arrives on the scene and drains the water by employing a flood control device. As Shayne and O'Hara walk back to the deck, Hagerman fires another shot at the detective. He hits O'Hara instead.

The ship's doctor is summoned, and the wounded agent is told that the bullet missed his lung "by a hair." With O'Hara out of commission, Shayne must solve the case singlehandedly. In an upbeat mood, O'Hara jokingly warns the sleuth to "watch out for silencers!" His last line in the film is an appropriate one: "Buenas Noches!" Moments after leaving O'Hara's bedside, Shayne learns that Hagerman has been found dead.

In Honolulu, Shayne manages to snag one of the jars from the basket Connie is fiercely guarding. After nearly cracking a tooth on one of the goodies, he pays a visit to the gown salon which Connie owns. Shayne addresses her as Helen—her real name. Angered by Shayne's tenacity, Helen points a pistol at the unflappable detective. Despite all her street smarts, Helen believes she was involved in a routine diamond heist. She can't quite fathom that the stones are industrial diamonds, intended to wind up in the hands of enemy agents. Shayne urges her to take a closer look. "There's nothing blue, white and perfect about these," he says. Just as Helen is about to disclose the identity of the ring leader, she is shot with a silencer. The gunman is none other than Nappy, who laconically explains that he killed Hagerman for being such a lousy shot. As Shayne is about to meet the same fate, he cries; "O'Hara! Don't shoot him in the back!" O'Hara, of course, is nowhere in sight, but the trick works nonetheless. Shayne hurls an object in Nappy's face, then knocks him to the floor.

With Merle back in the picture, Shayne finds himself facing prosecution for grand larceny. However, he patches things up with some sweet talk, a newspaper headline that screams, NAZI SPIES ROUTED BY RIVETER, and a marriage license. Merle is relieved to know that Mike didn't spend the money on some "dame" on a cruise ship. Unfortunately, this moment of bliss doesn't last very long. Suddenly, a corpse falls out of a closet with a cryptic note attached to it. With the challenge of a new case dangling before him, Mike announces that he's off to Manila. In typical fashion, Merle tosses a vase at the detective as he makes a hasty exit.

Full of atmosphere, with more twists than a six-headed snake, *Blue, White and Perfect* is a jewel. Lloyd Nolan carries the show with more than excellent support from George. Once again, it's a pity that George doesn't have more sides. Imagine George as Mike Shayne! It has been rumored that

George was to take over the Dick Tracy T.V. series (after Superman) from screen mate Ralph Byrd (*Jungle Goddess, Thunder in the Pines*).

George and star Lloyd Nolan have a stage irony insofar as he was a student at the Pasadena Playhouse a few years prior to George, and he played Biff Grimes in the Broadway hit of 1933, *One Sunday Afternoon*, which was made for the screen three times. George was a supporting player in the Jimmy Cagney version, *The Strawberry Blonde*.

Nolan's career spanned from the mid-1930s to the mid-1980s, with his last role on one of television's most popular mystery shows, "Murder She Wrote" starring Angela Lansbury. Nolan had a co-starring part on the late 1960s–early 1970s TV hit "Julia," starring Diahann Carroll. He was the first actor to portray the paranoiac Captain Queeg on stage in "The Caine Mutiny Court Martial" which debuted on Broadway in 1953. He can be seen in such favorites as *Johnny Apollo* (1940), *The Lemon Drop Kid* (1951), *Airport* (1970), and *Earthquake* (1974).

CAST: Lloyd Nolan, Mary Beth Hughes, Helene Reynolds, George Reeves, Steve Geray, Henry Victor, Curt Bois.

A TWENTIETH-CENTURY-FOX PICTURE; Executive Producer: Sol M. Wurtzel; Directed by Herbert I. Leeds; Screenplay by Samuel G. Engel; Based on the Story by Borden Chase, and the character "Mike Shayne" created by Brett Halliday; Director of Photography: Glen MacWilliams, A.S.C.; Art Direction: Richard Day, Lewis Creber; Set Decorations: Thomas Little; Film Editor: Alfred Day; Costumes: Herschel; Sound: Alfred Bruzlin, Harry M. Leonard; Technical Advisor: Det. Lieut. Frank L. James; Musical Direction: Emil Newman. Original theatrical release: December 24, 1941. Running time: 78 minutes.

SEX HYGIENE
Not to be screened after meals

This army training film is a ten minute documentary about venereal disease. Produced for the exclusive viewing of men in uniform, the film does not credit its cast or crew. It begins with a lengthy narrative, with words printed in black letters on a white background, just like the pages of a textbook. The viewer is warned this will be a "straightforward account of the effects of venereal disease which may result from illicit sexual intercourse." The commentary suggests that any soldier who does not keep himself in good condition is a "shirker," since he is requiring his comrades to do his work as well as their own. The film also tries to sell the idea that "medical science has definitely proved that a man can be healthy, and actually stronger, if he avoids sexual relations!"

A young sergeant (George Reeves), stands before his commanding officer to discuss the recent outbreak of venereal disease. In an effort to educate the

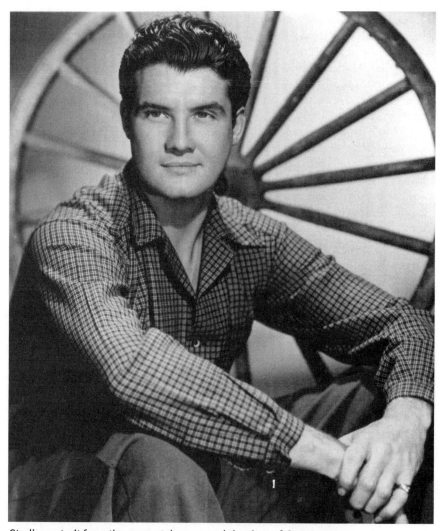

Studio portrait from the 1940s taken around the time of *SEX HYGIENE*.

men, Captain Brown has ordered the entire unit to view a film in the War Department theater. George is given the task of posting the order for all personnel to see. As Reeves walks away with the order in hand, his only line of dialogue is, "Yes, sir!"

Seated in the small theater, the men pay close attention to the medical officer, depicted on the screen, speaking directly to the camera. The doctor acknowledges the fact that all young men have strong sexual impulses. However, according to the Army, the best way to avoid contracting VD is total abstinence. We see some footage of organisms that cause such diseases as sleeping sickness, malaria, gonorrhea, and syphilis. After explaining how communicable diseases are transmitted, the doctor states that most men know more about their automobiles than their own bodies. Therefore, it is necessary to expound on the basic "plumbing" of male anatomy. (Keep in mind that in the 1940s, sex education was not part of the standard curriculum as it is today.) A large photograph of a man's body, naked from the chest down, is displayed. After a few words regarding the genitalia, the doctor moves on to the liver, stomach, bowel, and bladder. George and the other men have a few closeups as they listen intently to this utterly fascinating discourse.

When the subject shifts to actual symptoms of VD, the scare tactics begin. Most disturbing of all is the explicit footage of rotting flesh, seen on the genitals of the poor chaps who have been infected. This is followed by a review of the other possible manifestations, including sores, rashes, boils, puss, and scarring. Since insanity is also a complication, there's a shot of a restrained patient, undergoing some sort of torturous treatment, thrown in for good measure. The men are encouraged to seek medical treatment at once, should they notice the first sign of infection. "Do not permit yourself to be treated by a quack or druggist," the examiner warns. Proper methods of prevention, including the use of prophylactics, are also addressed.

The doctor concludes by saying, "It is hoped you will use your good common sense and continue to be good soldiers and citizens in the service of your country." This is followed by more textbook advice, after which the end title finally appears.

The graphic display of sexual folly rivals anything dished up on present day reality television. In fact, it manages to gross out contemporary programming in black and white. This is not a must for fans of George, and is only recommended for total completists. Sold in many genre magazines along with the training films on drug use, driving, dating, and other such nostalgic nonsense.

George, and a host of other Hollywood servicemen, made loads of these training films during the Second World War. A good many of these films have not survived, being recycled or destroyed. Two examples that did survive are *The Rear Gunner* (1943) with Burgess Meredith and Ronald Reagan (George is seen as a navigator and is unbilled) and *Airborne Lifeboat*, in which George appears as a pilot and is given billing. It's anyone's guess how many of these films George made, but one other film is listed on Internet Movie Database (IMDb) as a Reeves credit, *My Love Came Back* (Warner Brothers 1940). George plays "Sears," a character deleted from the final print. IMDb lists him as appearing in the trailer only. Maybe you readers have found more Reeves films?

Veteran actor Samuel S. Hines is the celluloid medical officer in this training film. He is best remembered for his numerous roles in Universal's horror series, Abbott & Costello features, Dr. Kildare dramas, and serials, westerns, and A-features. He was a lawyer before he began his acting career—ironic as he often played a lawyer or a judge.

SEX HYGIENE—OFFICIAL TRAINING FILM NO. 8-1238; War Department Restricted; Produced by The Signal Corps in collaboration with the Surgeon General through the cooperation of The Research Council, Academy of Motion Picture Arts and Sciences. Produced in 1941. Running time: 30 minutes.

THE MAD MARTINDALES

Nob Hill Nutters

Set in 1900, this saga centers around Kathy Martindale (Jane Withers), a spunky teenager with an absorbing interest in women's rights. Her father, Hugo (Alan Mowbray), is a great architect but a lousy manager of money. This is evidenced by the fact that the Martindales live in a magnificent Nob Hill mansion, but can't afford to pay the utility bills. Kathy and her older sister Evelyn (Marjorie Weaver) remain oblivious to their dad's squandering—until the water is shut off and the lights go out. In an effort to sort things out, Hugo takes a trip to Del Monte. Evelyn also escapes to the same locale, to address her problems "of the heart." Because her boyfriend, Peter Varney (Byron Barr), isn't the most romantic of young men, Evelyn dumps him in favor of a handsome violinist, Julio (George Reeves).

Back home, Kathy is stunned to learn that her father is seriously in debt, owing $2,500 in mortgage payments. Realizing that her father could lose the estate, Kathy discharges the domestic staff and pays them off with the priceless antiques Hugo has recklessly purchased. Kathy's boyfriend Bobby (Jimmy Lydon) then comes up with the idea of selling the household furnishings in order to pay off the debt. While Kathy is successfully working out her father's affairs, her older sibling isn't faring too well in the romance department. That's because Julio, having learned that the Martindales are broke, has no interest in marrying Evelyn.

When the investment counselor Mr. Hickling (played by the stern-faced Charles Lane), drops by to collect the back payments, he informs Kathy that her father still has an $8,000 debt on the books. This setback causes Peter to sympathize with Kathy, and he introduces her to his wealthy grandmother (Kathleen Howard), much to the chagrin of a jealous Bobby. Grandmother Varney takes a liking to young "Miss Martindale" and automatically assumes that she is Pete's fiancée. Kathy, in fact, does become enamored of Pete, especially after he presents her with a check from Grandma. Kathy, however, does not accept the gift.

When Evelyn returns home, she is shocked by the paucity of items in the Martindale home. By this time, Julio has cast aside all reservations about marriage. This is solely because Hugo is now involved in a property deal with Van Der Venne (Steve Geray), a man he met in Del Monte. Fortified with this information, Julio has come to call on Evelyn. But the Martindales are caught up in many entanglements which seem to be looming toward disaster. Ultimately, Pete's grandmother is the one who steps in and brings order out of chaos. Because she owns the controlling interest in the mortgage company, Mrs. Varney is able to leally expunge Hugo's debt. She also gives her approval for Pete and Kathy to tie the knot, despite the difference in their ages.

Having grown weary of all the Martindale madness, Julio decides to depart. So does Van Der Venne. Remembering that Hugo is a top-notch

George stares up at Jane Withers on the stairs in a rare still from *THE MAD MARTINDALES*. Anything related to this film is considered by collectors ultra-rare. In 2003, a videotape of this film reportedly sold for over $200 on eBay.

architect, Grandma finances his latest venture, and gives him the job of designing a honeymoon home for Pete and Kathy.

By 1942, playing accented playboys and aristocrats had become second nature to George, so there was nothing in this light-hearted farce that presented any challenges for him. According to early story outlines, George's character was to be called Mishka Rigo and Jane Withers' character was originally named Mabel. This film marked the second time George was paired with Marjorie Weaver, as the two of them had co-starred in Fox's *Man at Large* the previous year. Byron Barr (also known as Bryant Fleming), who played the role of Peter Varney, later changed his name to Gig Young and went on to achieve major stardom in motion pictures. In 1978, Young shocked the entertainment community when he apparently shot and killed his new wife, then himself. He was 64.

Another rare autographed photo of George and Marjorie Weaver in a scene from *THE MAD MARTINDALES.*

In real life, George and Gig were the best of friends! This is evidenced by photographs from the mid-50s of the two actors together, with groups of children. Gig outlived George by nineteen years, but ended up in the same situation as George, with a younger woman. Both thespians enjoyed wine, woman, and song, and maybe didn't make the best choices in life partners.

When the "E" Channel's 'Mysteries and Scandals' profiled Gig Young's murder/suicide, they noted that the gun had to be pried from Gig's hand, after his self-inflicted wound was discharged. Maybe George's gun was a little too oily to retain the death grip. Maybe? Maybe not.

In 1951, Gig Young was nominated for Best Supporting Actor in the riveting *Come Fill My Cup*, starring James Cagney; and in the same category in 1958 for *Teacher's Pet.* Young finally won Best Supporting Actor for his work in *They Shoot Horses, Don't They* in 1969.

Steven Geray, who worked with George in *Man at Large* and *Blue, White, and Perfect* is on board lending support. Geray co-starred in the Superman episode "The Deadly Rock."

The Mad Martindales is seldom seen, and VHS copies command high prices on eBay.

Alan Werker, the director of *The Mad Martindales*, was noted primarily for his "B" mysteries, but he occasionally tackled comedies. Werker's best remembered credits at Fox are *The Adventures of Sherlock Holmes* (1939), starring Basil Rathbone as the master sleuth, and the Vincent Price thriller, *Shock* (1946). Werker died in 1975 at the age of 78.

CAST: Jane Withers, Marjorie Weaver, Alan Mowbray, Jimmy Lydon, Byron Barr (Gig Young), George Reeves, Charles Lane, Kathleen Howard, Robert Greig, Steven Geray, Victor Sen Young, Emma Dunn.

A TWENTIETH CENTURY–FOX PICTURE; Produced by Walter Morosco; Directed by Alfred Werker; Screenplay by Francis Edward Faragoh; Based on the play by Ludwig Hirschfeld, Welsley Towner, and Edmund Wolf; Director of Photography: Lucien N. Andriot, A.S.C.; Film Editor: Nick DeMaggio; Music by Emil Newman. Original theatrical release: May 15, 1942.
Running time: 65 minutes.

THE LAST WILL AND TESTAMENT OF TOM SMITH

A Film for Uncle Sam, a Premonition, and a Cinematic Execution

Long sheets of crumpled paper illustrate the opening titles to this wartime propaganda short. Scattered among the credits are a few unobtrusive little drawings, supposedly scrawled by the title character. The narrator sets the tone: "This is the story of Tom Smith, prisoner of war. This is the story of a man in a prison cell. This is the story of death in Japan."

The camera takes us inside the grim cell where Tom Smith (George Reeves) is gazing through a barred window. We hear his thoughts as he contemplates the irony of his situation. Here is a man incarcerated in a place that reeks of death. And yet, he can behold the beauty of the cherry blossoms visible from his tiny cell window. A few moments later, a guard delivers a grim message: Tom is to be executed in twenty minutes. Tom is stunned, of course, but doesn't lose control. He explains that he is merely an aviator, caught in the duty of service to his country. The guard, however, isn't moved by Tom's sincerity and he quickly disappears. Resigned to his fate, Tom decides to spend the last twenty minutes of his life writing his last will and testament.

The condemned man begins by memorializing the date: April 18, 1943. Tom realizes he has nothing in the way of material things, such as stocks, bonds, or pictures, that he can bequeath to anyone. He can leave nothing behind, except words. The first person to enter Tom's thoughts is Grace (Barbara Britton), the girl he had hoped to marry after the war. A flashback to their first meeting, set in a sunny countryside, is short and sweet. Tom wills Grace "a Sunday in June."

Tom begins to recall his roots, especially the kids on his block; he wills them the "chance to be the things they want to be." Tom remembers how he had always wanted to fly; these thoughts segue into a flashback of his first airborne view of the land below. "I also leave behind me the American earth. All of it—the way I first saw it—solid, real, green," he writes.

Tom remembers his grandfather. Another flashback introduces the wheelchair-bound "Gramps" (Lionel Barrymore). On the front porch, Gramps expounds that "freedom" and "dignity" are more than just words in a textbook; there is a price that must be paid for these things. He also suggests that young men owe something to those who have passed before them. Tom listens respectfully, then interjects some of his own reflections. Tom and Gramps then chat briefly with the mailman (Walter Brennan), who hands

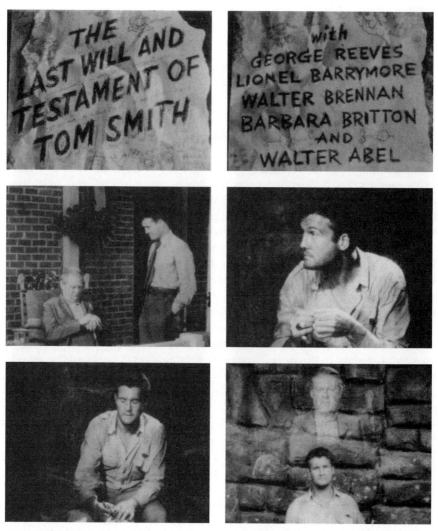

Several frame enlargements from the public domain film produced for the National War Fund by Paramount Pictures and distributed by RKO.

A Japanese soldier confronts George in his prison cell in a scene from the wartime short *THE LAST WILL AND TESTAMENT OF TOM SMITH.*

them a mail-order catalog, a rather innocuous thing in contrast to the seriousness of their discussion.

With this flashback over, Tom decides to leave Gramps "the freedom to say what he thinks." Suddenly, Tom realizes he does have one tangible item of value—a dime. A close up of the gritty coin reveals the word Liberty emblazoned on it. We continue to hear Tom's thoughts: "That's funny. I never noticed that on a dime before . . . in God we trust!" Tom grasps the importance of faith. "Yeah . . . you gotta believe, or you ain't nobody!"

The guards arrive. The time has come. With his hands tied behind him, Tom is brought to the prison yard. While positioned against a wall, Tom hears his grandfather's voice. A ghostly aberration of Gramps suddenly appears over Tom's head. This image speaks some soothing words: "Are you ready, boy? Are you calm?" Gramps implies that life, which is often a battle itself, can also be calm and dignified. Tom promises his grandparent that "we will return to this forsaken place to fill the sky with our wings and bombs, and burn this evil from the face of the earth." But there is one last bequest Tom needs to make. "You, sitting there in America," he declares. "I leave all of you the last minute of me . . . here . . . facing twelve guns." One of the officers yells, "Ready?" But Tom continues: "He is saying 'ready.' Are you ready out there?" Tom is shot down by the firing squad, but we still hear him: "What was that word on a dime? Liberty!" To be certain the sentence has been carried out effectively, one of the soldiers walks over to Tom's body and puts a gun to his head. After the weapon is fired, the camera focuses on Tom's lifeless hand—still holding the dime.

Back home, the mailman reluctantly approaches Gramps with a letter. The old man, however, already knows what is in the envelope. Gramps goes on to say that all of us have a job to do, emphasizing that no one is too old, too young, or too busy to fight. (A shot of the familiar poster for the National War Fund is shown in this sequence.) The mailman walks away, softly reading the names on the letters from his mailbag, a clear indication that many diverse individuals will be affected by this war.

The narrator's dialogue is as profound as Gramp's: "All over the world, countless Tom Smiths are giving. What will you give?" The camera moves in on Barrymore, who points to the lens and says, "It's up to you!"

It's funny how little things have changed from 1943 to 2005. The delivery of hideous events has changed, but not their effect. The horror of war remains so, and modern technology and more compassionate attitudes have virtually changed nothing. This short is a time portal into the psyche of the baby boomers' parents who survived the terrors of daily life during World War II.

CAST: George Reeves, Lionel Barrymore, Walter Brennan, Barbara Britton, and Walter Abel.

PRODUCED BY PARAMOUNT AND PRESENTED BY RKO for the benefit of the National War Fund; Directed by Harold S. Bucquet; Screenplay by Stephen Longstreet; Associate Producer: Richard Blumenthal; Director of Photography: Theodor Sparkuhl, A.S.C.; Musical Score: Gordon Jenkins; Art direction: Hans Dreier and Roland Anderson; Edited by Lee Hall; Director of Make-Up: Wally Westmore; Sound Recording: William Thayer and Don Johnson; Set Decoration: Rita Lower. Original theatrical release: September 9, 1943.
Running time: 10 minutes, 30 seconds.

BUCKSKIN FRONTIER

Scoping Out the B-Western Range

Stephen Bent (Richard Dix) is a businessman determined to build a railroad extending beyond the Santa Fe cutoff, right through the property of Jeptha Marr (Lee J. Cobb). Marr argues that Bent and the railroad company will prosper, while he and the other ranchers bear the brunt of higher taxes and loss of property. Bent assures the residents that higher taxes also mean higher land values, and that the railroad can transport their livestock quickly and inexpensively. This represents a threat to Marr, who owns a freight hauling business in addition to a substantial cattle empire. Undaunted, Bent tries to convince one of Marr's associates, Gideon Skene (Albert Dekker), that the railroad is the way of the future. But despite many words of reassurance and good faith, Marr and Gideon take measures to keep Bent, whom they regard as a "parasite," off the land in question. When Bent and his young surveyor, Jeff Collins (George Reeves), attempt to scope out the territory, they are forcibly ejected by Gideon.

Bent and Gideon are also at odds with each other over Marr's attractive daughter, Vinne (Jane Wyatt), who has caught the eye of both men. Realizing that Bent is a force to be reckoned with, Marr resorts to dealing with Champ Clanton (Victor Jory), an unscrupulous railroad competitor. Gideon, however, is leery over this alliance and shifts over to Bent's team. Doing his best (or his worst) to impede the railroad's progress, Clanton ruins Bent's reputation with the bankers. But even this doesn't deter the unflappable railroad exec, as he is being subsidized by a wealthy "old friend," the not-so-old Rita Molyneaux (Lola Lane). Both camps tussle back and forth, until the headline of *The Pawnee Press* reveals the inevitable outcome: "Missouri Central Wins Fight!"

When sabotage fails to close down the railroad project, Clanton begins to consider cold-blooded murder, a plan sternly nixed by Marr. Later, at the construction site, Bent receives word that Clanton and his mob are about to open fire. Horrified to learn that his daughter is also at the site, Marr rounds up a gang of ruffians capable of halting Clanton's attack. A brutal gun battle ensues, during which Bent and Clanton finally duke it out. Their well-choreographed brawl (clearly the best scene in the film) is witnessed by Vinnie, Rita, and a wounded Gideon. Bent delivers a devastating blow to Clanton's jaw, which sends the scoundrel to the bottom of a river. Having finally achieved his goal, Bent makes amends with Marr and offers him a position on the railroad company's board of directors.

Despite a good cast, a plausible plot, and a few good action sequences, *Buckskin Frontier* is an exercise in dullness. George appears in only two scenes, one of which affords him a mere 38 seconds of screen time. If Buckskin bears more than a superficial resemblance to *The Kansan*, there are several reasons. Both films were produced by Harry Sherman for United Artists in 1943 (the same year George worked for Sherman in the Hopalong Cassidy programmers). Both films featured the same roster of stars, headed

George and Richard Dix featured in a lobby card scene from *Buckskin Frontier*.

by Richard Dix. And both films, unfortunately, failed to provide George with a decent supporting role.

1943 must have been a frustrating year for George (although he might not have thought so at the time). From the heights of *So Proudly We Hail* to the B-western budget range of Iverson's Ranch, Reeves certainly experienced the highs and lows of the picture business. He should be commended for his professionalism and believability despite weak, unfocused material like this.

While 1944's *Winged Victory* would bring George a meatier role, he would not see A-list cinema work again. Instead, Reeves would see stardom in an infant medium, television, which was seen as a threat by the film colony.

Trivia department: George plays "Jeff Collins" in this film. He would play a character by the same name five years later in the Lippert programmer *Thunder in the Pines*.

CAST: Richard Dix, Jane Wyatt, Albert Dekker, Lee J. Cobb, Victor Jory, Lola Lane, Max Baer, Joe Sawyer, Harry Allen, Francis McDonald, George Reeves, Bill Nestell.

UNITED ARTISTS PRODUCTIONS; Produced by Harry Sherman; Directed by Lesley Selander; Associate Producer: Lewis J. Rachmil; Director of Photography: Russell Harlan, A.S.C.; Screenplay by Norman Houston; Additional Dialogue by

Bernard Schubert, From the Story "Buckskin Empire" by Harry Sinclair Drago;
Music Score: Victor Young; Art Director: Ralph Berger; Film Editor: Sherman A.
Rose; Associate Editor: Carrol Lewis; Assistant Director: Glenn Cook; Sound: Jack
Noyes; Wardrobe: Earl Moser; Set Decorator: Emile Kuri; Sound Recording by
Sound Services, Inc. Original theatrical release: February 17, 1943.
Running time: 78 minutes.

HOPPY SERVES A WRIT
A Villain on the Open Range, and a Soggy Subpoena

Hoppy's sidekick, California Carlson (Andy Clyde), is the latest victim of a
stagecoach holdup. California and Johnny Travers (Jay Kirby), both Texas
lawmen, are understandably eager to recover the wad of $500 bills lost in the
heist. But their boss, Sheriff Hopalong Cassidy (William Boyd), quickly
reminds them that the outlaws, who have crossed the state line into
Oklahoma, are now out of their jurisdiction. Nevertheless, with horse thievery and cattle rustling growing out of control, Hoppy rides into Oklahoma
with a plan to outsmart the scoundrels. Disguised as Mr. Jones, a soft-spoken
cattle dealer, Hoppy's first stop is the ranch of Ben Hollister (Forbes Murray)
and his lovely daughter Jean (Jan Christy). The Hollisters coldly inform their
visitor that he'll find no cattle for purchase here—or in Mason City, his
intended destination. Jean's boyfriend Steve Jordan (George Reeves) is especially inhospitable and practically runs "Jones" off the property.

It is at the nearby hotel that Hoppy encounters the master culprits: Tom
Jordan (Victor Jory) and his younger brothers Greg (Hal Taliaferro) and
Steve (Reeves). The catalyst for Tom and Hoppy's first clash is a game of
poker. After some very brief cat-and-mouse dialogue, the two men are soon
embroiled in a jarring fist-fight, from which Hoppy emerges practically
unscathed (remember, he's the hero). Here we have a prime example of the
1940s wartime sensibilities, and the use of suspension of belief! The fight
would have rendered both parties (in real life) butcher shop leftovers, let
alone having anyone walk away from the fracas. But it's a dynamic fight!

Then California and Johnny make the mistake of showing up in town.
Sure enough, one of the bandits from the robbery recognizes California
("the old buzzard") and instantly links him to the mysterious stranger. While
Hoppy is busy tracking down the stolen currency, California gets himself
abducted by the Jordan gang. The old guy is "roughed up" considerably—
until Hoppy and Johnny can come to his aid. Hoppy then finds the bulk of
the stolen bills in Steve's belongings, though Jean and her father are in the
clear. After deliberately allowing Steve to escape, Hoppy concocts a little
cattle rustling scheme of his own.

The trick is to get the desperados back over the state line where they can
be arrested. So Hoppy arranges for the herd to ramble right smack into the

William Boyd encounters Robert Mitchum in another exciting scene card from *Hoppy Serves a Writ*. Courtesy of Chuck McCleary.

George featured with William Boyd on a lobby card from *Hoppy Serves a Writ*. Courtesy of Mike Hawks.

Lone Star State. The plan works. As the outlaws pursue the herd, we are treated to the inevitable shoot-out between the two factions. Jordan and his brothers attempt to escape via the river, but Hoppy lassos them right into custody. When the threesome demand to see the requisite warrant for their arrest, Hoppy assures them that he's had it in his possession for quite some time. California wants the pleasure of bringin' 'em in, so Hoppy allows him to serve the warrant. (The film could have been titled Hoppy Causes a Writ to be Served!) In a comedic bit, California drops the document in the water, but manages to salvage it and his dignity as the villains are brought to justice.

Hollister thanks Hoppy for "cleaning out the territory." And with Steve out of the way, Johnny and Jean can have a little time to express their true feelings for one another. Very little time, in fact, as Hoppy and California have already hit the trail.

Amid the typical shoot-outs, fist-fight, chases, and comic buffoonery found in most B-Westerns, George has some fairly good sides in this, one of the better Hopalong Cassidy entries. He delivers his lines with an uncompromising sternness, and is totally believable as the jealous boyfriend in his scenes with Jan Christy. With his character on the wrong side of the law, we also get to see George portray an abusive type, as evidenced by the sequence in which he and the other "boys" take turns smacking the hell out of poor old California. Not the type of work you'd expect from a future Superman, but a good performance from a highly versatile actor.

Trivia department: A brief clip from *Hoppy Serves a Writ* can be seen in the A&E Biography entry: "George Reeves, Perils of a Superhero," first shown in 2000.

CAST: William Boyd, Andy Clyde, Jay Kirby, Victory Jory, George Reeves, Jan Christy, Hal Taliaferro, Forbes Murray, Robert Mitchum, Byron Foulger, Earle Hodgins, Roy Barcroft.

UNITED ARTISTS PRODUCTIONS; Produced by Harry Sherman; Directed by George Archainbaud; Screenplay by Gerald Geraghty; Based on a Story by Clarence E. Mulford; Associate Producer: Lewis J. Rachmil; Photography: Russell Harlan, A.S.C.; Musical Director: Irvin Talbot; Art Director: Ralph Berger; Edited by Sherman A. Rose; Assistant Director: Glenn Cook; Sound: William Wilmarth; Wardrober: Earl Moser; Set Decorations: Emile Kuri. Original Theatrical Release: March 12, 1942. Running time: 67 minutes.

BORDER PATROL
Bullets and Burritos

A lone rider flees a pair of gunmen, as Hoppy (William Boyd), California Carlson (Andy Clyde), and Johnny Travers (Jay Kirby) are contemplating crossing the U.S./Mexican border. The trio hear a shot and see the rider

Lobby card featuring Andy Clyde, Jay Kirby, William Boyd, Claudia Drake, and Duncan Renaldo in a scene from BORDER PATROL. COURTESY OF CHUCK MCCLEARY.

being pursued by the duo, and they join the chase. The lone rider is shot, and Hoppy and his friends listen as the dying caballero whispers the names Don Enrique Perez and Inez La Baroa.

As Hoppy asks the cowboy why he was shot, Senorita Inez (Claudia Drake) appears on horseback. Johnny spots her as she draws down on them, accusing them of the murder of her ranch hand. Still holding the three at gunpoint, she demands that Hoppy and company return with her to her rancho in Mexico for justice. Hoppy protests by telling her that she can't force them to leave the Texas side of the border. Hoppy tells her that he thinks the dead man had a message for her from Don Enrique, but he died before he could relay it.

They acquiesce and travel with her to Mexico. At the government office, they present their credentials to the Commandant (Duncan Renaldo), proving the trio are deputized Texas Rangers. The Commandant reveals that Mexicans traveling to Texas have been disappearing at an alarming rate, and that Don Enrique, Inez's fiancee, is the latest victim to vanish. He is also an officer in the Mexican Border Patrol. At dinner, the Commandant tells Hoppy that his people began disappearing after accepting employment at the Silver Bullet mine in Texas, nestled in the Hills of Missing Men, which is rumored to be haunted.

The next day, Hoppy and his cohorts leave for the Silver Bullet mine. Inez trails Hoppy, California, and Johnny.

Arriving at the mine, Hoppy and company are met by Quinn (Robert Mitchum), with another man who warns them off before opening fire on the Rangers. A fierce gunfight erupts. Hoppy ropes Barton (Cliff Parkinson) by the feet, and extracts a confession out of him about the murder of Inez's man. The gunman swears to Hoppy there was a warrant for the dead man, and he was only pursuing a wanted fugitive.

The Rangers, plus the captured man, reach the town of Silver Bullet, where they come up against Krebs (Russell Simpson), the mayor and sheriff of Silver Bullet. He informs Cassidy that he and his party are trespassers, and that he is the law in Silver Bullet. Cassidy responds by disclosing that a Texas Ranger and his deputies can go anywhere in Texas, under the law.

Krebs accuses Hoppy of killing Inez's ranch hand, who he claims is Don Enrique. This is a red herring. Krebs arrests Cassidy on murder, robbery, and a plethora of other charges. California deduces that Sheriff/Mayor Krebs just happens to be the judge in Silver Bullet, along with his other civic duties.

Inez arrives in the middle of the trial, only to be met by Krebs, who tells her that Hoppy and his friends are on trial for the theft of Don Enrique's horse.

In his private chambers, Krebs accuses Hoppy and his pals of killing Don Enrique and then following Inez's ranch hand Ramone and killing him as well. Krebs convinces Inez to testify against Hoppy and his Texas Rangers. She identifies them as the thieves and the murderers. Barton is the next to testify. He states that he saw Don Enrique killed after he inquired about the missing men in Silver Bullet. Barton fingers Hoppy, and Hoppy counters with Barton's confession that he was in league with the killers of Ramone.

The trio is convicted by a jury of felons, and Hoppy is led off to jail, whispering to Inez to get Krebs to show her the Silver Bullet mine.

After the trial, Inez confronts Krebs and forces a visit to the mine. Meanwhile, at the mine we finally get to see Don Enrique (George Reeves) as he is enslaved like the rest of the miners and missing Mexicans in Krebs' subterranean sweat shop. Barton rides into the mining camp and warns the foreman that Krebs is bringing Inez for a quick inspection of the mine and its workers.

After hearing this news, Don Enrique insists on staying to be seen by Inez. He is cracked on the shoulder and led away with the rest of the workers to the mine, half dazed. Krebs brings Inez to the mine where she hears Enrique's voice coming from a deserted shaft that, according to Krebs, had not been worked in years.

She then offers to cook a farewell dinner for Hoppy and his hanging party (just something to remember her by). Krebs insists that Inez not poison them, and that their hanging must be legal. Through her culinary endeavors, Inez finds out that there are forty men on the chuck wagon feeding list that aren't acknowledged by Krebs. Krebs samples the prisoner's last supper, proclaims it a culinary triumph, and wishes there was more of this exquisite meal left over, for his own dinner.

California breaks a tooth on his burrito in the jail cell. The burritos and the meal contain a gun and bullets to allow the heroes to escape. Another shoot-out erupts, and the heroes are at large. Krebs gives chase, and at the mine after a severe gun battle, Don Enrique is freed, but the party is trapped in the mine. Hoppy forces the villains to drive all the captured workers out of the mine by hiding them in their wagons.

Once again a fierce gun battle explodes. Krebs and his men are defeated, but Krebs makes his escape on lone horseback. Hoppy captures Krebs, and then he makes sure all the migrant workers are paid fairly for their labor in the Texas mine, the Silver Bullet.

An above average western, with loads of fights, rootin' tootin' gun battles, and great scenery filmed in the Alabama Hills just outside Lone Pine, California. But for Reeves fans, a bit disappointing as he's only in the last third of the show. His Latin American dialect is somewhat dated, but his appearance rescues the picture from the routine zone into which so many western films fall.

While this will not be one on the 'top ten' list of most Reeves fans, if you like westerns, it's loads of fun!

CAST: William Boyd, Andy Clyde, Jay Kirby, Russell Simpson, Claudia Drake, George Reeves, Duncan Renaldo, Pierce Lyden, Robert Mitchum, Cliff Parkinson, Earle Hodgins (uncredited), Merrill McCormick (uncredited), Bill Nestell (uncredited).

A HARRY SHERMAN PRODUCTION/RELEASED BY UNITED ARTISTS; Directed by: Lesley Selander; Characters created by: Clarence E. Mulford; Script: Michael Wilson; Executive Producer: Harry Sherman; Associate Producer: Lewis J. Rachmil; Cinematography by: Russell Harlan; Musical Director: Irvin Talbot; Film Editor: Sherman A. Rose; Art Direction: Ralph Berger; Set Decoration: Emile Kuri; Second Unit Director: Glen Cook; Sound: William Wilmarth; Stunts: Ted Wells; Wardrobe: Earl Moser. Original theatrical release: April 2, 1943. Running time: 65 minutes.

THE LEATHER BURNERS
Rustlers, Ranchers, and a Reel Life Spouse

With the problem of cattle rustling getting out of hand, Johnny Travers (Jay Kirby) summons his pal Hopalong Cassidy (William Boyd) for help. Fresh from Arizona, Hoppy and his sidekick California Carlson (Andy Clyde) encounter Dan Slack (Victor Jory), a crank who alleges that the ranchers are interfering with the water connection to his Buckskin Mine. To remedy this he wants to hire Hoppy and California to guard the railroad tracks. Johnny also wants to engage Hoppy—to investigate the problem he's having with rustlers. To everyone's surprise, Hoppy declines Johnny's offer and accepts the job from Slack (in order to keep an eye on the scoundrel, of course).

George Reeves disarms Forbes Murray with an assist from Jay Kirby in a staged publicity photo used to promote *THE LEATHER BURNERS*.

At the railroad office, Sharon Longstreet (Ellanora Needles, billed as Shelley Spencer), confers with her financial advisor, an attorney named Harrison Brooke (George Reeves). "I wish I could give you a better report on the financial condition of your railroad," says the mild-mannered Brooke. With a twinge of admiration in her voice, Sharon says she thought the young lawyer was brilliant enough to turn all the red figures into black. "I'm not that much of a magician," Brooke admits. Slack enters the office and introduces Hoppy and California as the new railroad guards. Sharon, however, says she can't afford to pay their salaries. Slack quickly reassures her that he will "foot the bill," and walks out of the office. Brooke sternly informs Hoppy that Slack is attempting to seize control of the railroad and was responsible for the killing of Sharon's father, though he has no proof of this.

Hoppy and California bunk down at the Palace Hotel, and are told a tale by the creepy clerk about a ghost in the Buckskin Mine—the ghost of Sam Bucktoe, the prospector who struck gold 30 years ago in the Buckskin Mine.

Slack learns the truth about his newly appointed "guards" when he is shown a wire that Hoppy addressed to the Marshal. In the telegram, Hoppy requests a basic background assessment of Slack. Not one to be outsmarted, Slack sends a phony telegram back to Hoppy. But Hoppy instantly recognizes the "reply" as a fake, as it doesn't include the special code word that the Marshal always cites. Hoppy manages to capture the crooked telegraph operator, Lafe Bailey (Hal Taliaferro), who is in fact employed by Sharon. Hoppy deliberately allows Lafe to escape, then trails him close enough to learn the direction in which the cattle are being led. When Lafe is reported dead, Slack sees to it that Hoppy becomes the prime suspect.

Hoppy has no alternative but to confront Sharon. He convinces her that he had nothing to do with the death of the telegraph operator, and that an unsavory character named Bart (Forbes Murray) is actually assisting Slack. Together, Hoppy and Sharon stumble upon the rustler's corral, though they still haven't determined the location of the missing cattle.

Later, Hoppy and California discover an alternate entrance to the Buckskin Mine; it is here that Slack and the not-so-dead Sam Bucktoe (George Givot) are hoarding the stolen cattle. Deep within the mine, Hoppy and California overhear the duo recounting their nefarious plots. Bucktoe, a power-mad eccentric believed to be dead, actually had designs to acquire Johnny's vast properties. Blaming his "partner" for the failure of this and other schemes, Bucktoe turns on Slack. He eventually kills him, and lets the cattle loose, while Hoppy and California are still trapped inside the mine.

Johnny (who now realizes Hoppy's good intentions), organizes a posse that includes Brooke and a team of ranchers to infiltrate the mine where Hoppy and Slack's henchmen are shooting it out. Also in jeopardy is Sharon's little brother, Bobby (Bobby Larson), who is nearly trampled during the raging stampede. When Johnny arrives on the scene, he shoots Bart. The resultant cave-in spells the end for Bucktoe. Hoppy, California, and Bobby make it out of the mine safe and sound. With his problem finally solved, Johnny says he will focus his attention in another direction, namely on the highly desirable Sharon. But Johnny catches a glimpse of the railroad heiress kissing Brooke, her true hero, who was injured during the fracas. With nothing else to hold him back, Johnny agrees to ride off with Hoppy en route to Bar 20.

The horror element of Bucktoe's ghost being alive makes this Hoppy adventure more atmospheric than most Western programmers. Effective use of Bronson Canyon and caves (located in the heart of Hollywood) adds to the ambiance of the show. Bronson Canyon (originally Brush Canyon, a rock quarry) made its cinematic debut in 1917 and has been featured in all types of motion pictures up to the present day. It is featured in such favorites as *The Vampire Bat* (1933), *Flash Gordon* (1936), *The Phantom Empire* (1935), *Superman* (1948), *Invasion of the Body Snatchers* (1958), *Return of Dracula* (1958), and a host of other features and serials.

George Givot's portrayal of Sam Bucktoe amplified the horror angle of this show. He resembles Glenn Strange in both the *Mad Monster* and the Bowery Boys flick *Master Minds* (1949), with a limp identical to Lon Chaney Jr.'s in the three Universal Mummy films of the mid-40s.

Ellanora Reeves/Needles/Spencer in real life had been married to George for three years when this picture was shot. Ellanora is the female lead of this Western adventure, and is an Anne Nagel type, who has the strength and presence of a highly competent actress, miscast in a B-picture. She has as much or more screen time than George, but the two end the show lip-locked. A better than average entry in the series.

CAST: William Boyd, Andy Clyde, Jay Kirby, Victor Jory, George Givot, Shelley Spencer, Bobby Larson, George Reeves, Hal Taliaferro, Forbes Murray, and Robert Mitchum (uncredited).

UNITED ARTIST PRODUCTION; Produced by Harry Sherman; Directed by Joseph E. Henabery; Screenplay by Jo Pagano; Based on the Story by Bliss Lomax, and characters created by Clarence E. Mulford; Associate Producer: Lewis J. Rachmil; Photography: Russell Harlan, A.S.C.; Music Score: Samuel Kaylin; Musical Director: Irvin Talbot; Art Director: Ralph Berger; Edited by Carrol Lewis; Assistant Director: Glenn Cook; Sound: William Wilmarth; Wardrobe: Earl Moser; Set Decorator: Emil Kuri. Original Theatrical Release: May 28, 1943. Running time: 66 minutes.

BAR 20

Musical mules, and Reeves vs. Mitchum on the Range of Love

A Wells Fargo stagecoach is held up. Hopalong Cassidy (William Boyd), his sidekicks California (Andy Clyde) and Lin Bradley (George Reeves) are riding along when they hear shots being fired. Hoppy and his boys shoot it out with the bandits and scare them away. Mark Jackson (Victor Jory), one of the passengers, says that the thieves got away with $10,000 worth of jewels belonging to Richard Adams, the fiancé of Marie Stevens (Dustin Farnum). Marie sadly points out that her wedding gown was also stolen, a fact echoed by Jackson, the best man. Marie's mother (Betty Blythe) thanks Hoppy for his assistance and orders the driver (Earle Hodgins) to head for home.

After a sumptuous supper at the Stevens' ranch, Hoppy learns that the holdup was the work of a notorious gang headed by Quirt Rankin. Hoppy then broaches the subject of purchasing some cattle from the Stevens herd, and is prepared to make payment with the $4,000 he is carrying. Though the family is in need of money, Mrs. Stevens declines the offer, claiming that the herd is Marie's only asset. Richard Adams (Robert Mitchum), the intended groom, arrives on the scene and reports that he, too, was the victim of a holdup. He also mentions that he received a ransom note pertaining to the jewels. Though a large sum of cash is needed to recoup the gems, Richard will not allow Marie to sell any cattle to Hoppy. At this point, everyone begins to suspect one another.

Later, when Hoppy and his men are robbed by the same gang, it becomes apparent that Jackson is connected to Quirt. Hoppy finds Richard's gun at the scene, but the young man says that the weapon had been confiscated by the outlaws when he was held up. Moreover, Richard is

William Boyd, Andy Clyde and George in a scene from *BAR 20*.

angered by the fact that Hoppy seems to be implicating him in the robberies. In fact, Hoppy does suspect Richard because no one (with the exception of the "best man") knew he was carrying a large sum of money.

Jackson meets up with his partners and retrieves the watch and money that were "stolen" from him. Jackson intends to purchase land from Richard, with the money that was just stolen from Hoppy. Richard, in turn, plans to use the money from the property sale to recover the jewels and wedding dress. But Richard has another problem: Lin is clearly smitten with the alluring Marie. Utilizing his ineffable charm, Lin tries to score points with Marie by warning her that Richard may be involved with Quirt. (This is George's best scene in the picture.) But Marie is unfazed and informs Lin that Richard thinks the same thing of him!

Hoppy and company secretly follow Richard when he sets out to respond to the ransom demand. Not realizing that Hoppy is watching his every move, Richard tells a scruffy looking desperado that he won't pay up until he gets the jewels. Afterward, Lin catches up with Richard and orders him to "reach" for it. Lin then rides away with $3,000 that really belongs to Hoppy. As the jewels are being divvied up by the thieves, Hoppy finally manages to capture the elusive Quirt (Francis McDonald).

Jackson and one of his cohorts, Slash (Douglas Fowley), decide to do away with Quirt, fearing that he may spill the beans. Slash fires at Quirt as he is riding along with Hoppy, but the villain survives long enough to disclose that Richard is in the clear, and that Jackson is actually the mastermind of the racket. Richard, who has always doubted Hoppy's honesty, is now convinced that the lawman is responsible for Quirt's death. When confronted, Hoppy defends himself by stating that he came back to give the jewels to Marie. And with his money reclaimed, why would he risk a return to the territory if he'd killed someone? Hoppy also says he recorded the serial numbers of the bills in order to identify them. Richard is quick to point out that Hoppy could have recorded the serial numbers today. Lin, however, reminds everyone that the outlaws still have $1,000 of Hoppy's money. Hoppy wouldn't know the serial numbers on those bills unless he'd seen them before.

Setting up a clever trap, Hoppy lets it be known that Quirt is still alive, unconscious from loss of blood, but out for revenge nonetheless. Pretending to be the dying rogue, Hoppy wraps himself in a blanket and positions himself neatly and quietly in the back of a wagon. In the throes of a major shootout (there has to be one in every western), the gang attempts to silence "Quirt" permanently—with a knife. But Hoppy and his team manage to outshoot the villains. Hoppy then lassos Jackson, catching him with enough evidence for prosecution. Richard and Marie finally make it to the altar, and Hoppy gets to purchase the cattle before riding off into the distance.

Bar 20 is a fast-paced, entertaining little western, even for those who are not exactly fans of the genre. It balances a tightly constructed plot, great location, and just the right amount of slapstick. Director Lesley Selander put

William Boyd, Andy Clyde, George, and Francis McDonald in a scene from *BAR 20*, photographed in the Alabama Hills just outside of Lone Pine, California.

George's talents to good use in the role of Lin Bradley, the amiable, good-looking sidekick. (Six of the other entries in the "Hoppy" series feature Jay Kirby in this capacity. Kirby's first "Hoppy" was *Undercover Man* from 1942.) *Bar 20* also contains some choice moments for young Robert Mitchum, who can be seen in the other four Hopalong Cassidy programmers in which George appeared.

CAST: William Boyd, Andy Clyde, George Reeves, Dustin Farnum, Victor Jory, Douglas Fowley, Betty Blythe, Robert Mitchum, Francis McDonald, Earle Hodgins.

UNITED ARTISTS PRODUCTIONS; Produced by Harry Sherman; Directed by Lesley Selander; Screenplay by Morton Grant, Norman Houston and Michael Wilson; Based on characters created by Clarence E. Mulford; Associate Producer: Lewis J. Rachmil; Photography: Russell Harlan, A.S.C.; Musical Director: Irvin Talbot; Art Director: Ralph Berger; Edited by Carrol Lewis; Assistant Director: Glenn Cook; Sound: Jack Noyes; Wardrobe: Earl Moser; Set Decorations: Emile Kuri. Original Theatrical Release: June 1, 1943. Running time: 55 minutes.

COLT COMRADES
A Drop of Water is Worth More than Oil on the Range

This show starts with Dirk Mason (Robert Mitchum) robbing a railroad station and killing the timekeeper in cold blood. Mason, after riding a hundred miles, fleeing Hoppy and company, pleads with Jeb Hardin (Victor Jory), a cattleman, for sanctuary. Hardin shoots at Mason, missing him, and Mason runs across the street into a saloon, only to be spotted by Hoppy, Johnny, and California.

A gun battle ensues between the heroes and the desperado. Hoppy captures Mason and is about to turn him over to the sheriff when the head of the vigilantes, Joe Brass (Douglass Fowley), demands that Mason be turned over to him. The sheriff (Russell Simpson) arrives at the saloon and confronts the vigilante. Mason steals the sheriff's six-gun and attempts his escape, only to be shot by Brass who claims self defense.

Outside the Post Office, Hoppy, Jeb Hardin, and Joe Brass disagree on the division of the reward money for Mason. Hardin says he'll relinquish his and Brass' part of the reward if Hoppy will invest $5,000 in the town out of his share. Back at the saloon, Hoppy proposes that he, Johnny, and California retire their guns and buy a farm in the area.

Hoppy returns to Hardin's office, reasoning that Hardin holds the majority of real estate in the town. Outside the office, Brass tries to cut a deal with Hoppy for a quarter of the reward, leaving Hardin out of the profits. Hoppy brushes Brass aside and enters the office.

Hardin offers the boys the Whitlock Ranch, owned by Lin Whitlock

Lobby card from *COLT COMRADES*. George is third from the right, next to Andy Clyde, his face partially blocked by Victor Jory's hat. COURTESY OF JERRY MEZEROW.

(George Reeves) and his sister Lucy (Lois Sherman, a.k.a. Teddi Sherman). Hardin owns the mortgage and the water rights to the ranch and has been squeezing the Whitlocks out by withholding water, threatening to foreclose.

Hoppy agrees to look the ranch over, and the three cowpokes ride to the ranch. Finding no one home, they enter and much to their delight find fresh cooked chicken. The Whitlocks arrive during their feast. Hoppy and his friends partner up with the Whitlocks. Hoppy, California, and Johnny go into town to run errands, and most importantly, to pay the water bill owed to Hardin.

In the saloon, California is approached by oil swindler "Wildcat Willy" (Earle Hodgins), who relieves him of the $500 for the water bill. California returns to the ranch with Wild Cat Willy and his drilling equipment where they are met with scepticism from Hoppy and Lin Whitlock. Lin reveals Wild Cat as a well-known flimflam man in the area.

Two weeks later, California and Wild Cat are still drilling with not a drop of oil to show for their labor. Hardin turns off the water to the ranchers in the valley. Hoppy and Lin return to the ranch with McVarney (Herbert Rawlinson), who has been cut off as well. Along with Johnny, they ride to the dam to try to restore the water to the valley.

At the dam, they see that Joe Brass and his vigilantes are controlling the water. An altercation breaks out, and Hoppy and company win the fight. Johnny opens the dam, sending the water into the valley. Hoppy insists that

William Boyd, Andy Clyde, Jay Kirby, Lois Sherman, and George with a gun aimed at the fried chicken thieves in *COLT COMRADES*.

Johnny turn off the water, as he could be arrested on a complaint sworn out by Hardin.

Back at the ranch, California's oil well turns out to be a water well, solving the major problem. In town, McVarney asks if it's true that Hoppy, Lin, and Johnny brought in a water well. Lin tells McVarney that there's enough water to irrigate the fields and water a thousand head of cattle.

Hoppy, Lin, and Johnny pay a visit to Hardin (who, coincidentally, controls the cattle business in town) to sell their cattle to repay their debt to him. He tells them the cattle market is glutted, and he can't sell their beef. Hoppy offers Hardin one-hundred head of cattle to square the debt, but Hardin refuses, telling Hoppy, Lin, and Johnny that he'll have their ranch by hook or crook.

Hardin plots to frame Cassidy for cattle rustling to turn the ranchers against him. McVarney and the ranchers come to the well on the Whitlock ranch to water their herds. Hardin and Brass, with the vigilantes, arrive as the ranchers begin to question what to do about him. Hoppy lays the case for the ranchers on Hardin.

Hardin claims that Whitlock's herd is stolen, and that Lin Whitlock is in league with Hoppy to mislead the ranchers. Hardin shows the ranchers how Lin altered the brands on McVarney cattle to match the Whitlock brand. Hardin attempts to take Cassidy into custody, but Hoppy responds that they would not reach the jail alive, and draws his six-guns. Hoppy shoots into the air, scattering Hardin's and the ranchers' horses, as he, Lin, and Johnny ride off.

Hardin and the ranchers give chase. Hardin's vigilantes corner Hoppy, Lin, and Johnny in the rocks above the ranch. Hardin realizes that he's a sitting duck. He leaves two men on guard to make sure the trio can't escape, and returns to town. Hoppy, Lin, and Johnny make a break after dark and hightail it back to the ranch.

At the ranch, Wildcat tells Hoppy that Dirk Mason was killed by Joe Brass to keep Mason from squealing on Hardin, who pulled the post office hold-up to secure the cattle contracts for the ranchers. Hardin hid the contracts, filling the cattle orders himself; ripping off the ranchers once again.

The next day, California arrives in town with a message from Cassidy for Hardin. Hoppy, Whitlock, and Johnny will give themselves up if Hardin brings the sheriff, and guarantees they won't be lynched. Hardin tells Brass to go after Cassidy without the sheriff, and then takes California hostage. Hoppy double crosses Hardin by making a surprise appearance in town, taking Hardin hostage and ransacking his office in search of the cattle contracts. Hoppy finds the contracts and plans to use this evidence to vindicate himself and the Whitlocks.

Meanwhile, back at the ranch, Hardin has Hoppy and company pinned down in a gunfight. Wildcat distributes the contracts as the posse led by Lucy Whitlock rides to Hoppy's rescue at the Whitlock ranch.

A fire erupts in the ranch kitchen from the spent slugs flying in the shootout, and lights the stove on fire. Hoppy is wounded retrieving water from the well to put out the fire. Hardin seizes his chance, and charges the ranch house with Brass. Hardin gets whooped by a one-armed Hoppy and Lin has a knock-down drag-out with Brass, as the ranger reinforcements and posse arrive. After the smoke settles, a wounded Hoppy receives a telegram pressing him back into service. Hoppy, California, and Johnny ride off to greater adventures.

Solid performances by all, especially Victor Jory as the villainous Jeb Hardin. George has much more screen time in this Hoppy adventure, and turns in good work despite the one-dimensional material with which he has to work.

CAST: William Boyd, Andy Clyde, Jay Kirby, Teddi Sherman, Victor Jory, George Reeves, Douglas Fowley, Herbert Rawlinson, Earle Hodgins, Robert Mitchum.

A UNITED ARTISTS PRODUCTION; Directed by Lesley Selander; Characters by Clarence E. Mulford; Story by Bliss Lomax; Screenplay by Michael Wilson; Executive Producer: Harry Sherman; Associate Producer: Lewis J. Rachmil; Cinematography: Russell Harlan; Film Editor: Fred W. Berger; Art Direction: Ralph Berger; Set Decoration: Emile Kuri; Assistant Director: Glenn Cook; Sound: Jack Noyes; Wardrobe: Earl Moser; Musical Director: Irvin Talbot. Original theatrical release: June 18, 1943. Running time: 67 minutes.

SO PROUDLY WE HAIL

And the Envelope, Please

With its sterling cast and stirring production values, *So Proudly We Hail* is one of the best remembered films of the war years. A true triumph for producer-director Mark Sandrich and Paramount Pictures, the film garnered no less than four Oscar nominations. The studio press book describes it as "a tribute to those gallant girls who fought side by side with their men, teasing, loving, inspiring them . . . and never letting them down." According to the advertising copy, George's role "covers every emotion imaginable, and Reeves handles them with the ability and finesse of a big star."

At a landing site in Melbourne, a plane delivers eight Army nurses "still in their ragged field uniforms." One of them, Lt. Janet Davidson (Claudette Colbert), is in a state of shock and is carried from the aircraft on a stretcher. As the women sail back to the States, Dr. Harrison, (John Litel) becomes increasingly disturbed by Janet's deteriorating health. As Janet stares into space, the doctor considers reading her a letter from someone named John. But before doing so, he wants to know what caused this woman to lapse into her current mode of unresponsiveness.

The story is told in flashback, beginning in San Francisco, where the nurses and other military personnel embark for Hawaii. The presence of men on the ship sets the stage for romance, and the first nurse to find love is the feisty Lt. Joan O'Doul (Paulette Goddard). She falls for a muscle-bound Marine named Kansas (Sonny Tufts), who is good for a few laughs during the long journey. But the attack on Pearl Harbor casts a grim shadow over everything, and the crew is ordered to join a convoy "Somewhere in the Pacific." Soon, the women find themselves facing the first of many challenges when a neighboring ship is torpedoed. The survivors, most of whom are either wounded or seriously burned, are intercepted and brought aboard for treatment. One young woman with minor burns is Olivia D'Arcy (Veronica Lake), who also happens to be a nurse. She joins the team, but isn't a team player. Exhibiting signs of emotional instability, Olivia is actually harboring a grudge against the Japanese, as her fiance was killed at Pearl Harbor. She makes it known that she would like to personally "punish" the enemy. (With the introduction of Lake's character, the topic of racial prejudice is lightly touched upon.)

Also among the wounded is Lt. John Sommers (George Reeves), a young medical technician. Though he is reeking from oil, and desperately in need of soap and water, he refuses to let Joan give him a bath. The resourceful nurse brings the problem to Janet's attention. "You're going to have a bath and don't be coy." Janet snaps. The handsome lieutenant, however, cannot be swayed. "No female is going to bathe me," he protests. Janet reminds him that his mother bathed him when he was a child. "Only until I was old enough to knock her down," he recalls. After some small talk and a few scrubs across his chest and back, John begins to enjoy the attention he's receiving. "Since you like this so much, I'm going to let you do it every day,"

Publicity still from the 1940s.

he murmurs. Janet gives him an incredulous look, then hands him the wash cloth so he can finish the job.

At Christmas time, John sends Janet a gift with a note that reads: "In memory of that first wonderful day when I was so hot and lathered." At first, Janet is reticent about fostering a relationship, preferring to remain totally dedicated to her work. But when John points out that everyone has important work to do, Janet's cool indifference gives way to warm enthusiasm.

They land on Bataan. Janet learns that the 4th Medical Unit, to which John is assigned, is based on the front line. As a warehouse in Limay is converted for hospital use, Janet meets the no-nonsense Captain "Ma" McGregor (Mary Servoss), a little woman with a big heart concealed under

George and Claudette Colbert in *SO PROUDLY WE HAIL*.

her tough exterior. Each nurse seems to have her own specialty. In a slice of prophecy, Joan, for instance works well with the children and reads them stories about America's favorite action hero, Superman. One little boy asks, "If Superman is good, why isn't he here?" The quick thinking nurse answers, "He just landed with the Marines. We call him Kansas!" When the boy eventually sees Joan and Kansas together, he asks, "Is that Superman?" With a subtle smile, Joan says, "He'd better be!"

During one of their encounters, Janet and John get caught in an air raid and are forced to spend the night in a fox hole. By this time, the two of them have a deep emotional investment in each other. The next day, Ma reprimands Janet for spending the night away from the base, and threatens her with a dishonorable discharge. But before any repercussions can develop, Limay must be evacuated. Janet, Joan and Olivia are among the last nurses to leave. Because Janet has taken the time to retrieve a special nightgown, she causes Joan, Olivia, and herself to be trapped inside a building during an attack. With a grenade concealed in her blouse, Olivia walks into the approaching enemy, and is killed in the process. Her sacrifice makes it possible for the other girls to escape.

With the hospital now situated in a jungle, the nursing unit is burdened with even more pressures. To alleviate some of the tension, John sends over a pet monkey. But even a lively animal can't bolster anyone's morale when Ma's son, Lt. McGregor (Dick Hogan) loses his legs. In one of the most poignant moments in the film, Ma comforts her son just before he dies. Janet and the other nurses continue to grow weary. When Kansas reports that the front line has collapsed, Janet asks that the facility be relocated. Shortly after her request is denied, another bombardment erupts. Nothing is spared, not even the make-shift operating area where a life-saving procedure is taking place.

The men and women paddle their way to Corregidor, where a huge tunnel provides an ostensibly quiet setting for treating the sick and wounded. Before the women can become even remotely complacent in their new surroundings, the ground attacks resume with full force. To make matters worse, the supply of quinine is depleted. John, who is recovering from leg injuries, informs Janet that he and his men will leave for Mindanao in order to procure the much needed medicine. He will depart in just nine hours. Janet tries to talk him out of it, but she fails. As a result, Janet informs Ma that she intends to break regulations one more time in order to marry John. After exchanging vows, the couple spend their honeymoon in a fox hole, feasting on peanut butter and wine. While nestled in each other's

Mark Sandrich directing George and Claudette Colbert.

Studio portrait from *So Proudly We Hail.*

arms, John and Janet realize how little they know about each other. As John recalls a little place he owns in the country, Janet contemplates the life she hopes to share with her husband one day. With their time expended, they bid each other good-bye on the dimly lit beach. "Wait for me here," says John, "I'll be back." Janet assures him that she'll be there when he returns.

A short time later, the nurses are rattled by more bad news. Because Corregidor cannot hold out much longer, the nurses are being dispatched to Australia. This latest setback results in a tearful farewell between Joan and Kansas. Janet, however, refuses to go. She informs Ma that she cannot go, as she promised John she'd be waiting for him on Corregidor. Ma tells her to stop acting like "a hysterical school girl." When Janet refuses to comply

George and Claudette Colbert in a scene from *So Proudly We Hail*.

with orders, Ma tells her that John's company is considered "officially lost." This disclosure is the catalyst for Janet's breakdown.

With the flashback over, we are back to the setting that opened the film. Dr. Harrison thanks the women for their courage and for sharing their stories. In an attempt to prod Janet back to vitality, the doctor begins to read John's letter. In his letter, John discerns something good in just about everything, even this war which he loathes so much. He touches upon several personal issues, including the little country home he had described on his wedding night. Eventually, the doctor's voice fades into John's and his soothing words release Janet from her state of shock. The picture ends on a note of optimism: bright clouds projected on a screen, presumably to indicate a brighter tomorrow.

This is the film that should have made George Reeves a star! For once, the Hollywood hype machine was right in reporting that Reeves expresses every emotion possible. Another film of this potency directly on the heels of *So Proudly We Hail* would have sealed the deal for George's star status. But George was off to the wild blue (on stage and screen) with *Winged Victory* and was absent from Hollywood at a crucial time in his career.

Reeves fans can 'Monday Morning Quarterback' his life and career to death, but the fact of the matter is, had George stayed in Hollywood for another six months (and made another "A" picture), his whole life would have been different. Perhaps he wouldn't have played the "Man of Steel."

Studio portrait used to promote *SO PROUDLY WE HAIL*.

In Gary Grossman's SERIAL TO CEREAL, it's reported that George Reeves was promised stardom by director Mark Sandrich, but Sandrich died when George was in the service, and George never shone like this in another motion picture; the zenith of his film career!

The Best Supporting Actor Oscar should have been his!

CAST: Claudette Colbert, Paulette Goddard, Veronica Lake, George Reeves, Barbara Britton, Walter Abel, Sonny Tufts, Mary Servoss, Ted Hecht, John Litel,

George joins in a sing-along with Walter Abel (right) in *So Proudly We Hail*.

Dr. Hugh Ho Chang, Mary Treen, Kitty Kelly, Helen Lynd, Lorna Gray, Dorothy Adams, Ann Doran, Jean Willes, Lynn Walker, Joan Tours, Mimi Doyle, James Bell, Dick Hogan.

A PARAMOUNT PICTURE; Produced and Directed by Mark Sandrich; Written by Allan Scott; Acknowledgments: The War Department, The Army Nurse Corps, The American Red Cross; Special Thanks: Colonel Thomas W. Doyle, U.S.A., Commanding Officer, Combat Team 45th Infantry, Philippine Scouts, on Bataan, and First Lieutenant Eunice Hatchitt, Army Nurse Corps of Bataan and Corregidor; Musical Score by Miklos Rozsa; Director of Photography: Charles Lang, Jr. A.S.C.; Art Direction: Hans Dreier, Earl Hedrick; Special Photographic Effects: Gordon Jennings, A.S.C.; Process Photography: Farciot Edouart, A.S.C.; Edited by Ellsworth Hoagland; Make-Up Artist: Wally Westmore; Sound Recording: Harold Lewis, Walter Oberst; Set Decorator: Steve Seymour. Original theatrical release: September 9, 1943. Running time: 126 minutes.

THE KANSAN
Outlaw for a Day

It's hard to believe that as late as 1943 (after *So Proudly We Hail*), George would appear in a picture that only afforded him two brief shots (sans dialogue) and no billing. But that's the case regarding his performance—if you could call it that—in *The Kansan*. The cast, headed by Richard Dix, is a rather diversified one. It's refreshing to see a young, demure Jane Wyatt playing the hero's love interest. Wyatt, like Reeves, would find her greatest fame on television in the 1950s and 1960s. From 1954 to 1960, she co-starred with Robert Young on the now-classic "Father Knows Best" series, and then in the mid-60s she assumed the role of Mr. Spock's human mother in an episode of the "Star Trek" series. Be prepared, though, for some offensive racial stereotyping in this little B-western. Willie Best, one of the era's most prolific African American character actors, appears as "Bones," the perpetually frightened hotel lackey employed by Wyatt's character.

The film opens with the sun shining brightly on the little town of Broken Lance. All is peaceful until Jesse James (George Reeves) and his gang appear out of nowhere and attempt to rob the bank. James and his boys meet their match in John Bonniwell (Dix), a sharp-shooter who thwarts the robbery, but gets wounded in the process. John finds himself recuperating in a hospital ward where he meets Eleanor Sagar (Wyatt), the owner of the town's hotel. When the patient hears a celebration brewing outside his window, he can't fathom what all the fuss is about. Sagar informs John that the cheers are intended for him, as he's just been "elected" marshal.

John learns that his new position is attributable to Steve Barat (Albert Dekker), a slick banker who owns most of the land and businesses in the territory. While Steve is ostensibly grateful to John, it is obvious that he had him appointed for the purpose of having a lawman at his beck and call. Whenever anyone crosses the banker, he promptly demands that John arrest the offending party, with no questions asked. Though he condemns the unscrupulous activities of others, Steve Barat is actually the biggest swindler of them all. With the help of several corrupt officials, he has mastered the art of milking the town dry. But when the new marshal refuses to fall in line and follow suit, Steve realizes the need to get rid of the man he put in office.

In an effort to discredit the marshal, Steve plots the hold-up of a bank messenger, with assistance from his equally conniving brother, Jeff (Victor Jory). Their scheme falls flat, and it is the marshal who ultimately wins the war of wits. When Steve is in court, ready to claim victory in one of his many lawsuits, John presents evidence that the banker has been indicted on larceny charges in New York. After this setback, Jeff (who is Eleanor's former beau) turns the tables on a rival gang of cutthroats who have targeted Broken Lance. There's a climactic gun battle, and John is shot once again. Back in his old hospital bed, John listens to the roar of approval emanating from the streets. This time, however, Eleanor informs him that the crowd is cheering the announcement of their engagement.

Studio portrait of George from the 1940s.

George Reeves as Jesse James would have been an interesting concept, had a longer prologue for this film been developed. Had the screenwriter Harold Shumate, and the original writer of 'Peace Marshall,' Frank Gruber, which the film was based on, crafted a more Jesse James mythological screen scenario, George might have been given a larger role. Probably another disappointment for George, given the all-star cast who carry the bulk of the film, beginning with Richard Dix who was nominated for the 1930/31 Best Actor in *Cimarron*. Dix was magnificent in Val Lewton's classic *Ghost Ship* (RKO 1943), and a haunting specter in Columbia's Whistler series (based on the radio program).

Reeves' invisible performance is showcased by a host of notable genre performers. Albert Dekker, who had a long and varied career, most notably with the film *Dr. Cyclops* (1939) where he portrayed a bespectacled madman who shrank his contemporaries, is especially effective in what could have been a mundane western exercise. Dekker himself had the distinguished honor of out-bizarring George Reeves in death. On May 5, 1968 he was found in his Hollywood apartment in a most peculiar hanging position in the lavatory, obscenities scrawled on his body in lipstick. His death remains unsolved to this date.

Also included in the cast was Robert Armstrong, who portrayed Carl Denham in the 1933 productions of *King Kong* and *Son of Kong*. 1943 also saw Armstrong in Universal's *The Mad Ghoul* and the serial *Adventures of the Flying Cadets* (Universal 1943) with Dead End Kid Bobby Jordon. In 1949 he would reprise a hybrid of his Carl Denham character in *Mighty Joe Young*.

Victor Jory three years earlier had portrayed the popular hero *The Shadow* in Columbia's 1940 serial (as referenced in Chapter One) as well as Columbia's serial production of *The Green Archer*. Rod Cameron starred as Rex Bennett in two breathtaking Republic serials, *G-Men vs. The Black Dragon*, and *Man Hunt in the African Jungle*.

Douglas Fowley, the character actor who seemed to turn up everywhere, from Bela Lugosi's only color movie *Scared to Death* to the camp *Cat Women of the Moon* (co-starring Victory Jory), to a touching TV episode of "Andy Griffith" where he plays the hopeless but loveable hobo, rounds out a strong cast. Fowley also worked as a dialogue director.

CAST: Richard Dix, Jane Wyatt, Albert Dekker, Eugene Pallette, Victor Jory, Robert Armstrong, Beryl Wallace, Clem Bevan, Hobart Cavanaugh, Francis McDonald, Willie Best, Douglas Fowley, Rod Cameron, Eddy Waller, Raphael Bennett, and George Reeves (unbilled).

A UNITED ARTISTS PICTURE; Produced by Harry Sherman; Directed by George Archainbaud; Screenplay by Harold Shumate; From the story "Peace Marshal" by Frank Gruber; Associate Producer: Lewis J. Rachmil; Director of Photography: Russell Harlan, A.S.C.; Music Score by Irvin Talbot; Art Director: Ralph Berger; Film Editor: Carroll Lewis; Assistant Director: Glenn Cook; Sound by Jack Noyes; Wardrobe: Earl Moser; Set Decoration: Emile Kuri; Song: "Lullaby of the Herd," Lyrics by Foster Carling, Music by Phil Ohman, sung by The King's Men. Original theatrical release: September 10, 1943. Running time: 82 minutes.

WINGED VICTORY

From the Footlights to the Wild Blue Yonder

In this screen adaptation of Moss Hart's play, "all the boys in uniform are members of the U.S. Army Forces," as the opening title affirms. Hart also penned the screenplay for the film, which Fox wisely placed in the competent hands of director George Cukor. Sergeant George Reeves, who had portrayed Lieutenant Thompson in the 1943 Broadway musical, reprises his role in this glossy, star-studded movie.

In addition to its illustrious cast, *Winged Victory* showcases the state-of-the-art aircraft and weaponry of the Second World War. It is basically a "feel good" story about a group of young cadets in training for their wings, with Pvt. Lon McCallister standing out as the central character. Lt Thompson (Reeves) is the affable instructor given approximately five minutes of screen time, which isn't much considering the length of the film (two hours plus). His big moment occurs at the celebration held on the eve of graduation. When asked to address his former trainees, the lieutenant plays it cool and seems reticent to speak up. However, without too much prodding, he agrees to say a few words to the graduating class. Reflecting on his first impressions, Thompson tells the guys they were the "raunchiest bunch of cadets" he'd ever seen, a comment that elicits a fair amount of guffaws. All joking aside, he reassures the men that, much to his surprise, they have "made it" through the rigorous training process. Thompson also acknowledges how rewarding it is to shape the careers of young pilots, calling to mind one particular kid who has kept in touch all through his assignment in the South Pacific. According to Thompson, his only regret is that he doesn't get to

George and Elisabeth Fraser reading with the touring company of *WINGED VICTORY.*

Print advertisement for *WINGED VICTORY*.

serve in combat alongside the men he has trained. This scene could have come off as maudlin. Yet, George's treatment is so sincere that you want to give him a standing ovation! Showing their appreciation and approval, the men break into a few bars of "For He's a Jolly Good Fellow," which is followed by much applause and much beer. Lt. Thompson is seen one more time in the film, during the graduation sequence, where he proudly presents the new pilots with their wings.

In April of 1944, a magazine profile on George Reeves entitled G.I. Greasepaint (written by Frank Warren) outlined Sergeant Reeves' involve-

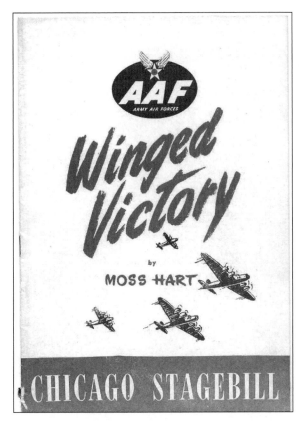

A rare playbill from the Opera House theatre in Chicago where the play ran from December 17, 1944 to January 3, 1945. George's *MOLE MEN* co-star and friend Walter Reed was a cast member in this production.

ment in Moss Hart's stage play and soon to be motion picture *Winged Victory*. When Reeves enlisted in the Army, he virtually retired from acting. His focus was to be on his duties as an anti-tank training student and nothing else. While on furlough, he was given permission to participate in the short subject, *The Last Will and Testament of Tom Smith* (with Walter Brennan and Lionel Barrymore).

Moss Hart had toured Air Force bases for material for *Winged Victory*, and during the casting process he saw Tom Smith and offered Reeves any lead he wanted. Due to Reeves' age at the time (29), Reeves opted-out for the role of flight instructor Thompson. The article goes on to describe Reeves' life, saying that acting is a part time distraction, and Reeves would be continuing his anti-tank training, while serving as a supply sergeant in Manhattan (Greenwich Village), where he and his wife Ellanora lived. It further states that the film production will begin in June in Hollywood.

This article can be viewed in its entirety on Lou Koza's CD-ROM, *Saving George Reeves, Part II*.

Star Edmund O'Brien went on to film noir fame with an unforgettable portrayal of the paranoia riddled victim in 1950s *DOA*. In 1954 he essayed another man on the outside, in George Orwell's *1984*, co-starring Michael Redgrave (father of Vanessa and Lynn).

Studio portrait for *WINGED VICTORY.*

Genre fans know Witner Bissel as Whit Bissell, co-star of many 50s Sci-Fi classics, which include *Creature From The Black Lagoon* (Universal 1954), *Invasion of the Body Snatchers* (AA 1956), *Target Earth* (AA 1954), *I Was A Teenage Werewolf* (AI 1957), and *I Was A Teenage Frankenstein* (AI 1957).

A footnote to Reeves' and Bissell's careers: the 1957 season of Superman was filmed at ZIV Studios at the same time *I Was A Teenage Frankenstein* was being filmed, with Reeves' first Lois Lane (Phyllis Coates) co-starring with Bissell, who played Dr. Frankenstein in this Herman Cohen production.

Lee J. Cobb, whose real name was Leo Jacoby, played a doctor, and was nominated for Best Supporting Actor in 1954 for his work in *On The Waterfront*, and in 1958 for the *Brothers Karamazov*. He had a bit part in the

Bela Lugosi serial *The Phantom Creeps* (Universal 1939). Some of his other classic portrayals were *The Three Faces of Eve* (1957), *Twelve Angry Men* (1957), *Exodus* (1960), *How The West Was Won* (1962), *Our Man Flint* (1966), *In Like Flint* (1967), *MacKenna's Gold* (1969), and the shock revulsion classic of the 1970s, *The Exorcist* (1973).

CAST: Sgt. Mark Daniels, Sgt. Edmond O'Brien, Pvt. Lon McCallister, Cpl. Don Taylor, Cpl. Lee J. Cobb, Sgt. Peter Lind Hayes, Cpl. Alan Baxter, Cpl. Red Buttons, Cpl. Barry Nelson, Cpl. Rune Hulfman, Cpl. Bernard J. Tyers, Cpl. Phillip Bourneuf, Cpl. Garry Merrill, Cpl. Witner N. Bissell, Sgt. George Reeves, Pvt. George Petrie, Pfc, Alfred Ryder, Cpl. Karl Malden, Pfc. Martin Ritt, Cpl. Harry Lewis, S.Sgt. Fred A. Cotton, Cpl. Henry Rowland, Lt. Gilbert Herman, S.Sgt. Sascha Brastoff, Cpl. Archie Robbins, Cpl. Jack Slate, Pfc. Hendry Slate, Jeanne Crain, Jane Ball, Jo-Carroll Dennison, Judy Holliday, Geraldine Wall.

A TWENTIETH CENTURY FOX-PICTURE, in Association with the U.S. Army Air Forces; Produced by Darryl F. Zanuck; Directed by George Cukor; Stage Play and Screenplay by Moss Hart; Continuity Design: Sgt. Harry Horner; Director of Photography: Glen MacWilliams, A.S.C.; Music: Sgt. David Rose; Choral Director: Leonard DePaur; Art Direction: Lyle Wheeler, Lewis Creber; Set Decorator: Thomas Little; Associate: Al Orenbach; Film Editor: Barbara McLeon; Costume: Kay Nelson; Make-Up Artists: Guy Pearce, Ben Nye; Special Photographic Effects: Fred Sersen; Sound: Eugene Grossman, Roger Herman. Original Theatrical Release: December 20, 1944. Running time: 130 minutes.

CHAMPAGNE FOR TWO
A Bubbly Bill for George

Although this two-reel musical short didn't present any challenges for George, he probably enjoyed making it, given his fondness for Latin American music. The film, which was shot in color, opens with some fancy footwork on the dance floor of a posh night club, owned by Malone (George Reeves). Lita (Isabelita), Malone's energetic wife, adds some sparkle to the proceedings as she performs in a style reminiscent of Carmen Miranda's. Afterward, Lita joins her mate for a champagne celebration. Since it is their first wedding anniversary, Malone surprises Lita with a trip to Havana. There's a quick change of plans, however, with the arrival of the elderly Mrs. Cowdy (Ida Moore), who demands to speak to the boss. Cowdy, a diminutive cleaning woman, tells Malone that she's overheard some gangsters making plans to hold up the club. The club owner offers Cowdy some cash for her trouble, but she refuses to accept it. Mildly alarmed, Malone notifies the authorities.

The following morning, Malone auditions the new act, which consists of a comic bullfight routine. Later, Malone decides to invite Cowdy to the club for dinner, hoping she can identify the crooks before any ruckus ensues. Malone instructs her to give a signal when the gangsters show up. He then breaks the news to Lita that their trip will have to be delayed due to "business."

That evening, Mrs. Cowdy and her husband Ben (Griff Barnett) arrive for dinner. She haughtily informs the host that she and her husband are guests of the boss. Ben isn't the least bit shy about ordering the most expensive items on the menu, including champagne for two. Following dinner, Lita offers her rendition of the song, "Ho! Ho! Jose."

It's getting late, and Malone realizes that there hasn't been the slightest hint of a signal from Mrs. Cowdy. In fact, Malone's manager says, "The only signal your friend gave was to the waiter—for more champagne!" Malone calmly asks Mrs. Cowdy, "Do you see them?" Without hesitation, she answers, "No! You can arrest me now." The old gal admits that the whole thing was a lie; there isn't going to be a stick-up. She is quick to point out that her husband knew nothing about her little scheme. Incredulous, Malone asks, "How can you stick your neck out with a trick like this—just for a dinner?" Mrs. Cowdy explains that she and her husband haven't much time left. For year, they've been dreaming of an evening like this, but the tab was simply beyond their means. Malone remains cool, taking the whole thing in stride.

The ancient song "Let Me Call You Sweetheart" is played, the couples take to the dance floor. Ben says that the Malones are wonderful people, and he'd like to invite them over for dinner. Finally, Malone whispers the words Lita has been waiting to hear: "We're flying to Havana just as soon as we can pack!" The two of them rub noses as the picture fades out.

Isabelita and George in *CHAMPAGNE FOR TWO.*

Short subject films were beginning to wane in 1947, but this little ditty about a felonious old biddy in some ways speaks more about the real George than his other roles. Always generous to a fault, always the jovial guy who pays the bills, "living large" as friend and co-star Jack Larson once described him to us. It's too bad that George and whomever couldn't have rubbed noses and had a happy ending like this short.

CAST: Isabelita, George Reeves, Ida Moore, Griff Barnett, Billy Daniels, Douglas Wright & Co., The Guadalajara Trio.

A PARAMOUNT PICTURE; Produced by Harry Grey; Directed by Mel Epstein; Screenplay by Jack Roberts; Based on a story by Billy Rose; Music Score: Van Cleave; Music Direction: Irvin Talbot; Music Associate: Phil Boul; Vocal Arrangements: Ken Lane; Song, "Ho! Ho! Jose" by Jay Livingston & Ray Evan; Dances Staged by Billy Daniels; Director of Photography: Stuart Thompson, A.S.C.; Art Direction: Hans Dreier, Albert Nozaki; Edited by Everett Douglas; Costumes by Waldo Angelo; Make-Up Supervision: Wally Westmore; Set Decoration: Sam Comer, Stanley J. Sawley; Sound Recording: Don McKay, Philip Wade; Original Theatrical Release: June 13, 1947. Running time: 19 minutes.

VARIETY GIRL

By George, is that him in the third row to oblivion?

When sound motion pictures revolutionized Hollywood in the late 1920s and early 1930s, the major studios began showcasing their contract stars in musical-comedy reviews. MGM, the studio with the biggest names, established the pattern with such novelties as *The Hollywood Revue* (1929), and *Hollywood Party* (1934). Paramount jumped on the bandwagon with its *Paramount on Parade* (1930), and kept the genre alive during the war years and beyond. Four years after the release of *Star Spangled Rhythm* (1942), the studio began lavishing most of its creative energies on *Variety Girl*. The film is a star-studded tribute to Variety Clubs International, the "heart of show business" charity that has been bringing assistance to children since 1928.

Looking at *Variety Girl* today, it seems that everyone on the Paramount lot, with the exception of the janitorial staff, is featured in this 93 minute extravaganza. Even George Marshall, the director of the film, gets into the act. The publicity trailer pumps it up as "a big-time story of a small-town girl, behind the scenes in Hollywood." This is true enough, but it's also a story of mistaken identity, with one budding performer (played by Olga San Juan) passing herself off as another (Mary Hatcher, in her screen debut). As a whole, the film is simply a hook on which to hang a succession of musical numbers (including "new" songs by Frank Loesser), vaudeville-style comedy sketches, and elaborate sight gags. There's also a contribution by producer

IT'S THE BIGGEST FESTIVAL OF FAMOUS STARS IN ALL SCREEN HISTORY!

GALA MUSIC! LAVISH COSTUMES! SPECTACULAR DANCING!

PLUS A WONDERFUL STORY BRIMMING WITH LAUGHTER AND YOUNG LOVE!

Sterling Hayden · John Lund · Howard Da Silva
Billy De Wolfe · Cecil Kellaway
and Spike Jones and his Orchestra

THESE ARE JUST A FEW OF
42 GREAT STARS YOU'LL SEE

in

Variety Girl

STAR SPANGLED ENTERTAINMENT FROM PARAMOUNT

Produced by DANIEL DARE
Directed by GEORGE MARSHALL

Print advertisement for *Variety Girl* featuring a cavalcade of studio stars from Paramount. George might easily have been one of them.

George Pal, in the way of a clever sequence with the Puppetoons. (This was several years before Pal gave us *Destination Moon* and *War of the Worlds*.)

So what does all this have to do with George Reeves? Very little, if anything. Some sources affirm that George appears in this movie (as himself) while others maintain that he does not. The uncertainty is intensified by a color photo that was originally published in the June 1947 issue of Fortune magazine. It is a group shot that includes George, dressed like an old-time vaudevillian, standing proudly among his fellow thespians. Like every other actor at the studio, George was pressed into service by the publicity department. But looking for George in the film itself can be downright frustrating. Many believe that he can be spotted in the finale, where a plethora of stars cavort across the stage while singing a tune called "Harmony." And if you look very close at the third row, you will see a dark-haired young man who looks something like the male lead in *So Proudly We Hail*. Unfortunately, the camera is a great distance away, and the young man zips by very quickly. Maybe it is our George. Maybe not. Considering that Reeves was at Paramount during the filming of *Variety Girl*, and obviously had some connection to the film, we are including it among his credits.

For viewers with a cinematic sweet tooth for this fodder, this will entertain. For Reeves fans, it is another of life's rich canvas of mysteries. Of interest is future Captain Midnight television star Richard Webb's billed cameos. One would surmise that George, who co-starred in *So Proudly We Hail* for the studio four years earlier, would have had more reason to be a credited feature player than an invisible extra. The show's regular players include a young DeForest Kelley, whose character is central to the movement of the piece. Also soggily on board is George's frequent screen mate Frank Ferguson (Lady In Black), who is soaked more times than Jimmy Olsen in an hour and a half.

Cast: Bing Crosby, Bob Hope, Gary Cooper, Ray Milland, Alan Ladd, Barbara Stanwyck, Paulette Goddard, Dorothy Lamour, Sonny Tufts, William Holden, Joan Caulfield, Burt Lancaster, Lizabeth Scott, Sterling Hayden, Gail Russell, Diana Lynn, Veronica Lake, Robert Preston, William Bendix, John Lund, Barry Fitzgerald, Macdonald Carey, Howard DeSilva, Cass Daley, Olga San Juan, Patric Knowles, Billy De Wolfe, William Demarest, Mona Freeman, Cecil Kellaway, Virginia Field, Richard Webb, Frank Faylen, DeForrest Kelley, Glen Tryon, Frank Ferguson, Cecil B. DeMille, Mitchell Leisen, Frank Butler, George Marshall, Nella Walker, Torben Meyer, Jack Norton, Elaine Riley, Charles Victor, Gus Taute, Harry Hayden; Specialty numbers by Pearl Bailey, Spike Jones and his City Slickers, Jim Mulcay, Mildred Mulcay; and Introducing Mary Hatcher.

A PARAMOUNT PICTURE; Produced by Daniel Dare; Directed by George Marshall; Original Screenplay by Edmund Hartmann, Frank Tashlin, Robert Welch, and Monte Brice; Director of Photography: Lionel Linden, A.S.C. and Stuart Thompson, A.S.C.; Special Puppetoon Sequence by Thornton Hee and William Cottrell; Music Score and Direction: Joseph J. Lilley; Music Associate: Troy Sanders; Special Orchestral Arrangements: Van Cleave; Music Score for Puppetoon Sequence: Edward Plumb; Songs by Johnny Burke, James Van Heusen, Allan Roberts, and

Doris Fisher; New Songs by Frank Loesser; Edited by LeRoy Stone; Stars' Gowns: Edith Head; Production Gowns: Dorothy O'Hara; Chorus Costumes: Waldo Angelo; Musical Numbers Staged by Billy Daniels and Bernard Pearce; Make-Up Supervision: Wally Westmore; Assistant Director: George Templeton; Art Direction: Hans Dreier and Robert Clatworthy; Special Photographic Effects: Gordon Jennings, A.S.C.; Process Photography: Farciot Edouart, A.S.C.; Puppetoon Sequence in Technicolor Executed by George Pal; Sound Recording by Gene Merritt and John Cope; Set Decoration: Sam Comer and Ross Dowd. Original Theatrical Release: August 29, 1947. Running time: 93 minutes.

THE SAINTED SISTERS
Flim Flam Sisters With a Peekaboo Scam

Set in the gaslight era, *The Sainted Sisters* begins with a humorous forward: "In 1781, Yorktown was taken by General Washington. In 1865, Richmond was taken by General Grant. And in 1905, Oswald T. Lederer was taken by two dames."

Lederer (Harold Vermilyea) is an old geezer who has been swindled by two sisters (confidence women by profession) to the tune of $25,000. After realizing he's been had, Lederer makes a full report to the authorities, who promptly issue a circular identifying the female felons as Helen and Evelyn Smith. Their true identities are Letty and Jane Stanton, two stunningly attractive blondes who have a saintly look about them. Letty (Veronica Lake) is the feisty and strong-willed sister, while Jane (Joan Caulfield) is the more compassionate and straight-laced one. As the sisters head for the Canadian border, their buggy catches fire and they are forced to make a stop in the tiny town of Grove Falls, Maine. In the middle of the night, the girls sneak into the home of Robbie McCleary (Barry Fitzgerald), a pleasant but somewhat shifty Irishman who builds cemetery monuments for a living. Robbie is mildly bewildered by the presence of the two intruders and orders them to leave. But Letty, putting her feminine wiles to good use, sweet talks Robbie into accepting $1.00 as payment for a night's worth of lodging. The next morning, Robbie's attitude changes after catching a glimpse of the huge bank roll his "guests" are hoarding.

Robbie introduces the sisters to his friend, Vern Tewilliger (William Demarest), the town's lackadaisical sheriff. Vern manages to dodge most of his duties by nursing a supposedly injured leg, set in a huge cast that never comes off. Robbie and Vern bemoan the fact that their lives are made miserable by Hester Rivercomb (Beulah Bondi), a stingy biddy who delights in foreclosing on the many properties she owns. Hester is so conceited that she has commissioned Robbie to construct an ornate tomb for her eventual passing which, according to the townsfolk, can't occur soon enough.

In need of a wagon wheel, Letty and Jane are directed to the little shop owned by Sam Stokes (George Reeves), the town tinker. Sam greets the sis-

Print advertisement for *SAINTED SISTERS*. *"Pity poor George Reeves... he's in love with both of the most kissable sisters in history!"* says the ad copy.

ters rather coldly—until he gets a good look at them. "Why didn't you tell me they were so doggone pretty?" he asks young Judd Tewilliger (Darryl Hickman). Sam offers to drive the sisters to Moosehorn. But Robbie, having seen the incriminating circular, seizes the girls' money and blackmails them into remaining in town. Worse yet, Robbie uses the girls for domestic labor, requiring them to pump water, milk animals, and serve him breakfast in bed.

The girls find a map depicting a spot where their money might be buried. Robbie catches the duo after a rigorous digging in the cemetery,

Veronica Lake, Joan Caulfield, and George in *Sainted Sisters*.

bringing an end to any plans to skip town. Before leaving the cemetery, Robbie and the sisters overhear the prayers of a pathetic woman, the widow Davitt (Dorothy Adams), as she stands over the grave of her husband. She is in desperate need of a cow in order to save the family farm. The next day, a cow mysteriously turns up in the widow's backyard. This is attributable to Robbie, who purchased the animal with some of the cash he is "holding" for the girls. Soon, nearly everyone in Grove Falls is praying for, and receiving, something urgently needed.

Angered over the way they are being exploited, the sisters take a dip in the river, decked out in their spiffy 1890s swimsuits. They encounter Sam as he busily calculates the water flow, noting how the current would be vital to the electrical power plant he hopes to build some day. All Sam needs to accomplish this dream is $30,000, a sum his Aunt Hester could easily invest, but will not.

The sisters beg Robbie for their money so they can move on. But he dangles a newspaper in their faces, confirming their worst fears. Moments later, the townspeople congregate in front of Robbie's place, demanding to see Letty and Jane. The girls assume that the mob has finally learned the truth about them. However, all the folks want to do is thank the sisters for their generosity. Letty makes it clear that she and her sister had nothing to do with the many gifts that have been handed out. Nevertheless, everyone in town (with the exception of Hester) seems to be in love with these two angels of charity. Sam, in particular, is smitten with both girls and applies for a "blank marriage certificate," as he can't decide which sister he would

Publicity
photographs for
Sainted Sisters.

George and Joan Caulfield in *SAINTED SISTERS*.

like to marry. Vern suggests he make separate trips with the girls to Crown Point, the most romantic spot in town. Sam follows the sheriff's advice and enjoys romantic interludes with both Stantons—first with Jane, then Letty. This, of course, causes a rift between the sisters, especially when Jane expresses a desire to remain in Grove Falls.

A public forum is held at the town's bank. The topic of discussion is Sam's proposal to establish a power plant that would pump new life in the lackluster town. But Aunt Hester is the only person who could finance such a project, and she refuses to fork over the $30,000. She will, however, put up half the money—but only if the town can raise the other half. After Hester's money is placed is a safe-deposit box, Letty makes a moving (and totally insincere) speech about how much the town means to her and Jane. As a result, Letty is entrusted with the key to the safe-deposit box, much to the approval of the unsuspecting crowd.

Letty tells her sister that Robbie has hidden the money in Hester's unfinished burial plot. She also tells Jane that she intends to run off not only with their money, but also the town's. When Jane objects to this, Letty slaps her across the face, threatening to tell Sam everything about their unsavory past. All such plans, however, are thwarted by Sam, who has finally decided which sister he wants as his bride. "Jane," he says softly. "I want you to be my sister-in-law!" Sam and Letty kiss passionately.

Shortly after the girls "rob" the cemetery, Robbie's house is struck by lightning. Sam enters the blazing structure to rescue Robbie, who is

Veronica Lake and George in *Sainted Sisters*.

nowhere in sight. Soon, everyone on the scene worries that the sisters might be trapped in the fire. Even Hester, in a rare display of emotion, gets involved in the action. "Save those girls!" she yells at Vern. Without hesitation, the sheriff rips off his cast and darts into the house, looking for the sisters. Ironically, when Vern manages to extricate himself from the smoldering house, he trips over a fire hose and breaks his leg!

During all this mayhem, Robbie is down at the river, confronting the sisters as they prepare to depart. Jane bids him a tearful farewell. Letty then steps forward and gives Robbie the town's money and the key to the safe-deposit box. The girls disclose their plans to go to New York, where they will accept whatever the law has in store for them. In a small boat, the sisters sail down the river, disappearing into the night.

Barry Fitzgerald and George in *SAINTED SISTERS*.

Veronica Lake and Joan Caulfield (seated, center) with George on the right in a scene from *SAINTED SISTERS*.

George and Joan Caulfield in a scene from *SAINTED SISTERS*.

Time goes by. It is the holiday season and a big electrical sign illuminates the sky: "Merry Christmas . . . The Town of Grove Falls." The streets now glisten with the bright lights of progress, all due to Sam's innovative vision. A wagon suddenly pulls up in front of th sheriff's office. "It's the sisters!" yells someone in the crowd. Letty and Jane are back, courtesy of the prison warden they have befriended (or perhaps bamboozled). Jane gets a big kiss from the town's bank executive (one of her many admirers), and Letty finds herself in Sam's arms. Several light bulbs on the town's sign are blacked out, with the remaining letters declaring "The End."

While not quite an "A" budget show, this is a film which should have put George's career back on track. He excelled in this type of film in the early 40s, and his acting chops had not diminished in 1948. The problem was that this genre had run its course, as audiences moved into the atomic age. Nonetheless, a thoroughly entertaining film when viewed today.

CAST: Veronica Lake, Joan Caulfield, Barry Fitzgerald, William Demarest, George Reeves, Beulah Bondi, Chill Wills, Darryl Hickman, Jimmy Hunt, Kathryn Card, Ray Walker, Clancy Cooper, Dorothy Adams, Hank Warden, and Harold Vermilyea.

A PARAMOUNT PICTURE; Produced by Richard Maibaum; Directed by William D. Russell; Screenplay by Harry Clock, N. Richard Nash; Adapted by Mindret Lord; Based on a story by Elisa Bialk, and a play by Elisa Bialk and Alden Nash; Director of Photography: Lionel Lindon, A.S.C.; Process Photography:

Farciot Edouart, A.S.C.; Set Decorations: Sam Comer and Grace Gregory; Music
Score: Van Cleave; Costumes: Edith Head; Edited by Everett Douglas; Make Up
Supervision: Wally Westmore; Sound Recording by Philip Wisdom and Gene
Garvin; Assistant Director: Francisco Day. Original Theatrical Release: April 30,
1948. Running time: 89 minutes.

JUNGLE GODDESS
Monkey Shines in the Poverty Row Jungle

In Larry Ward's Noel Neill biography *Truth, Justice, and the American Way
(The Life and Times of Noel Neill the Original Lois Lane),* Noel recalls that
George might have had an edge over other super hopefuls in the casting of
the Superman television show. "I don't think George got the job purely on
talent alone, although he was more than qualified. I knew he had taken up
with Toni Mannix, the wife of MGM boss Eddie Mannix, some years prior
to Superman. I also knew that she had promised to make him a star if he
divorced his wife, which he did." If this is true, did Toni arrange for George
to appear in this B-feature and its companion piece *Thunder In The Pines*?
Was this part of Mrs. Mannix's star power bootcamp, or was this obsessive
love gone nuts? Probably both!

Actors returning from World War II had varying experiences reviving
their careers, and George didn't have the greatest cinematic track record
after World War II. While George delivers a believable performance, this was
not a career building choice.

At a little pub in Johannesburg, two aviators mull over an intriguing
newspaper story about the late Peter Vanderhorn, whose will has just been
probated. The estate is offering a huge reward for the "discovery" of Greta
Vanderhorn, the descendant's daughter, who's been missing since her plane
crashed over the Zambesi territory in 1939. Motivated by greed, Bob
Simpson (Ralph Byrd) decides to cancel his next scheduled flight in order
to pursue the missing heiress. However, he has a tough time selling this idea
to his straight-laced partner, Mike Patton (George Reeves). Although the
pilots have a joint ownership in their plane, Bob has the controlling interest.
He wins the argument.

From the cockpit of their tiny plane, Mike and Bob are able to spot the
wrecked aircraft. After an uneventful landing in the jungle, they begin to
explore what appears to be uninhabited territory. But as the men approach
the wreckage, they come face to face with a band of natives. Bob is so startled that he shoots and kills one of the younger tribesmen. The pilots are
immediately captured and brought before the ruling goddess, who happens
to be none other than Greta Vanderhorn (Wanda McKay). Clad in a two-
piece leopard skin number that underscores her long blonde locks, Greta
coldly states the "the penalty for murder is the same here as anywhere else—
death."

Title lobby card for *JUNGLE GODDESS*.

The trial, such as it is, begins with the ominous sound of pounding drums. The "verdict" is announced by Greta. Since Mike didn't harm anyone, and in fact tried to avert violence, his life will be spared. He'll be permitted to leave the region after justice has been served. This means that Bob, the "white devil," will be executed on the next full moon, just eight nights away. After the sentencing, Greta summons Mike to her hut. In private, Greta is anxious to know what happened to her father. Mike informs the young heiress that her father is dead.

Mike, in turn, asks Greta how she achieved the dubious honor of being the "White Goddess" of the jungle. In a flashback to her school girl days in 1939, Greta is alarmed by a radio broadcast about the impending war in Europe. In order to be with her father, Greta boards the next available flight to South Africa. But the tiny plane carrying her crashed in the jungle. Miraculously, Greta is the only survivor. The natives, who have obviously never seen a white woman, bow to Greta and whisk her off to a hut where a young girl is dying. When the girl makes a startling recovery, the event is attributed solely to the "power" of this mysterious woman. All the natives, with the exception of the witch doctor (Smoki Whitfield), are grateful to "Monta Greta," as she comes to be worshiped.

Greta assured Mike that there will be no execution, and advises him to obey all her commands, no matter how bizarre they may seem. Understandably, she does not like Bob, and expresses displeasure over his caustic behavior. Mike assures her that while his buddy is "a little trigger-

Wanda McKay and George in *JUNGLE GODDESS*.

Wanda McKay, George, and Ralph Byrd in *JUNGLE GODDESS*.

happy," he is otherwise all right. Greta vows to get both men, and herself, back to civilization. Meanwhile, the natives begin to prepare the lethal snake poison that will be used to execute the condemned prisoner.

Bob suspects that Mike is planning to leave him behind, an accusation that begins to sour their already tenuous friendship. As their comradeship diminishes, Mike finds himself becoming the object of Greta's admiration. She invites him to dinner. "Greta, I'm so hungry I could eat a horse," says Mike. "You are," quips Greta. As they dine on this "tasty" delicacy, Mike explains that Bob still has possession of his compass and pistol. Something in Greta's hut catches Mike's eye," a carving made from a rare element used in the production of atomic energy. Mike shows the specimen to Bob, noting the possibility of a future return to the territory in order to conduct an expedition.

Overzealous about the prospect of wealth, Bob opts to make an immediate break just before dawn. Mike explains that Greta has already worked out an escape route for the three of them. "Who said anything about Greta?" snaps Bob. "It's tough enough getting through that jungle without being slowed down by a dame." With more than a twinge of anger in his voice, Mike asks, "Suppose they kill her?" Bob has a quick answer: "She doesn't have to be alive for us to collect the reward!" Not quite believing his ears, Mike says he'll attribute Bob's lack of compassion to the predicament he's in. "Nobody can be that much of heel," he concludes.

Mike and Greta decide that their departure should occur while the natives are away on their hunting expedition. While they are mapping things

Behind the scenes photograph from *JUNGLE GODDESS*.

George and Wanda McKay enjoy a quiet moment in *JUNGLE GODDESS*.

George and Ralph Byrd in a sinister scene from *JUNGLE GODDESS*.

Wanda McKay watches as George and Ralph Byrd struggle for the only gun in the jungle. Smoki Whitfield as the witch doctor was also featured in several of Monogram's "Bomba, the Jungle Boy" features and will appear in the "Drums of Death" episode of the *ADVENTURES OF SUPERMAN* a few years later.

out, Bob tries to trick Greta's assistant, Wanama (Armida) into helping him escape on his own. Mike quickly gets wind of this and has a clash with Bob over the pistol. During their struggle, the weapon discharges and seriously wounds the native guard. The shooting causes Mike, Bob, and Greta to make an immediate departure. However, the natives are soon on their trail, due in part to the angry witch doctor. During the run through the jungle, Greta injures her ankle. She offers to stay behind and let the pilots leave without her, so as not to imperil their lives. Bob thinks this would be a splendid idea. Mike, however, won't hear of it. The three of them wind up spending a night in the jungle. While Mike and Greta enjoy the cozy campfire, Bob snores away.

The next morning, Bob attempts to get the pistol away from Mike while he's asleep. The two of them get into a fist fight, which culminates with Mike getting knocked out. As Greta tries to revive him, the natives begin to close in swiftly. With the compass and pistol in his possession, Bob makes a hasty

The natives bow to the jungle goddess as George and Ralph Byrd arrive at the village.

retreat. But he makes the mistake of firing at several animals, arousing the natives. Eventually, Mike and Greta make it safely to the plane, but are attacked by a vengeful Bob. As the men go another round, the witch doctor hurls a spear into Bob's back. Mike shoots the witch doctor and says, "Poor devil," referring to his former partner. "He must have gone completely out of his mind." With all attention focused on the fallen native, Mike and Greta soar away in the plane, contemplating the life they will enjoy together.

While an improvement over *Thunder in the Pines*, *Jungle Goddess* still falls short on many levels. As with most of these low budget jungle pictures, generous amounts of poorly matched stock footage left over from previous decades were used to cut costs. *Jungle Goddess* is no exception. With an over-talkative script, a severe lack of action, and an off-track role for Ralph Byrd, this show is interesting, yet pedestrian. A strange mix.

Byrd is believable as a good guy gone bad, and Reeves maintains a degree of professionalism far above this show's plausibility. A starring role, but aimed at the same age group as Superman, this must have been a frustrating period for George. But the worst was yet to come over at Columbia, courtesy of Sam Katzman.

If one is a fan of Monogram's 'Bomba, The Jungle Boy' series, or Sam Katzman's 'Jungle Jim' films (Reeves co-starred in the opener) starring Johnny Weissmuller at Columbia, *Jungle Goddess* might be right up your alley (or vine).

CAST: George Reeves, Wanda McKay, Ralph Byrd, Arminda, Smoki Whitfield, Dolores Castle, Rudy Robles, Linda Johnson, Helena Grant, Fred Coby, Onest Conley, Zach Williams, Jack Carroll.

A LIPPERT RELEASE of a William Stephens Production; Produced by William Stephens; Directed by Lewis D. Collins; Original Screenplay by Jo Pagano; Photography: Carl Berger, A.S.C.; Edited by Norman A. Cerf; Assistant Director: Melville Shyer; Art Director: Martin Obzina; Set Decorations by Alfred E. Spencer; Sound by Glen Glenn; Music by Irving Gertz; Original Song: "There's No One In My Heart But You" by Irving Bibo, ASCAP. Original Theatrical Release: August 13, 1948. Running time: 62 minutes.

THUNDER IN THE PINES

Dick Tracy, Superman, Atom Man, and Lex Luthor
Get Lost In the Woods!

With its picturesque locations and rustic settings, *Thunder In The Pines* was originally released in "glowing sepia tone," (as was the first Columbia Superman Serial, released the same year), a gimmick duly publicized on the posters and lobby cards issued for its distribution. With George starring as a rugged logger who almost wins the girl, it's a film most likely to found in

The ad campaign featured "in glowing Sepia-Tone" as a hook to draw an audience to *THUNDER IN THE PINES*, an otherwise ordinary action picture.

the video collection of every Reeves fanatic. While *Thunder in the Pines* isn't quite on a par with *Jungle Goddess* (the other Lippert programmer that teamed George with Ralph Byrd) it is still an entertaining little picture.

"TIMBER!" That's the "thunder" heard throughout the pine woods of Twin Rivers County. At a little place called the Sky Light Café (it's actually a saloon), two former GIs are horsing around at the bar. Jeff Collins (George Reeves) has his pal Boomer "Baby Face" Benson (Ralph Byrd), clenched in a headlock. When they're not cutting down trees, these guys revel in guzzling down beer, fighting, and chasing women. Though they don't know it, the buddies also share something else: a mail-order bride named Yvette. They met her in France during the war, and she's been writing love letters to both of them ever since. She's also accepted passage money from Jeff and Boomer, though neither is aware of this.

Nick Roullade (Lyle Talbot), the owner of the saloon and logging magnate, is contractually obligated to produce and deliver a substantial number of logs. A shifty, cigar-smoking entrepreneur who cheats at cards, Nick offers Jeff an opportunity to make some ready cash. But Jeff turns him down, insisting that he and his partner only work for the "established and legitimate" lumber companies. "Besides," says Jeff, "we don't work for people we don't like!" Boomer, however, becomes interested in the job after drooling over a photo and letter he's just received from Yvette, announcing her imminent arrival. Later that day, Jeff receives the exact same photo and letter.

Boomer approaches Nick for the job that had been offered to Jeff. "You've got yourself a deal," says Nick without hesitation. Seconds later, Jeff shows up to accept the same position. "He can't work without me," says Jeff. "I'm his brains!" Taking the competitive nature of these guys into account, Nick turns the "deal" into a contest. In addition to the base salary, he'll pay a $1,000 bonus to the first man who can deliver a half million board feet by the first day of April. Jeff and his crew are assigned to the northern territory, while Boomer and his men tackle the southern region.

At the train station, Jeff and Boomer are bedazzled by the alluring figure of Yvette Charad (Denise Darcel). The two of them are soon at each other's throats when they realize they're vying for the same woman. Yvette, however, brings the clash to a halt by slapping the men into compliance. In her endearing French accent, Yvette informs Jeff and Boomer she'll run off to Canada if they don't stop their "silliness." When she makes her debut at the saloon, Yvette quickly runs afoul of Nick's girlfriend, the tough and worldly Pearl (Marion Martin). In an attempt to "punish" the guys who've been fussing over Yvette, Pearl serves up a wild mixture of bourbon, gin, vodka, beer, tequila, and bitters. While the male patrons can hardly sip the stuff, Yvette swallows it without a flinch and asks for a refill!

Jeff and Boomer's story makes the front page of the local newspaper. The headline informs us that the victor will also win the "French Beauty." With the competition in full swing, Boomer encounters some difficulty in getting his logs into the river. As he continues to lag behind schedule, Nick offers some assistance in the way of a hard drinking ex-con named Hammerhead Hogan (Greg McClure). Complicating matters for both camps is the "late thaw" that has been predicted this season. Because of the lingering frigid temperatures, both teams must resort to the use of explosives to loosen the frozen logs.

Yvette, now working as a barmaid, begins to question Bernard, the bartender (Vince Barnett), about Nick's financial status. Yvette begins to play up to Nick, who quickly succumbs to her aristocratic charms. The two of them take a motor trip up to the woods for a progress check. During this visit, Nick has a private exchange with Hogan, asking if the job can be completed by May. To his astonishment, Hogan says he thought the deadline was supposed to be the first day of April. Nick, however, obviously has something nefarious up his sleeve. With a beseeching grin on his face, Nick pulls out one of his oversize cigars and asks, "Have you got a match?" A short time later, Hogan is seen sabotaging Boomer's dynamite supply. He also attempts to ruin the other team's dynamite, but is caught immediately and roughed up by Jeff. Although Jeff had been in the lead, he begins to experience his share of problems. Boomer, on the other hand, successfully utilizes a fresh supply of dynamite and is able to "bust up" the jammed logs. Boomer wins the contest.

A defeated Jeff walks into Nick's office (the back room of the saloon) to collect his earnings. As they wait for Pearl to arrive with the cash, Jeff and Nick pass the time with a game of poker. When Pearl returns from the bank, she looks every inch the woman scorned. She quickly notices that Nick is cheating again, and takes great delight in fogging up his hidden mirror. With

Lobby card from *Thunder in the Pines*.

Lobby card from *THUNDER IN THE PINES*.

Jeff now getting an honest deal, he not only beats Nick out of a large pot, but ownership of the Sky Light as well. Boomer turns up at the saloon, wanting to know where his "bride" can be found. "Why don't you ask her husband?" says Pearl, sarcastically. Believing his pal has double-crossed him, Boomer is ready to tear into Jeff. But Pearl steps in and unmasks Nick as the unlikely groom. Jeff and Boomer realize they've been used by Yvette, who was only interested in snagging the richest guy in town. Ironically, Nick is now the poorest guy in town, having lost all his assets to Jeff in the poker game.

Pearl also discloses that Nick hired Hogan for the sole purpose of sabotaging Boomer's dynamite. Now Jeff and Boomer squabble over who's going to take the first punch at Nick. A barroom brawl erupts, with Nick receiving exactly what he deserves. "Hey Baby Face," says Jeff during the fracas, "Don't break up the place. We own it." After the commotion dies down, Jeff and Boomer resume their headlock stance. That is, until a young woman (with a missing leg) walks in. "Do you know who the owner is?" she asks. Boomer points to Jeff and says, "He is." With a big grin, Jeff says, "No. We are!" Partners till the end, Jeff and Boomer signal Bernard to draw three beers. The closing gag shows Bernard, on the barroom floor, dousing his bald head with the beer spewing from a large keg.

This triumvirate of superheroes and villains in a low budget film could have been a more rewarding experience for the viewer, but amid the stock shots and disposable writing, the co-stars get hopelessly lost in the pines.

Three years after this and its companion piece *Jungle Goddess*, Reeves would be introduced to American audiences as the second live action Superman.

Ralph Byrd was already typed as Chester Ghould's leading cinematic cop in the four Dick Tracy serials at Republic Studios, and two features at RKO in 1947, a year before landing at Lippert Studios. Featured in Tracy-like serials such as *Blake of Scotland Yard* (Victory 1937) and the top notch Lugosi serial, *SOS Coast Guard* (Republic 1937), in the early 1950s Byrd starred once again as Dick Tracy in the short-lived Dick Tracy TV series. Byrd died of a heart attack on August 15, 1952, and in a weird twist of fate, it was rumored that George Reeves would take over as Dick Tracy in a new TV series, after production shut down on the ADVENTURES OF SUPERMAN.

While Reeves and Byrd were type cast, Lyle Talbot was a versatile character actor whose resumé was long and varied. In Sam Katzman's second Superman serial installment, *Atom Man vs. Superman* (Columbia 1950), Talbot did double duty as Lex Luthor and the mysterious Atom Man.

A second leading man at Warner Brothers in the 1930s, Talbot ended up in two forgotten horrors, *The Thirteenth Guest* and *Shriek in the Night* while out on loan. In the "Forgotten Horrors (the Definitive Edition)" authors George E. Turner and Michael Price comment that "The Thirteenth Guest is outstanding by any standard." Years later, Talbot was featured in Ed Wood's *Plan 9 From Outer Space* (DCA 1959). He was a frequent visitor to TV screens in the 50s. He was a regular on Ozzie & Harriett, and played Mr. Denason on Leave It To Beaver, on which his son Steve Talbot played the Beaver's buddy Gilbert Bates.

CAST: George Reeves, Ralph Byrd, Greg McClure, Michael Whalen, Denise Darcel, Marion Martin, Lyle Talbot, Vince Barnett, Roscoe Ates, Tom Kennedy, Arno Tanney, Joey Ray.

A LIPPERT RELEASE; Produced by William Stephens; Directed by Robert Edwards; Screenplay by Maurice Tombragel; Original Story by Jo Pagano; Photography: Carl Berger; Assistant Director: Milville Shyer; Art Director: Martin Obzina; Musical Score and Direction: Ralph Stanley; Music Supervision: David Chudnow; Sound by Glen Glenn; Set Decorations by Alfred E. Spencer; Edited by Edward Mann. Released: December 24, 1948. Running time: 61 minutes.

JUNGLE JIM

Jungle Sam Katzman's Stock Shot Jungle,
and His Dilapidated Ape Men!

When former Olympic swimmer Johnny Weissmuller grew too old (and too pudgy) for his Tarzan loincloth, he took on the role of Jungle Jim. Between 1948 and 1955, Weissmuller starred in 16 programmers as the unflappable jungle hero, often described as "Tarzan with clothes." Interestingly, there are

Publicity
photographs from
JUNGLE JIM.

George and Johnny Weissmuller in *JUNGLE JIM*.

a few similarities between the "Jungle Jim" and "Superman" properties. Both characters appeared in newspaper comic strips before landing on the big screen, via producer Sam Katzman, at Columbia Pictures. Following their low-budget film adaptations, both characters made the switch to television. In 1956, a time when the Adventures of Superman was still flying high, Jungle Jim re-emerged in 26 half-hour TV episodes, much to the delight of the kiddie audience.

In this first entry in the film series, Jungle Jim tries to save a native who is about to become the next meal of a hungry leopard. Despite Jim's intervention, the young man is killed. Jim notices a vial, decorated with hieroglyphics, clenched in the victim's hand. He brings this unusual finding to the attention of Commissioner Marsden (Holmes Herbert), who orders an analysis. A short time later, the commissioner relays information about the vial to Bruce Edwards (George Reeves), an American photographer. Reckless enough to have squandered all his money, Edwards is living a hand-to-mouth existence, taking pictures of natives and selling his work for little remuneration. "It's a living," he muses. "It keeps me in food and drink. Mostly drink, of course!" Edwards seems mildly interested in the story about the vial, but goes on his way without wavering.

A dowdy government archeologist, Dr. Hillary Parker (Virginia Grey), is brought into the case. She cites three reasons why an expedition must be

George and Holmes Herbert in a scene from *JUNGLE JIM*.

conducted. First, the vial is ancient and therefore of great archeological value. Second, the fact that the vial is made of gold has fostered the belief that an entire collection might be out there, just waiting to be unearthed. The third and most important reason involves the contents of the vial. The dark, gummy, substance, known to induce paralysis and death, has great curative powers when properly administered to polio patients. Knowing that certain witch doctors use the stuff on the tips of their poison arrows, Jim leads Dr. Parker and company towards the Temple of Zimbalu.

The expedition team includes Jim's sidekick Kolu (played by future Superman villain Rick Vallin), and a sexy native girl, Zia (Lita Baron). They encounter all the exotic dangers of the jungle—gators, insects and wild beasts. But nothing startles Jim more than the discovery of Edwards, taking a peaceful snooze, during a nocturnal excursion. Dr. Parker, unbeknownst to Jim, has invited Edwards to join the group in order to keep a photographic record of the expedition. Jim, however, has serious reservations about the photographer. Sure enough, as the company trudges near the edge of a precipice, Edwards shows his true colors. Pretending to be tired and dizzy, Edwards stumbles into Jim, nearly knocking him to his death. Jim knows it was not an accident. "I'll be more careful," Edwards promises. "So will I," says Jim suspiciously.

Dr. Parker, Kolu, and Zia find themselves held captive at the very temple they've been seeking. Jim, in fierce pursuit, battles with the natives in his efforts to rescue the threesome. But in the midst of all the mayhem, Edwards calmly enters the scene, brandishing his press camera. Apparently, the natives regard the photographer as a god, solely because of his "power" to produce images on paper. (Exactly how he is able to develop prints in the jungle is not explained, of course.) "Don't expect me to use my magic to save your necks," he sneers at Dr. Parker. Desperately in need of money, and greedy enough to kill for it, Edwards has no qualms about watching his former comrades get slaughtered.

The native chief, feeling a bit slighted about not appearing in any of the photos, wants Edwards to use his "magic" one more time. But while Edwards is busy dumping loads of treasure into his case, Jim's pet crow uses its beak to remove the lens from the camera. The photographer is nabbed and brought before the chief. "Take picture—now!" he grumbles. Realizing that he can't take photos without the lens, Edwards tries to rationalize the situation. "Camera broken . . . no can use," he explains. But the chief doesn't understand these words and becomes highly insulted. As a result, the natives are now out for Edwards' blood. Although another full-scale fracas breaks

Lita Baron, Virginia Grey, George, and Johnny Weissmuller trek thru the Columbia backlot in *JUNGLE JIM*.

The cast and crew celebrate Virginia Grey's birthday party on the set of *JUNGLE JIM*.

out, Jim manages to free his fellow explorers and a group of prisoners who have been dangling from their feet for quite some time (the most bizarre, yet somehow humorous, aspect of the film).

Edwards gets hold of a gun and begins firing it madly. In an effort to escape, he goes so far as to kill one of the natives with his own spear. Nevertheless, the inevitable showdown between Jim and Edwards finally arrives. But before Jim can deliver the long awaited comeuppance, a native knocks Edwards into a deep pit of flames. Finishing the task at hand, Jim overpowers two of the last standing natives by knocking their heads together (á la Superman). With the expedition concluded, Jim is able to provide Dr. Parker with the treasure and the drug for polio.

Weissmuller's interpretation of Jungle Jim is the least satisfying of all three renditions of the character in other than the print media. In the dynamic 1937 Universal serial, Jim is an astute, educated hero with command of the English language. The same holds true with the radio show, which was a favorite of the airwaves in its day.

But when it came to Katzman's stock shot and plastic jungle, the part of Jim was not given to an actor, but was awarded to a personality. It is possible that Weissmuller's part was written down with as little dialogue as possible, to accommodate his semantic deficiencies, or mask his horrendous acting skills.

His characterization is nonexistent, and his line delivery is worthy of an award on the paint drying channel. It is to George's credit that this film is of any interest in 2005. His costars turn in highly professional performances, especially Lita Baron and future Superman co-star Rick Vallin.

This is not the way to start a series, but true to his form, Katzman squeezed a box office profit.

CAST: Johnny Weissmuller, Virginia Grey, George Reeves, Lita Baron, Rick Vallin, Holmes Herbert.

A COLUMBIA PICTURE; Produced by Sam Katzman; Directed by William Berke; Story and Screenplay by Carroll Young; Based upon the King Features Syndicate newspaper feature "Jungle Jim"; Director of Photography: Lester White, A.S.C.; Art Director: Paul Palmentola; Film Editor: Aaron Stell; Set Decorator: Sidney Clifford; Musical Director: Mischa Bakaleinikoff. Original theatrical release: December 31, 1948. Running time: 73 minutes.

THE MUTINEERS
Yo, Ho, Ho with Ramar and George

The Mutineers starts out as an atmospheric murder mystery set ashore. After the first reel, however, the film drifts into a shipboard melodrama with just enough action to keep it afloat. Sam Katzman, the czar of low-budget features and serials, produced the film for Columbia Pictures, who later reissued it under the title *Pirate Ship*. Though he receives third billing, George has the most desirable role as the ruthless, girl-slapping gangster who masterminds the piracy of an ocean freightliner. Jon Hall, the star, seems a bit wooden in his performance (even under Jean Yarborough's inspired direction) as the hero who saves the day and the ship. Matt Willis, a Columbia stalwart best remembered as the werewolf in the studio's *Return of the Vampire*, appears here as one of the mates.

The plot unfolds with the murder of Captain Jim Duncan (Lyle Talbot), the amiable skipper of the Island Princess. Because some counterfeit bills were found in the wallet of the slain captain, the authorities begin to dig into his past. This angers Nick Shaw (Jon Hall), the first mate, who refuses to believe his friend could have been involved in anything shady. Shaw sets out to uncover the truth on his own.

Posing as an ailing businessman, Thomas Nagle (George Reeves) boards the Princess, bound for Lisbon, with a cache of firearms and scads of counterfeit money. With the help of his mob, Nagle plots to highjack the vessel to Marseille, where he can readily sell the guns and exchange the fake currency for the real thing. When Shaw discovers the hidden cargo, he gets into a well choreographed fist fight with "Butch" (Tom Kennedy), one of Nagle's henchmen. Nagle conceals the weapons in his cabin, then instructs his moll,

George (far left) listens to Jon Hall in *THE MUTINEERS*.

Norma Harrison (Adele Jerkins), to find out what Shaw "is all about." When the attractive blonde meets Shaw for the first time, she coyly asks for a match, then a cigarette. In the most flirtatious possible way, she delivers the best line of dialogue in the film: "Isn't it strange how the best things in life are either a sin or make you fat?"

Nagle knows he's going to need a seasoned navigator. So he begins patronizing Shaw, and deliberately loses a large sum of money to him in a high stakes poker game. When Shaw realizes his winnings are counterfeit, he knows he's pinpointed the murderer. During the poker game sequence, and in other scenes throughout the film, Reeve's interpretation of Nagle is effectively underplayed. For instance, when Nagle informs the alcoholic Captain Stanton (Frank Jaquet) that he is hijacking the vessel, his tone of voice is as calm and pleasant as when he utters "good morning!" To the astonishment of the crew, Shaw goes along with Nagle's outrageousness, just long enough to learn his intentions and devise a strategy to take back the ship. But Nagle is not easily fooled. Even though he is the jealous type, Nagle encourages Norma to continue her romantic byplay with Shaw. "Play up to him," he tells her sarcastically, "and let your conscience act as a stop light."

To counteract the mutiny, Shaw sets fire to an oil drum, then rounds up his men during the ensuing distraction. The battle against the mutineers is unintentionally comical, with the crew using streams of water from the ship's fire hoses in addition to their guns. Inevitably, Shaw and Nagle find themselves heading their own factions. The first mate and his men occupy the main deck. Nagle and his motley crew are down below, in the engine room, where they have access to the controls, radio equipment, and food

Always the romantic, George with Adele Jerkins in *THE MUTINEERS*.

supply. Until he can be assured of total control, Nagle orders the ship to a halt. In order to get the ship moving, Shaw and his men stitch together large pieces of canvas which serve as sails in lieu of the inaccessible engines.

As the stalemate rages on, Nagle's henchmen detect the ship to be moving about three knots per hour. In desperation, Nagle offers Shaw a fifty-fifty split of the "profits." Before any deals can be discussed, Nagle and his thugs have something else to worry about: their area of the ship has been cut off from the flow of fresh air. Communicating through the tube, Shaw finally confronts Nagle about the murder of Captain Duncan. With the camera focused on the first mate, Nagle's voice blares from the tube. He shouts at Norma, "You told him!" Several loud slaps are heard, followed by a gunshot, then a scream. Moments later, the patrolmen from the Lisbon Harbor arrive on deck; they inspect the engine room, where Nagle's lifeless body is sprawled on the floor. Rogers (Pat Gleason), one of the thugs, surrenders a pistol to one of the officers. "I told him not to hit her," he says solemnly. As the authorities escort the mutineers off the ship, Norma once again asks Shaw for a match, then a cigarette. This time, however, she doesn't flirt with him. She simply turns her back and walks away as the picture goes to black.

Despite his stiff performance, Jon Hall had a varied and successful career in motion pictures and television. Hall, a native of central California (Fresno), began life in 1915 as Charles Lockner, changing his moniker to Lloyd Crane before settling on the professional name Jon Hall. He was a screenwriter, producer, and director, as well as being a stage and screen leading man. His career paralleled George's as he was on television with Ramar of the Jungle. His life also mirrored George's when he took his life on December 13, 1979 by shooting himself, after a long battle with cancer.

Highlights of his picture work include: *Charlie Chan in Shanghai* (1935), *The Lion Man* (1936), *The Mysterious Avenger* (1936), *The Clutching Hand* (1936 serial), *The Hurricane* (1937), *The Invisible Agent* (1942), *Arabian Nights* (1942), *White Savage* (1943), *Ali Baba and the Forty Thieves* (1944), and his last picture, Beach Girls and the Monster (1963).

Adele Jerkins is also on board to provide the boilage factor. She sizzled the screen in 1951 with Abbott & Costello in *A&C Meet the Invisible Man*, and Roger Corman's first science fiction show, *Day the World Ended* (1956).

CAST: Jon Hall, Adele Jerkins, George Reeves, Noel Cravat, Don C. Harvey, Matt Willis, Tom Kennedy, Pat Gleason, Frank Jaquet, and Lyle Talbot.

A COLUMBIA PICTURE; Produced by Sam Katzman; Directed by Jean Yarborough; Screenplay by Ben Bengal, Joseph Carole; Story by Dan Gordon; Director of Photography: Ira H. Morgan, A.S.C.; Art Director: Paul Palmentola; Film Editor: James Sweeney; Set Decorator: David Montrose; Musical Director: Misha Bakaleinikoff. Reissued as *Pirate Ship*. Original theatrical release: April 22, 1949. Running time: 60 minutes.

SPECIAL AGENT
Riding the Rails, with Reeves—well, sort of

Special Agent is an old-fashioned cops-and-robbers yarn that should interest anyone who likes vintage trains. In fact, the forward title declares that the story is "based on material in the official file of American Railroads." It's a film that takes itself very seriously (despite an archaic plot) and looks as though it could have been the prototype for such early TV fare as 'Racket Squad' and 'Dragnet.'

The narrator (Truman Bradley, later host of the popular 1950s television series Science Fiction Theater) explains that for more than a hundred years, the Special Agents have tracked down train wreckers, hold-up men, baggage thieves, and a variety of other "criminally minded" people. While an agent's job is thought to be exhilarating, it is actually boring most of the time. Such is the case with Johnny Douglas (William Eythe), a young agent paying his dues in a rural California community. "Nothing ever happens in Santa Marta—except you," he complains to Lucille Peters (Laura Elliot), an attractive railroad secretary with a disarming smile and innocent charm. (Elliot later changed her name to Kasey Rogers, and went on to portray Louise Tate on the popular TV series Bewitched.)

Johnny's boredom does not last long. The passengers aboard "old number 6," a combination freight and passenger train, are shocked when they hear an enormous explosion in Tunnel 13. While the ancient locomotive sits idle in the darkness, three men are shot and killed. The victims are Pop Peters, the engineer and Lucy's father, Jake Rumpler, the fireman, and Dan Simmons, a U.S. Postal clerk. After being briefed, Johnny has the dreaded task of informing Lucy that her father has been murdered. Lucy, in turn, breaks the tragic news to Mrs. Rumpler (Virginia Christine, who co-starred with George in 1953's Superman episode "Lady in Black" as the Lady herself. She later was a spokesperson for Folger's coffee), who is left with two fatherless boys. Johnny and a team of investigators learn that two registered postal sacks, containing a $100,000 payroll, were stolen from the rail car.

The men who perpetrated this crime are brothers and have sought refuge in a nearby mine shaft. The younger brother, Paul Devereaux (George Reeves), injured his ankle during the heist and was only able to carry one of the postal sacks. The heavier sack (with the bulk of the loot) has been hidden at the top of a mutilated tree in a remote location. Paul is a choir-boy-gone-wrong type of guy. Rugged on the outside, sensitive on the inside. When his conscience begins to nag, he expresses regret over the fact that three men were murdered. His brother Edmond (Paul Valentine), the one who actually fired the shots, exhibits not the slightest sign of remorse. Edmond coldly states that it was necessary to eliminate the men because they were potential witnesses (they saw Paul's face when his mask fell off). An embittered man, Edmond's chief rationale is that the victims were much like the scoundrels

Laura Elliot, George, William Eythe, Paul Valentine, and Carole Matthews, the lead players of SPECIAL AGENT.

who deprived the Devereaux family of its wealth. Moreover, Edmond clings to the wayward belief that the stolen money can re-establish the family name, something he has promised to do for Grandpa Devereaux (Frank Puglia).

Johnny devotes all of his energy to cracking the case, which has now escalated into "the greatest criminal manhunt in the history of California railroading." The young agent begins to enlist the aid of several top criminologists, presenting them with odd pieces of evidence, such as grains of salt and a copy of Tolstoy's "War and Peace." As the investigation continues, several witnesses provide clues from which a pair of composite sketches are drawn.

At the Devereaux farm, just outside Santa Marta, Grandpa receives some devastating news. The old man is told, rather bluntly, that he can no longer run his cattle on the acres of land that once belonged to him. However, Edmond and Paul promise to repurchase the land with the $100,000 they have supposedly "made" from a recent business venture. But before anyone can sign on the dotted line, one of the residents identifies the criminals on the police sketches to be the Devereaux boys. This news quickly reaches the ears of Paul's girlfriend, Rose McQuery (Carole Matthews). She alerts Paul, who flees into the night with Edmond, just as the sheriff and his men are about to close in. When Grandpa learns the truth, he begins to sob quietly and pathetically, taking the blame for filling the boys' heads with nonsense about restoring the family name.

In a desperate effort to partially vindicate himself, at least in the eyes of his sweetheart, Paul steals a car and turns up at Rose's house unexpectedly.

Like most of the VHS copies of this film, here is George in a dark, moody scene from *SPECIAL AGENT*.

Laura Elliot and George in *SPECIAL AGENT*.

He tells the young woman that he never intended to hurt anyone, and certainly didn't kill anyone. He comes dangerously close to getting caught by Johnny, who drops by to ask Rose a few questions. Suspecting that Rose might know more than she's willing to let on, the agent mentions the possibility of someone collecting the substantial reward money. Rose, however, remains loyal to Paul and the search for the missing brothers rambles on.

With the Devereaux boys at large for what seems like forever, the authorities begin to doubt Johnny's competence. And in the absence of progress, all documents regarding the Devereaux matter get stashed in the same filing cabinet with the other unsolved crimes. But the case is back on the front burner when the two Rumpler boys discover the missing sack hidden atop the mutilated tree. Johnny and the sheriff's department replace the currency with torn strips of paper and small rocks; they wait in silence for one of the brothers to fall into their trap. During the night, Paul climbs up the tree and retrieves the sack, not realizing that he is being watched. When

Paul Valentine (left) and George are out-gunned by William Eythe in *SPECIAL AGENT*.

Paul returns to the mine shaft, Edmond accuses him of attempting to abscond with the cash. The brothers get into a scuffle, which is cut short by the arrival of Johnny and the other lawmen. During the confrontation, Edmond is shot and killed on the spot. Paul is taken into custody and the case is finally concluded. From this day forward, Special Agent Douglas never complains about things being dull in the sleepy town of Santa Marta.

A bit dated for today's eyes and ears, Special Agent is a prime example of 1949's version of Your Government At Work, whether it be in the skies or riding the rails. Unfortunately, the only way to see this film is on the collector's market, where an unacceptably dark print is all that is available. A real shame, because this picture is an unusual entry for railroad noir fans, if there is such a thing. (We are told there are.)

CAST: William Eythe, George Reeves, Laura Elliot, Paul Valentine, Tom Powers, Carole Mathews, Frank Puglia, Virginia Christine, Raymond Bond, John Hilton.

A PARAMOUNT PICTURE; Produced by William H. Pine and William C. Thomas; Directed by William C. Thomas; Screenplay by Lewis R. Foster and Whitman Chambers; Based on material by Milton Raison; Director of Photography: Ellis W. Carter; Art Direction: Lewis H. Creber; Film Editor: Howard Smith; Sound Recording: Tom Lambert; Set Decoration: Alfred Kegerrs; Narrated by: Truman Bradley; Music Score by Lucien Cailliet. Theatrical release date: July 22, 1949. Running time: 70 minutes.

SAMSON AND DELILAH

Mr. DeMille, George is Ready for his Close-Up!

Though it has been re-made more than once, many historians consider this Cecil B. DeMille production to be the definitive telling of the famous story from the Old Testament. Lavish sets, scanty costumes, and brilliant casting characterize this Technicolor epic which turned out to be one of Paramount's biggest hits, and is still today a popular selection on home video.

The setting is Palestine, 1000 BC, where Samson (Victor Mature), a humble Danite, becomes known as the strongest man alive. Though capable of killing a lion with his bare hands, the mighty Samson is as susceptible to women as any other man. And he has ruffled quite a few feathers by falling in love with Semadar (Angela Lansbury), a Philistine woman whom he intends to marry. But Samson and Semadar are never united in marriage. She is killed during a fracas at what was supposed to be their wedding cele-

Hedy Lamarr and Victor Mature in Cecil B. DeMille's epic masterpiece.

bration. However, Semadar's sister Delilah (Hedy Lamarr) has an unrelenting passion for Samson, and uses every one of her feminine wiles to snag him. She fails.

As Samson's reputation grows, he runs afoul of the Saran of Gaza (George Sanders), a tyrant who is in love with Delilah himself. As a result, the young Danite is voraciously hunted and captured by a large army. Adhering to his unwavering faith, Samson prays for the power to overcome the insurmountable force that has surrounded him. His prayers are duly answered, as evidenced by the wind and lightning that instantly materialize (a nice DeMille touch). In one of his most amazing displays of power, Samson defeats the entire army and emerges totally unscathed, his body glistening with the sweat of victory.

Later, one of the wounded soldiers (George Reeves) is sprawled at the feet of the Saran, delivering a first hand account of the ordeal he has barely survived. "Never did mortal man fight like this," the messenger testifies. "His strength was greater than any instrument of war!" (Reeves has about one page of dialogue which he conveys with his usual gusto.) But the Saran does not believe the messenger, especially when he describes the atmospheric manifestations, and the fact that Samson's only "weapon" was the jawbone of an ass!

Believing herself to be a woman scorned, Delilah offers to turn Samson over to the Saran (for a hefty price), with the understanding that no blade shall touch his skin and his blood will not be spilled. Through treachery and deception, Delilah learns that the secret of Samson's strength is his long hair. Moments after she shears off his locks, a totally powerless Samson is apprehended by the Saran's henchmen. He is brutally blinded and subjected to the most heinous form of slavery. Then, after realizing what she has done, Delilah foolishly seeks to win Samson's love by extricating him from the daily torture he is enduring.

The most impressive sets and special effects are saved for the final reel of the film, in which Samson is put on display at the temple where he is to be scourged. Delilah secretly attempts to help him escape. But with Samson's strength fully restored, he topples the columns of the structure on which he had positioned himself. A domino effect ensues, and soon the entire temple is destroyed, bringing death to Samson, Delilah, and hundreds of spectators.

Samson and Delilah plays a pivotal role in the storytelling process of Billy Wilder's classic Hollywood fable *Sunset Boulevard* (Paramount 1950). It is on the Samson set that Norma Desmond reunites with her silver screen creator, Cecil B. DeMille. In an emotional tidal wave, Norma is re-introduced to her old studio and its remaining inhabitants, only to glaze over and return to a world only she lives in.

In this celluloid reality, DeMille's production assistant Gordon Cole merely wishes to rent Miss Desmond's exotic car. An effective use of the movie within a movie fiddle, and a glimpse at the shooting on *Samson and Delilah* on Paramount's Stage 18!

While George performs well in this epic, it must have been intensely frustrating to be slogging through bit parts to pay the rent.

CAST: Hedy Lamarr, Victor Mature, George Sanders, Angela Lansbury, Henry Wilcoxon, Olive Deering, Fay Holden, Julia Faye, Russell Tamblyn, William Farnum, Lane Chandler, Moroni Olsen, Francis J. McDonald, William Davis, John Miljan, Arthur Q. Bryan, Laura Elliott (Kasey Rogers), Victor Varconi, John Parrish, Frank Wilcox, Russell Hicks, Boyd Davis, Fritz Leiber, Mike Mazurki, Davison Clark, George Reeves, Pedro DeCordoba, Frank Reicher, Colin Tapley.

A PARAMOUNT PICTURE; Produced and Directed by Cecil B. DeMille; Screenplay by Jesse L. Lasky, Jr. and Fredric M. Frank; From Original treatments by Harold Lamb and Vladimir Jabotinsky; Based on the History of Samson and Delilah in the Holy Bible, Judges 13-16; Music by Victor Young; Color by Technicolor; Technicolor Director: Natalie Kalmus; Associate: Robert Brower; Director of Photography: George Barnes, A.S.C.; Director of Photographic Effects: Gordon Jennings, A.S.C.; Unit Directors: Arthur Rosson, Ralph Jester; Art Direction: Hans Dreier, Walter Tyler; Process Photography: Farciot Edouart, A.S.C., Wallace Kelley, A.S.C.; Holy Land Photography: Dewey Wrigley, A.S.C.; Choreographer: Theodore Kosloff; Dialogue Supervision: Frances Dawson, James Vincent; Assistant Director: Edward Salven; Edited by Anne Bauchens; Costumes: Edith Head, Gile Steele, Dorothy Jeakins, Gwen Wakeling, Elois W. Jenssen; Set Decoration: Sam Comer, Ray Moyer; Special Photographic Effects: Paul Lerpae, A.S.C., Devereux Jennings, A.S.C.; Make-Up Supervision: Wally Westmore; Research: Henry Noerdlinger, Gladys Percey; Sound Recording by Harry Lingdren, John Cope. Original Theatrical Release: December 21, 1949. Running time: 130 minutes.

THE GREAT LOVER

Superman, Murdered by Topper, with Mr. Magoo Watching

The Great Lover opens with a nighttime view of a glitzy hotel in the heart of Paris. The camera pans up to one of the lavish suites where an elderly gentleman, C.J. Dabney (Roland Young), is cautiously closing the window and drapes. Seated nearby is a strapping young American, Williams (George Reeves), who is happily counting a wad of cash he's just won in a poker game with Dabney.

Despite the fact that he's lost a large sum of money, Dabney remains a congenial host and uncorks a bottle of champagne. "As the French so aptly put it—c'est la vie," he says softly. The men sip their drinks as they recount the events of the evening. Williams takes great delight in confessing that he knew his opponent was a card shark from the outset. He dispenses a rather smug assessment of Dabney: "A retired millionaire. Plays cards for the fun of it. Loves to lose! I had you pegged from the minute you fumbled with those cards!"

Dabney feigns indifference. "It was a nice try anyway," he says in mock sadness, also mentioning how his techniques "always worked so well" in the

Another rare photograph of Roland Young and George in THE GREAT LOVER.
COURTESY OF THE ACADEMY OF MOTION PICTURE ARTS AND SCIENCES.

past. "But not tonight," says Williams gleefully. Williams plops himself in a chair, unaware that Dabney is positioned behind him, carefully fashioning a knot in the cloth that had been wrapped around the champagne bottle. "Don't feel too bad," Williams continues. "You can't win all the time. As the French so aptly put it . . ." Before Williams can finish his mimicking discourse, Dabney swiftly tightens the linen around the young man's neck. The camera focuses on one hand, clutching desperately at thin air, as the life is choked out of Williams. (The hand close-up reveals the pinky ring that George will still be wearing a few years later, as Clark Kent, on the ADVENTURES OF SUPERMAN.)

Dabney isn't merely an eccentric card shark; he's a killer card shark who always utilizes the same method of strangulations. His distinctive knots are

Roland Young and George in the opening scene of THE GREAT LOVER.
COURTESY OF THE ACADEMY OF MOTION PICTURE ARTS AND SCIENCES.

not lost on Police Inspector Higgins (Jim Backus), who is hot on Dabney's trail, knowing that another "innocent" young American will soon be targeted. Enter Freddie Hunger (Bob Hope), a bumbling newspaper man who is the equally bumbling scoutmaster of The Boy Forrestors. As luck would have it, Dabney, Freddie, and his overly studious troops, are all on the same ocean-liner bound for New York.

While on deck, Freddie meets and falls for the alluring Duchess of Alexandria (Rhonda Fleming), who is accompanying her father, Grand Duke Maximillian (Roland Culver) to the States. The Duke and Duchess, though seemingly regal, are in fact penniless. They are easily convinced that Freddie is a millionaire, thanks to a pack of lies effectuated by Dabney. The subject of money precipitates laughs in several ways. For instance, when Dabney needs to get Freddie out of the way, he asks him to procure change of a one hundred dollar bill. Freddie obliges. When he asks a passerby for change, he finds himself face to face with Jack Benny. Was it really the one and only Mr. Tightwad? "Nah," says Freddie to himself. "He'd never be traveling first class!"

The script provides Hope with many clever one-liners, and ample opportunities to deliver his exaggerated affectations and sexual innuendos, especially when he's enjoying the company of an attractive female. There's also much byplay between Freddie and the troop, mostly when the boys catch their leader engaging in such sordid acts as smoking, drinking, and gambling. One memorable scene has the boys coaching Freddie through his early morning calisthenics—while he's nursing a monumental hangover.

The real fun begins when the Duke loses a substantial sum of money to Freddie in a crooked game of poker. When Freddie realizes that Dabney is behind all the chicanery, the veteran miscreant starts to tie a knot in a cloth, mumbling his "c'est la vie" routine, just as he had done with Williams in the first reel. Dabney attempts to strangle Freddie, but his efforts are thwarted by the unexpected arrival of Inspector Higgins. The Inspector later takes Freddie into his confidence, and explains that more evidence is needed in order to convict a criminal of Dabney's caliber. A short time later, Higgins is found dead—with a knotted cloth by his side.

Dabney telephones the Duke and tells him that Freddie is the real culprit. Soon everyone, including the scouts, are hunting for Freddie, who has sought refuge in the ship's dog kennel. When the Duchess finds Freddie in hiding, she learns the truth about Dabney. The couple decide to search for some tangible evidence that can be used to bring the true criminal to justice. In the course of playing amateur sleuth, Freddie finds himself dangling overboard, on the end of a rope, and is nearly drowned. The scouts eventually rescue Freddie who, in turn, comes to the aid of the Duchess as she is about to be strangled by you-know-who. The authorities arrive on the scene just in the nick of time, and Dabney is finally apprehended. With the voyage over, Freddie attempts to bid the Duchess adieu, but she won't hear of it. They indulge in a kiss for the fadeout, while the scouts look on with dubious admiration.

With the death of Bob Hope at the age of one hundred, many historians and fans are re-examining his varied career. *The Great Lover* is a show that showcases Hope's talents, supported by an excellent cast and production values, and delivers on many levels. While George has no scenes with Hope, he is highly effective in what little screen time he has. The viewer is left wanting more, but ends up in a Bob Hope comedy/mystery instead of a full-fledged mystery. No matter, the George prologue sets up the film perfectly and believably. Too bad Hope, Reeves, and Benny didn't share a scene.

Roland Young, famous for being Topper in the Topper film series, is well cast as the gambler turned homicidal maniac. Jim Backus, who would later become a star as the voice of Mr. Magoo, was reportedly a friend of George's last girlfriend, Lenore Lemmon.

CAST: Bob Hope, Rhonda Flemming, Roland Young, Roland Culver, Richard Lyon, Gary Gray, Jerry Hunter, Jackie Jackson, Karl Wright Esser, Orley Lindgren, Curtis Lays Jackson, Jr., George Reeves, Jim Backus, Sig Arno, and Jack Benny (unbilled).

A PARAMOUNT PICTURE; Produced by Edmund Beloin; Directed by Alexander Hall; Written by Edmund Beloin, Melville Shavelson, and Jack Rose; Director of Photography: Charles B. Lang, Jr., A.S.C.; Art Director: Hans Drier and Earl Hedrick; Special Photographic Effects: Gordon Jennings A.S.C.; Process Photography: Farciot Edouart, A.S.C.; Set Decoration: Sam Corner and Ross

Dowd; Edited by Ellsworth Hoagland; Costumes by Edith Head; Make-Up Supervision by Wally Westmore; Assistant Director: John Coonan; Sound Recording: Harold Lewis and Walter Oberst; Music Score by Joseph J. Lilley; Songs by Jay Livingston and Ray Evans. Original theatrical release: December 28, 1949. Running time: 80 minutes.

THE ADVENTURES OF SIR GALAHAD

a Serial in 15 Chapters
King Katzman's Cardboard Round Table

Sound movie serials are a lost art. Gone are those lazy Saturdays spent at neighborhood theaters, where for a quarter you could enter a movie palace (in varying degrees of decay) and view a serial chapter, three or four short subjects, and a full length feature—and probably score some popcorn and candy to boot.

The audience would be made up mostly of kids whose Ritalin had worn off, and a few strange adults who hadn't yet played out their arrested development childhoods. If they were lucky, they would be treated to a Republic or Universal serial chapter to kick off the Saturday matinee. The Columbia serials of the late 1930s to mid-40s were passable entertainment, but the Columbia serials of the late 1940s to the mid-50s left much to be desired. This, George's only serial offering, isn't the worst Sam Katzman serial, but would easily fall into a 'top twenty' list of Katzman clunkers.

Sir Galahad could be the most convoluted rendering of the Camelot legacy ever committed to films.

CHAPTER ONE
THE STOLEN SWORD

Chapter One opens with veteran announcer Knots Manning's narration describing the days of old in Camelot, where knights vie for the right to sit with King Arthur (Nelson Leigh) at the Round Table. Galahad (George Reeves) proves himself, but before he assumes his chair at the Round Table, the magic sword Excalibur is stolen on his watch.

Galahad is denied knighthood until he retrieves and returns Excalibur to King Arthur. Meanwhile, Merlin the Magician (William Fawcett), aide and confidant to King Arthur, predicts doom and disaster for Camelot upon the loss of Excalibur.

A courier enters Arthur's court and informs Arthur that King Ulric's (John Merton) Saxons have invaded Britain. Merlin crows as his dire warnings become reality. Later, Morgan (Pat Barton) tells Galahad that Excalibur could be in the Enchanted Forest.

In Merlin's domain, the Enchanted Forest, Merlin bewitches, blinds, and burns him alive as a fitting cliffhanger to the first episode.

CHAPTER TWO
GALAHAD'S DARING!

Galahad is saved by the Lady of the Lake's (Lois Hall) magic, which is more powerful than Merlin's.

Galahad teams up with Sir Bors (Charles King), a knight of the Round Table, to protect Camelot. In an underground hide-out, the mysterious Black Knight presents Bartog (Don Harvey), a knight of King Ulric's court, with Excalibur to aid in conquering King Arthur's Britain.

Galahad and Bors see Bartog on a mountain road with Excalibur, and give chase. After a losing battle the pair split up, with Galahad following Bartog and Bors returning to Camelot to inform Arthur of their progress. Galahad spies on Bartog and Ulric in Ulric's tent, where Ulric promises Bartog Sir Lancelot's (Hugh Prosser) wealth and woman, for his success in obtaining Excalibur. Galahad is spotted spying, and subsequently trampled by Ulric's horsemen.

Charlie King as Sir Bors and George as Sir Galahad.

CHAPTER THREE
THE PRISONERS OF ULRIC

Cheating death by rolling out of the path of the raging horses and knights, Galahad reasons that he has no reason to return to Camelot. He and Bors meet a peddler on the road with a stubborn mule. With a nod and a wink, Galahad transforms Bors into an ugly woman to drive the peddler's wagon into Ulric's encampment. Ulric shows Bartog his newest weapon, a giant crossbow designed to defeat Arthur.

Bors in drag is stopped by Ulric's guards on the road and questioned. The plot thickens as Bors loses his skirts and is discovered as a spy.

Once again, Galahad eavesdrops on Bartog and Ulric, and Merlin materializes in Ulric's tent. Merlin discloses that he persuaded Arthur to fortify the wall Ulric intended to attack, and tells Bartog and Ulric to attack the South wall of the castle.

Galahad enters the tent, only to discover that Merlin has used his magic to adhere Excalibur to the table in Ulric's tent. Galahad rescues the de-dragged Bors from the Saxon soldiers. Galahad is captured by Ulric's knights as he is put before the giant crossbow and interrogated.

Bors attempts to aid Galahad, but in the fight between Bors and the Saxon warrior the crossbow is triggered, sending Galahad to his death.

CHAPTER FOUR
ATTACK ON CAMELOT

With a simple maneuver, Galahad escapes the fate of the crossbow. Galahad rejoins the fight, and he and Bors escape Ulric's encampment. Arthur orders the arrest of Galahad and Bors. Galahad and Bors surrender to Arthur's guards. In the Great Hall, Galahad reveals that Merlin is in league with Ulric, and has advised him to attack the South wall of Camelot, instead of the East wall. Arthur imprisons Galahad and Bors, where they are visited by Morgan, who proclaims that Merlin isn't the only one who can practice the art of magic in Camelot.

With the aid of Morgan, Galahad and Bors escape, only to be recaptured by Ulric's forces. Feigning allegiance to Ulric, Galahad produces a ring of Merlin's (which Morgan stole for him) and deceives Ulric into attacking the East wall of Camelot. Galahad and Bors are forced to ride with Ulric to continue the ruse, and are ambushed by King Arthur and his knights.

To prove his allegiance to Ulric, Galahad scales a cliff to battle Arthur's soldier, only to plunge to his death.

CHAPTER FIVE
GALAHAD TO THE RESCUE

Miraculously, Galahad survives the fall and continues the battle, and his true allegiance is revealed. Ulric challenges Galahad with Excalibur, and Galahad is victorious, retrieving Excalibur for King Arthur. Ulric and the

Saxon retreat. Dividing their forces, Lancelot and Galahad (now armed with Excalibur), and Bors are attacked by a Saxon bowman. Lancelot is taken prisoner in Ulric's cave.

Galahad dresses Bors as a tinker arms repairman, to decoy Ulric and his Saxons, while Galahad sneaks into Ulric's hideout and frees Lancelot and his knights, returning Excalibur to Camelot. Merlin charges that the sword is not Excalibur, or how would Ulric be so easily defeated? Merlin takes the counterfeit Excalibur from Galahad, as Galahad is condemned to death by beheading in Arthur's court.

CHAPTER SIX
PASSAGE OF PERIL

Arthur interrupts Galahad's execution. Arthur allows Galahad to defend himself. Galahad reveals that Ulric could not have had Excalibur or else how could he and Arthur not have been defeated? Further, Galahad maintains that Ulric's right hand man, Bartog, is the one who delivered Excalibur to Ulric, and speculates that Bartog could have kept Excalibur for his own gains.

Galahad and Bors hunt Bartog down, and are attacked by Ulric's Saxons. Galahad releases the Saxon soldiers' horses, and he and Bors proceed to Ulric's cave. In the cave, Ulric questions Bartog, while Galahad listens, unseen, in one of the cave's tunnels. Ulric accuses Bartog of giving him a fake Excalibur, and keeping the real Excalibur for himself. Bartog responds by telling Ulric that his confidant in Camelot (a black-hearted knight, the Black Knight) may have passed the fraudulent Excalibur.

Bartog convinces Ulric that he should journey to Camelot and confront the Black Knight about the authenticity of Excalibur. Galahad and Bors follow Bartog back to Camelot, where Bartog enters a secret passageway. Galahad follows Bartog, only to be trapped by a wall of swords.

CHAPTER SEVEN
UNKNOWN BETRAYER

Galahad uses his own sword to stay the closing wall of swords, as he wiggles out of the passageway. Outside the passageway, Galahad reunites with Bors, and they return to the passageway in pursuit of Bartog. Bartog is captured inside Camelot by Arthur's men, and taken to the dungeon as Galahad and Bors watch in silence.

Bartog is sentenced to death, but Galahad pleads for his life, citing his connection to the Black Knight, as the Black Knight gave the fake Excalibur to Bartog in the first place. Galahad reasons that the delay of Bartog's execution and rumors of torture on the rack, might cause the traitor to reveal himself, and the real Excalibur to be recovered.

The plan is that Galahad and Bors hide in the dungeon and wait for the traitor's Black Knight to contact Bartog. In the dungeon, Bartog and the Black Knight overpower Galahad and Bors and render them useless, only to be freed by Arthur's men.

Later in the forest, the Black Knight and Bartog forge an alliance against King Arthur and King Ulric. The Black Knight states he needs more than Excalibur, he needs Arthur's subjects to turn against Arthur. The Black Knight instructs Bartog to don the clothes of a monk, and meet an emissary at the Ram's Head Inn.

Bors finds out that a meeting of those who oppose Arthur is being held at the Rams Head Inn. Galahad, dressed as a woodsman, enters the Rams Head Inn as Bartog and the emissary Cawker (Pierce Lyden) conspire against Arthur.

Suddenly, Arthur's knights invade the Inn and discover Galahad despite his disguise. A free-for-all fight erupts, and the Black Knight appears and cuts the cord of a chandelier above Galahad's head, pinning him to his doom.

CHAPTER EIGHT
PERILOUS ADVENTURE

Galahad jumps out of the chandelier in the nick of time, and the Black Knight engages Sir Kay (Jim Diehl) IN A SWORD FIGHT. Galahad saves Sir Kay's life, only to be called a traitor, and Kay begins to fight Galahad.

Galahad and Bors escape. Later at the Black Knight's camp, the Black Knight informs Bartog that he must return to Camelot, as Arthur will miss one of his knights at his Round Table, of which he is one.

In King Arthur's court, suspicion shifts to Lancelot.

George up to his neck in quicksand.

Galahad and Bors gain entry into the rounds to the Black Knight's camp, as an informant tells Bartog that Arthur has sent a small band of men (led by Sir Kay and Lancelot) to recover some of Ulric's weapons; and that he is to attack Arthur's knights. Galahad overhears this plot on the road to the munitions. Kay and Lancelot spot Galahad and Bors. Suddenly, Bartog and the Black Knight's men attack. Lancelot and Kay confront Galahad and Bors. A battle ensues, and one of Arthur's wagons is commandeered by one of the Black Knight's men. Galahad gives chase, and boards the wagon, fighting the driver as the wagon plunges off a cliff, sending Galahad and the driver to certain death.

CHAPTER NINE
TREACHEROUS MAGIC

As the wagon careens down the mountain, Galahad and the outlaw roll off before the wagon crashes at the bottom of the cliff and breaks into pieces. In the fight, the knights lose both supply wagons. Bors and Galahad return to the Ram's Head Inn in the woodsmen's identities, where Bartog and Cawker plot against Arthur in the backroom. The pub patrons start a fight with Bors and Galahad, and Galahad escapes with Bors being captured by Bartog and Cawker.

In Camelot, Galahad is discovered by Lancelot, and Galahad tells Lancelot that the real Excalibur will be at the Ram's Head Inn at noon this day. Galahad asks Lancelot to arrange a meeting with Morgan.

Morgan arms Galahad with an invisibility ring, which had one usage, for emergencies. Lancelot aids Galahad's escape.

Galahad arrives at the Ram's Head Inn to rescue Bors, as the Black Knight appears with Excalibur. Galahad challenges the Black Knight and Bartog, and another fight breaks out. Excalibur neutralizes Morgan's ring, and causes Galahad to fall over the balcony to his certain demise.

CHAPTER TEN
THE SORCERER'S SPELL

Galahad's fall is broken by the rebels gathered below the balcony. He then flees the Black Knight's men.

Galahad discloses his plan to Bors, to inform Ulric that Bartog has betrayed him and had fallen in with the Black Knight. Galahad and Bors go to Ulric's cave. At the cave, Galahad fires an arrow with a message for Ulric, which tells the king if he wishes to possess Excalibur to meet him at Echo Canyon at dawn.

At daybreak, Galahad informs Ulric that Bartog has betrayed him, and that Bartog and the Black Knight have Excalibur. As Galahad and Bors make their escape, Merlin appears and renders Galahad and Bors unconscious, and Ulric captures the pair. Ulric ties Galahad and Bors to a tree. As Ulric's archers take aim at Galahad and Bors, Merlin appears. Merlin advises Ulric that Galahad speaks the truth. Merlin tells Ulric to let Galahad

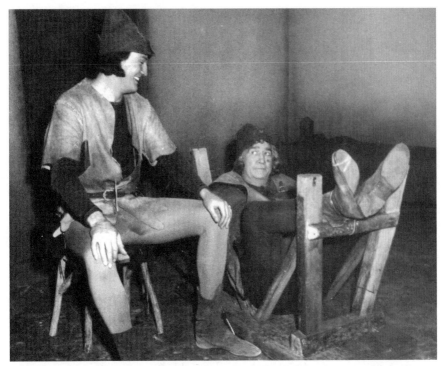

George with Charlie King in *THE ADVENTURES OF SIR GALAHAD*.

lead him to Bartog. Ulric forces Galahad and Bors to lead the attack against Bartog and the Black Knight, at the Ram's Head Inn.

A battle rages outside the Inn as the Black Knight appears on the balcony. The Black Knight descends and disarms Ulric, as Merlin appears in a puff of smoke. Galahad battles the Black Knight, but Merlin intervenes with his magic, and Excalibur is sent into the stratosphere.

Galahad gives chase after the Black Knight, with Ulric close behind in his pursuit. Galahad falls into a pool of quicksand, which engulfs him.

CHAPTER ELEVEN
VALLEY OF NO RETURN

Ulric and his men arrive as Galahad is sucked down into the pool of quicksand only to leave, certain that Galahad's fate is sealed. Sir Bors rescues Galahad from the quicksand with a tree limb. Resuming their chase of the Black Knight, Galahad and Bors discover the Black Knight's steed has thrown a shoe. The duo come upon the Black Knight's horse. Galahad and Bors discover Sir Modred, both in search of the Black Knight. Modred and Galahad form an alliance against the Black Knight.

Galahad, Bors, and Sir Modred enter a cave as an explosion reveals Excalibur in the cave wall. Galahad and Sir Modred fight over the sword in the wall. Merlin appears and removes Excalibur from the cave wall. Merlin disappears with Excalibur, and Modred and Galahad engage in a sword fight. Galahad defeats Modred and makes his escape with Bors.

In the forest, Bors spies a feast that disappears before his very eyes, only to encounter a sword-fighting tree that also disappears. Bors warns Galahad that no one ever comes back from "The Valley of No Return." Suddenly, Excalibur appears in a puff of smoke in a nearby rock. Bors and Galahad attempt to pull the sword from the rock, as Merlin appears behind them.

Merlin tells Galahad that his fate is sealed, as the Lady of the Lake appears and banishes Merlin. Galahad removes Excalibur from the stone, and Merlin reappears. By his magic, three knights materialize on steeds and charge Galahad. He fears not, because he has Excalibur. The knights trample Galahad into the sod.

CHAPTER TWELVE
CASTLE PERILOUS

Galahad meets the charge of the three knights, but at the point of impact, the knights and Galahad de-materialize. Bors is astonished, as he hears Merlin laugh.

Galahad reappears on the forest floor without Excalibur, at the Black Knight's camp. Galahad and Bors are captured by Bartog and Cawker. They escape their bonds, and Galahad overhears the Black Knight plotting with Bartok to kidnap Queen Guinevere (Marjorie Stapp). Cawker finds Galahad listening at the Black Knight's tent. He is re-tied to a tree, only to free himself, strike down Cawker, and escape.

On the road, the Black Knight and his men intercept Guinevere's party and begin to battle. The Black Knight threatens to use Excalibur on Queen Guinevere's pretty neck, if the Knights of the Round Table do not yield. Morgan le Fay (who is in Guinevere's party) is urged by the Black Knight to use her magic to aid their escape. She makes the Knights of the Round Table, Guinevere, Bartog, and the Black Knight all vanish before Galahad's and Bors' very eyes. Modred appears and arrests Galahad and Bors.

At King Arthur's court, Modred accuses Galahad of conspiring to kidnap Guinevere. Galahad questions Modred's whereabouts during the battle and kidnaping. Arthur warns Modred "No Knight has ever broken his word at the Round Table."

Arthur organizes a search party to find Guinevere. Galahad, Bors, and Modred stay behind at the castle, where Modred orders Galahad's death by the descending spiked ball.

CHAPTER THIRTEEN
THE WIZARD'S VENGEANCE

Modred's spiked ball is sent off course by the sudden entry of Sir Bors, saving Galahad by seconds. Galahad and Bors escape, locking Modred and his men in the dungeon. Modred breaks free of his imprisonment. Galahad and

"Holy Batman, Aunt Harriet! It's Sir Bors in drag!" Scene from Chapter Three of
THE ADVENTURES OF SIR GALAHAD with Charlie King and George.

Bors double back to the dungeon with Modred's guards on their trail.
Galahad and Bors are discovered th the catacombs. The archers fire on them
as they flee.

Outside the castle wall, Galahad and Bors observe Bartog arriving at
Camelot, to be met by the Black Knight. Inside, Bartog bargains with the
Black Knight for Lancelot's kingdom, and promises the death of King Arthur.
Bartog leaves Camelot on his mission with Galahad and Bors in hot pursuit.

Eluding Galahad and Bors, Bartog returns to the Ram's Head Inn,
where King Arthur is. Bartog is brought to Arthur, where he states that he
knows where Guinevere is being held, and asks amnesty for his crimes.
Bartog leads Arthur in search of Guinevere.

Galahad and Bors meet Merlin in the forest, and are informed that
Arthur is being led into an ambush by Bartog. Galahad and Bors ride to rescue Arthur, and enter the battle to save Arthur. Galahad is felled by an arrow
while fighting Cawker on a cliff, falling to his certain death.

CHAPTER FOURTEEN
QUEST FOR THE QUEEN

In a cheat ending, Cawker, not Galahad, is slain by the arrow meant for
Galahad, falling to his demise. Galahad spies Bartog returning to the Black
Knight's cave, and he and Bors ambush Bartog, with Bors knocking him
unconscious.

George lives by the sword in *THE ADVENTURES OF SIR GALAHAD*.

In the cave, Galahad finds the Black Knight's headgear. Arthur questions Bartog, and condemns him to death. Galahad approaches Arthur in the garb of the Black Knight, and engages Arthur with a plan to free Guinevere.

Galahad as the Black Knight knocks out Bartog's guard, and Bartog and Galahad set out to move Queen Guinevere, with Arthur in pursuit. They reach the hideout where Queen Guinevere has been moved by the real Black Knight. Bartog realizes that Galahad is a decoy. Galahad is knocked out, and Bartog escapes. Arthur arrives at the Black Knight's former hideout to find Galahad.

They return to the Ram's Head Inn, where Galahad suggests to Arthur that Modred could be the traitor in Camelot. Arthur banishes Galahad from his kingdom. Sir Bors loses faith in Galahad; and on his own, Galahad returns to Camelot, entering the underground chambers leading to the dungeon, where he finds an imprisoned Lancelot. A guard enters the cell as Galahad is about to free Lancelot.

After the fight, Galahad frees Lancelot, who informs Galahad that he and Guinevere were returned to Camelot by the Black Knight. Galahad goes in search of Guinevere, and overhears Modred arguing with Bartog, accusing Bartog of failure in his assassination attempt on King Arthur.

Behind a curtain Galahad hides, as Modred and Bartog quietly detect his presence. Modred pulls a cord and seals Galahad in a secret alcove, where one side is the curtain where Galahad is. Modred and Bartog run Galahad through with their swords, sealing his fate.

CHAPTER FIFTEEN
GALAHAD'S TRIUMPH

As Modred and Bartog lunge at Galahad, he dislodges the curtains from their rod, leaving the villains in a bundle on the floor. He returns to the dungeon to find Lancelot and tell him of information that must reach King Arthur. Galahad tells Lancelot that it is possible that Modred is the Black Knight.

Back in Camelot, Modred again disagrees with Bartog, but agrees to show Bartog Excalibur, which he has kept for the Black Knight. Modred opens a secret panel, and discovers Excalibur is missing, much to Bartog's pleasure. He baits Modred by suggesting that Modred will fail in his quest for Camelot, and suggests that Modred form an alliance with the Saxon King Ulric. Modred promises double Bartog's share of Camelot if he can arrange such an alliance with Ulric.

Merlin advises Arthur to abandon his search for Queen Guinevere and return to Camelot. Merlin appears on the road to Galahad and Lancelot, and explains that the Black Knight intends to destroy Arthur at Camelot. Further, he warns that Galahad is the only knight who can deliver Excalibur to Arthur in time to save the Queen and her kingdom. Merlin tells Galahad to make haste to the Enchanted Forest, where the Lady of the Lake will present Excalibur to Galahad.

Bartog and Ulric arrive at Camelot to be greeted by Modred, who tells them that the Black Knight will give them an audience. Ulric and Bartog find the Black Knight sitting on Arthur's throne. The Black Knight discloses his plan to conquer Arthur: the combined forces of both the Black Knight and Ulric will surround Camelot, allow Arthur to enter Camelot, and then strike.

In the Enchanted Forest, the Lady of the Lake presents Excalibur to Galahad, as the Black Knight and Ulric's men attack Arthur, who has returned to Camelot. Galahad arrives in Camelot and kills Ulric with Excalibur. He tosses Excalibur to Arthur, who defeats the Black Knight and in the process reveals that the Black Knight is truly Modred. Arthur kills Modred, and Galahad is finally admitted to the Round Table as Sir Galahad!

Merlin pledges no more magic, but Morgan le Fay casts a spell suspending Sir Bors helplessly over King Arthur's court. All laugh, as harmony is restored to Camelot.

While it's hard to fathom whether the movie goers in 1949 believed any of this Round Table hokum this did George Reeves' career no good. George and his fellow cast members turn in believable performances, but the script undermines all fifteen chapters. Serials are noted for action and adventure, and Sir Galahad has neither. There are no thrill-packed fights, and the chases are pedestrian at best.

A thoroughly forgettable entry in George's film catalog.

George spies on Bartog (Don Harvey) and Ulric (John Merton, Lane Bradford's father in real life) in an exciting scene from *The Adventures of Sir Galahad*.

George proves the sword is mightier than the script in a scene from *The Adventures of Sir Galahad*.

CAST: George Reeves, Charles King, William Fawcett, Pat Barton, Hugh Prosser, Lois Hall, Nelson Leigh, Jim Diehl, Don Harvey, Marjorie Stapp, John Merton, Pierce Lyden, Rick Vallin, Leonard Penn, Ray Corrigan.

A COLUMBIA PICTURE; Directed by Spencer Bennet; Screenplay: George H. Plympton, Lewis Clay, David Mathews; Assistant Director: R. M. Andrews; Photography: Ira H. Morgan; Music: Mischa Bakaleinikoff; Editor: Earl Turner; Producer: Sam Katzman. Original theatrical release: December 29, 1949. Total running time: 252 minutes.

THE GOOD HUMOR MAN
Funnyman, Stuntman, Future Superman

If there was ever a born loser, it is Biff Jones (Jack Carson), the unwitting hero of this fast paced romp. Biff is a good-hearted but bumbling ice cream salesman who is victimized by practically everything and everyone, including his customers. Biff's major source of happiness is his girlfriend, Margie Bellew (Lola Albright), who works as a secretary for Peerless Insurance Investigators. (The popular tune Margie, which accompanies the film's opening credits, is also used in the incidental scoring when the leading lady appears on screen.) Biff drops by the Peerless office regularly, so he can visit Margie and sell Good Humors at the same time. Margie's boss, Stuart Nagle (George Reeves), has an eye for Margie himself, and can't understand why such an appealing girl would waste her time on a mere salesman. When Biff accidentally dumps a load of ice cream all over Nagle's face and neck, the irate executive has him barred from the building.

Biff's other pleasure in life is the friendship he has fostered with Margie's young brother, Johnny (Peter Miles). The two of them preside over "The Captain Marvel Club," which is made up of neighborhood boys who meet in a neat clubhouse, usually garbed in capes identical to the one worn by the comic book hero.

Late one evening, Biff rescues an attractive blonde (Jean Wallace) who is being pursued by a gang of thugs. Biff meets her again the following evening, and agrees to guard her through the night in a rented house. The next morning, Biff is horrified when he finds the woman's lifeless body. Putting his Captain Marvel power of reasoning to good use, Biff concludes that he must have committed the crime in his sleep, and makes a confession to Inspector Quint (Frank Ferguson). But when Biff and the police return to the house, they do not find the corpse, or any discernable evidence of the woman's presence.

A short time later, the police are summoned to a nearby plant where the safe has been robbed, and the paymaster has been murdered. Nagle, who is present at the investigation, balks that his company will have to cover the $300,000 loss. Because a Good Humor truck had been admitted to the

George turns on the charm for Lola Albright in *THE GOOD HUMOR MAN*.

plant just prior to the crime, and Biff has already confessed to committing a homicide, the hapless salesman becomes the prime suspect.

Eventually, Biff and Margie find the body of the "dead" woman at the same house. When some unsavory characters enter the premises, Biff and Margie hide behind a chair. They listen carefully as one of the hoodlums brags about receiving his cut of the $300,000 that was stolen. After the men depart, Biff and Margie try to reach Inspector Quint. Suddenly, the mysterious woman, identified as Bonnie Conroy, is very much alive and orders Biff to drop the telephone. While aiming a pistol at the couple, she explains how the mob needed to gain access to Biff's Good Humor truck, knowing that the vehicle could easily accommodate a large safe, and mislead the police at the same time. When a fight breaks out, Biff and Margie overcome the woman and tie her up. Margie, believing that Inspector Quint is visiting Nagle, places a call to the Peerless office.

Nagle, seated at his desk in a darkened room, answers the phone and pretends to take a message for Inspector Quint who, of course, is nowhere in sight. Margie discloses all the information she and Biff have learned about the robbery/murder. Nagle, who is alarmed by this development, cooly instructs Margie to escort Biff to the clubhouse; he also warns her not to tell a soul where they are going. After hanging up, Nagle orders his men to take care of Biff.

That night, Biff and Margie engage in a wild slapstick battle with the gangsters in a school adjacent to the clubhouse. Here is where the style and expertise of director Lloyd Bacon really shines through. Bacon, who began his career as an actor in early silent films (he appeared in Charlie Chaplin's 1915 two-reeler, *The Tramp*), went on to become a highly respected director with a flair for comedy. (George had bit roles in two of his best remembered works: 1939's *Espionage Agent* and 1940s *Knute Rockne, All American*.) The script in this comic farce allows the characters to indulge in many elaborate sight gags straight out of the old Keystone Comedies. Props such as the school's playground equipment, swimming pool, and musical instruments seem to take on a life of their own and are put to use with great precision.

Johnny and the Captain Marvel club members dash over to the school in order to assist their leader. In fact, it seems that every kid in town is headed for the school, eager to converge right into the ensuing mayhem. Nagle shows up growling, "Where are they?" Margie is shocked to see that her boss is actually the mastermind of the racket. By this time, the melee has escalated to the auditorium, where the kids attack the thugs with pies and baseballs ("Take Me Out to the Ball Game" is appropriately heard on the soundtrack at this point). Inspector Quint arrives on the scene to make the arrests. Nagle, looking a total wreck with custard pie dripping from his face,

George takes a pie in *THE GOOD HUMOR MAN*.

Another fine mess for George in *THE GOOD HUMOR MAN*.

has had enough and begs Quint to take him in. The inspector obliges. The stolen cash, which had been concealed in Nagle's coat, is recovered by the police. A happy ending. But a slapstick comedy cannot close without a cute gag. Biff and Margie suddenly hear the "Margie" tune and wonder where it could be coming from. The camera pans down to Margie's ankles, which have a concertina hooked to them; as her ankles sway back and forth, the instrument bellows out the familiar melody. Biff and Margie smooch as the picture goes to black

Star Jack Carson worked with George in 1941 on *The Strawberry Blonde*, playing opposite James Cagney. He was married to his *The Good Humor Man* co-star Lola Albright, and made his first picture, *Stage Door*, in 1937. Highlights of his career are *Stand-In* (1937), *Too Many Wives* (1937), *Crashing Hollywood* (1938), *Queen of the Mob* (1940), *Hollywood Canteen* (1944), *Arsenic and Old Lace* (1944), *A Star Is Born* (1954), *Ain't Misbehaving* (1955), and *Cat On A Hot Tin Roof* (1958).

A native of Carmen, Canada, Carson was born on October 27, 1910. He succumbed to cancer on January 2, 1963, and worked in vaudeville and television as well as films.

Co-star Frank Ferguson is no stranger to George Reeves. Born on Christmas Day of either 1899 or 1908, Ferguson's first film in 1940 was the Reeves picture *Father Is A Prince*, followed by another George title, *Gambling*

On The High Seas that same year. He worked with George in an all star production of *Variety Girl* (1947). Other films include *They Won't Believe Me*
(1947), *The Walls of Jericho* (1948), *Abbott & Costello Meet Frankenstein*
(1948), *Walk A Crooked Mile* (1948), *West Point Story* (1950), *The Beast From
20,000 Fathoms* (1953), *Pocketful of Miracles* (1961), *Hush, Hush Sweet
Charlotte* (1964). His portrayal of Mr. Frank on Superman in "The Lady In
Black" is a long-time favorite with George Reeves fans.

Also in the cast was the man who brought Captain Marvel to life nine
years earlier in Republic's classic serial, *The Adventures of Captain Marvel*,
David Sharpe. Sharpe's first recorded appearance in films was 1929's
Masked Emotions. He was a player in Vaudeville and a circus acrobat, before
entering films as an actor/stuntman. According to friend Bob Burns, his first
unbilled appearance was in a Douglas Fairbanks, Sr. silent at the tender age
of seven. Readers interested in Sharpe's career and exploits would be
encouraged to pick up a copy of "Monster Kid Memories" by Bob Burns
and Tom Weaver (on Dinoship Press 2003). He was known as the crown
prince of the daredevils in Hollywood. His reputation for performing stunts
in over 3,000 films without injury made him a legend among his peers.

Some of his most breathtaking stunt work can be found in such serials
as *Dick Tracy Returns* (1938), *Daredevils of the Red Circle* (1939), *The
Adventures of Red Ryder* (1940), *The Mysterious Doctor Satan* (1940), *The
Adventures of Captain Marvel* (1941), *Dick Tracy vs. Crime, Inc.* (1941), *Spy
Smasher* (1942), *Perils of Nyoka* (1942), and *King of the Rocket Men* (1949).

His leaps, landings, and dives brought a realism to *The Adventures of
Captain Marvel* and *King of the Rocket Men* which has only been equaled in
the computerized special effects. With his talents and those of the Lydecker
Brothers (special effects), matinee theatergoers were thrilled every Saturday
for three decades.

David Sharpe was born in St. Louis, Missouri in 1910, and passed away
on March 30, 1980 from Lou Gehrig's disease, having left a rich legacy for
future stuntmen all over the world.

CAST: Jack Carson, Lola Albright, Jean Wallace, George Reeves, Peter Miles, Frank
Ferguson.

A COLUMBIA PICTURE; An S. Sylvan Simon Production; Directed by Lloyd
Bacon; Director of Photography: Lester White, A.S.C.; Art Director: Walter
Holscher; Film Editor: Jerome Thomas; Set Decorator: James Crowe; Assistant
Director: Paul Donnelly; Gowns by Jean Louis; Make-Up: Clay Campbell; Hair
Styles by Helen Hunt; Sound Engineer: George Cooper; Voice Effects by Sonovox;
Musical Score by Heinz Roemheld; Musical Director: Morris Stoloff.
Original theatrical release: April 6, 1950. Running time: 80 minutes.

One-sheet (above) and an ad cut from the pressbook for *Superman and the Mole Men*

SUPERMAN AND THE MOLE MEN

Superman? . . . What's That?

The "All-Time Ace of Action," as he was dubbed in Lippert's mismatched 1951 color poster, first debuted on the silver screen in Fleischer Studio's Superman cartoons. *Superman and the Mole Men* was the first attempt by D.C. Comics and Hollywood Studios to place the Man of Steel in a serious sci-fi story; to be as much an adult film as kiddie fare. *Superman* (Columbia 1948) and *Atom Man vs. Superman* (Columbia 1950), both starring Kirk Alyn, were staples of the Saturday Matinee set.

Variety headlines from May of 1951 spoke of a 30-year deal for Superman completed by Joseph Harris and Sy Weintraub of Flamingo Films, and Robert Maxwell of Maxwell-Carlin Associates. Fifty-two programs were to be made per year, and the content would also mark the first time complete Superman stories had been made.

On July 19 of 1951, National Comics allocated $400,000 for 26 half-hour Superman shows, shooting at RKO Pathe. On August 8, Variety announced that Whitney Ellsworth, editor of National Comics, had gone back to New York following meetings with the producers of Superman to release the series to television.

On September 16, 1951, it was announced in the New York Times and the Hollywood Reporter that two episodes out of 17 half-hour Superman shows were to be the bottom of a double bill on theater screens, to be released in late November. The two episodes would be held back from television for a year, following their theatrical release in October 1951. The fact is, Unknown People, Parts I and II, as they are known to TV audiences, were not released to television until the 1960s syndication runs. The feature, to be entitled *Superman and the Mole Men,* was to be distributed by Lippert, produced by Bernard Luber and Robert Maxwell, and directed by Lee Sholem. In the spring of 1953, the Adventures of Superman debuted. Although syndicated, in the major cities it usually appeared on the ABC affiliate, sponsored by Kellogg's cereals. The first run of the series consisted of 24 episodes, sans Unknown People I and II.

The 1951 feature *Superman and the Mole Men* begins with Lois Lane (Phyllis Coates) and Clark Kent (George Reeves), sent from Metropolis to Silsby to cover the story on the world's deepest oil well, which has been mysteriously shut down by Corrigan (Walter Reed), the oil mining engineer. After retiring to the Hotel Silsby, Lois and Clark swiftly return to the oil well. Once there, Lois encounters the Mole Men.

In the drilling shack, after everyone leaves, Kent takes the opportunity to cross-examine Corrigan. Kent baits Corrigan with "I guess you know why I hung around." Corrigan, with an air of indifference replies, "No, why?" Corrigan finally opens up to Kent, proclaiming "You're a newspaperman. You want a story? Well, I can give you one so big, so fantastic, you'd never dare print it!" Kent replies, "Whatever you can prove, I'll print."

Lippert campaign
manual (pressbook)
for the promotion of
a new film featuring a
strange visitor from
another planet in his
first full-length
adventure.

Walter Reed (left) and Steve Carr (right) in *SUPERMAN AND THE MOLE MEN*.

In 1978, Director Lee Sholem remembered filming this sequence for *Superman and the Mole Men*. "It's a crazy little thing! The interesting thing about *Superman and the Mole Men* was an insert shot that we did on the floor, under a cot—we pull back, and there was a man standing over Pop Shannon's body, looking at it. We went from one man to eight people who came in and out of the room and then these people, when they went through this particular scene they left the room, except for two guys (Walter Reed and George Reeves) who then went into another room. We had a feather wall, and we moved into another room of this laboratory, or whatever the hell it was, in the miner's hut. This was all done in one take in 45 minutes, and it ran just under a full reel. One take!"

Meanwhile, the creatures have discovered life above ground. They discover a snake, and recoil in fear.

Clark and Corrigan return to town and find Luke Benson's mob ready to flush out the invaders. As Benson (superbly portrayed by Jeff Corey) instructs his men, Kent interrupts, "They may look strange to us. We must look strange to them. As far as we know, they don't mean us any harm." After being shouted down, Kent tries a second time, pleading desperately "But don't you see, if you go around shooting at every shadow, someone is likely to get hurt?" and then promises (much to Lois Lane's chagrin) that he deal with the inner-terrestrials.

Suddenly, a scream breaks the night, and Benson exclaims, "Where did that scream come from?" In the original script, entitled *Nightmare*, much

George and Phyllis Coates.

original dialogue was either edited out or re-recorded. According to that script (final revisions were turned in on June 9, 1951), Eddy (Benson's right-hand man) exclaimed that it was up the street, and that he had seen something run out from behind Luke Benson's house. With Benson replying, "My wife, my kid—come on!" (Dialogue which was omitted from the final release print, as were all references to Luke Benson's family.)

Lois barbs Kent that he's made a fool of himself, as Kent shyly backs into the interior of the hotel for the convenience of transforming into Superman. Lois, in sheer disgust to Craig and Corrigan, "He always does that. He gets himself into a jam and then runs away."

Meanwhile in the deserted street, Kent runs into the familiar alley. He takes off and flies over the crowd. Director Sholem gives the audience Superman's birds-eye view as he flies over the mob to Benson's house. Superman lands and runs into the house to check on the child and her mother. Superman informs Benson that the woman and child are all right. Benson challenges Superman, and in the verbal barrage, Superman picks Benson up over his head, replying to Benson that his actions make it difficult for people to understand one another. Benson is relentless, and orders the mob to put the hounds on the scent.

Once again, the Silsby night air is broken by the sound of howling dogs, indicating that they have picked up the scent. Benson emerges from his house, exclaiming that the townsfolk may not mean anything, but for those

George with his pal, Walter Reed, in a scene from *SUPERMAN AND THE MOLE MEN*.

critters to go after a little kid ("my little kid," from the *Nightmare* script), that he aims to do something about it.

Veteran character actress Ann Doran had always believed she worked with George Reeves in more than one Superman episode. However, a careful review of the series could confirm only one appearance: in the 1951 episode "Night of Terror." Since she had been a frequent fixture at Columbia Pictures, where Kirk Alyn donned the famous cape and tights, it was suggested that she might have appeared in one of the serials. "No, no, it was definitely George Reeves," she would insist. Shortly after her death in 2000, a still photograph and lobby card were analyzed, revealing that Doran may have appeared in *Superman and the Mole Men* in the role of Luke Benson's

wife. The Variety review from December 12, 1951 lists Margia Dean as
Mrs. Benson.

At the back of the house, Superman shows Corrigan, Craig and Lois Lane
where the creatures entered the house, and explains that there is nothing left
to do, other than wait for routine decontamination on the mother and her
little girl. (The creatures glow in the dark, and are feared to be radioactive.)
Another wide variance from Unknown People to the *Superman and the Mole
Men* feature is a scene that is deleted from Unknown People. This is as Lois
Lane recovers from the rapid-fire events and the newspaperwoman in her
regains control. She states to Superman that she must get to a phone, because
this is the biggest story of the century. Superman explains that this kind of
hysteria—screaming headlines of "Monsters Invade Western Town," "Hideous
Creatures from the Center of the Earth Terrify Populace"—will only incite
panic throughout the country. But Lois counters, stating she is a newspaperwoman who has an obligation to report the facts. Superman reassures her that
"we've seen what can happen here tonight, and it must be stopped here if
stopped at all."

Lois reacts to Superman's warning, "Well, I guess so, but what about
Clark Kent? I'll bet he's phoning the story in this very minute." Superman
solemnly replies, "I'm quite sure he isn't."

For the second time of the evening, the dogs' shrill yelps pierce dead
silence. Through special effects man Danny Hayes' leather harness, the takeoff

Ray Walker, Walter Reed, Phyllis Coates, and George in *Superman and the Mole Men*.

Adrienne Marden, Frank Reicher, George, and John Baer in the hospital discussing the fate of the little captured creature in the operating room.

from behind Luke Benson's house is awkward. [*Author's Note*: Danny Hayes is credited only on the TV show, and Ray Mercer is credited with special effects for the feature.] These takeoffs, effective through sometimes jerky, were to prove to be troublesome in the shooting of the telefilm episodes. In the episode "Ghost Wolf," the harness broke, sending George Reeves crashing to the studio floor.

Below the dam, Luke Benson and his mob have spotted the creatures from the oil well on the spillway of the dam. This, in Unknown People Part I was where the conclusion of the episode takes place and Jack Narz's narration to "Stay tuned for a preview of Unknown People Part II" begins. After the preview, which has long since been excised from all TV prints in circulation the titles run out.

The feature continues. Sweeping over the dam with a light, Benson's men spot the little creatures. Superman lands suddenly and has a confrontation with Benson and his mob; one of them shoots one of the creatures off the parapet of the dam. Superman flies high above the mob and catches the mole man. In this sequence, as the mole man falls (with the background of the dam), an animated Superman flies to catch him. Cut to a close-up of George Reeves dangling by wires on a black backdrop, catching the midget mole man dummy.

Superman lands and determines his small luminous friend requires hospitalization, as the companion creature eludes Benson's mob. Again, accord-

ing to the *Nightmare* script, this chase sequence would seem to have played twice as long as the TV version. References are made to the death of Benson's prime hound Daisybelle, as the Mole Man is cornered in a shed, which is set afire. The creature finds his way through loose floorboards, burrows under the foundation of the shed, and runs under the moonlight to the oil derrick.

Back in Silsby a discussion which has been deleted from the TV two-parter is taking place in the Sheriff's office. Craig, Corrigan, and the Sheriff (Stanley Andrews) are debating the Sheriff's decision to call in the State Police to battle the problem of the Mole Men. Suddenly Benson and two of his men burst in, exclaiming that they got both the creatures, only to be informed that one is in their local hospital. Benson baits the Sheriff with

"I'm figuring on getting that critter and stringin' him up!" only for the Sheriff's reply, "Luke, you ain't stringin' up nothin' in this town unless it's a slab of bacon." Benson, hell-bent on taking the law into his own hands, exits, leaving the Sheriff and his deputy, Jim, to organize the opposition.

At the hospital, the superintendent verbally wrestles with Kent about Superman's right to bring such a monstrosity into the hospital. The superintendent is played by veteran actor Frank Reicher. Reicher was featured as Captain Englehorn in the RKO classics *King Kong* (RKO 1933) and *Son of Kong.*

Kent and intern Dr. Ried (John Baer) determine that the bullet must be taken from the creature's chest. With Kent assisting, Dr. Ried performs the operation. Outside, the Sheriff makes an attempt to arrest Luke Benson, only to be thrown into his own jail.

At the hospital, Kent and Lois are reunited. The operation is a success, and Kent remarks to Lois (indicating Dr. Ried), "There goes a young man with courage." Once again, Lois Lane reverts to bitchiness by snorting, "I wish I could say the same for you." Kent, who is obviously stung by the verbal jab, cracks back, "One of these fine days, Lois . . ."

Lois, not letting go of the verbal stranglehold she has on Kent, snaps "You always do that. Your start to say something and then you abruptly change your mind." Kent replies sheepishly, "I do?" with Lois probing, "What are you afraid of? What are you hiding? You give the impression you're leading a double life."

The Mole Men (*Jerry Maren, Tony Boris, John Banbury,* and *Billy Curtis*) protected by their iconic electrolux deadly raygun.

The dialogue differs between Unknown People and the feature. In the screenplay, Lois accuses Kent of "leading a Jekyll and Hyde existence."

Kent suddenly becomes aware of Craig and Corrigan running up the street. The mob is in hot pursuit. Kent once again disappears, to which Lois cracks, "He's scared to death—it's pitiful!" As the mob approaches, Lois exclaims, "I never thought I'd live to see anything like this." Superman appears at the hospital entrance. Lois, while standing by Superman, is shot at by one of the zealots. With her safely inside the hospital, Superman exclaims to the mob that he will give them one last chance to stop acting like Nazi Stormtroopers.

In a scene reminiscent of Republic Studios *The Adventures of Captain Marvel* (1941), Superman takes the entire mob's arsenal by force. In a departure from the TV shows, the script describes Superman as he collects the guns strewn about the street with super speed. A second creature has now appeared with two more mole men from the oil well, carrying a weapon which is an Electrolux vacuum cleaner with a funnel attached to the front.

As the creatures creep through the darkened Silsby, Superman spies them from his vantagepoint at the hospital. The creatures merely want their friend and to be allowed to return to their own world in peace. As Superman is retrieving their friend, Benson appears in an alleyway. The creatures turn their deadly machine on Benson. Superman gives them their injured friend before standing in front of Benson, blocking the rays. After the ordeal, Benson gasps to Superman, "You saved my life." Superman's cold response, "It's more than you deserve."

George and three of the mole men on a mission to rescue the fourth.

A mob is forming at the Silsby Hotel led by Jeff Corey and confronted by words of reason from George and Walter Reed in *SUPERMAN AND THE MOLE MEN*.

Superman assists the creatures in returning the wounded one and themselves to the oil derrick, which they descend, forever leaving Silsby. Corrigan, Lois, and Craig arrive, informing Superman that the woman and her daughter checked negatively for exposure to radiation, and that the creatures only had harmless phosphorescence on their bodies. The creatures set the well afire, to which Lois Lane prolaims, "It's almost as if they were saying "We'll live our lives, you live yours."

According to the *Nightmare* script, there was an alternate ending, which took place after the well fire. It began in P.R. man Craig's car the next day. Lois is in front, with Kent in the back. Lois: "Too bad you missed it, Clark. It was the most amazing thing to see them go back to their own world and destroy the well!" "It must have been," replies Kent. Lois repeats her soliloquy by the well, with Craig acknowledging that he was glad it was over, but boy, what a nightmare. "It could have been a lot worse," replies Lois. As the car moves down the road, Craig suddenly slams on the brakes. He gets out of the car and grabs a handful of sod, savagely flinging it at the signboard: Silsby, Home of the World's Deepest Oil Well. He reacts with great satisfaction and returns to the driver's seat, much to the amusement of Kent and Lois.

Superman and the Mole Men press sheets bore the ballyhoo of "Comic Strip Hero in his first full-length action adventure." Released on December 4, 1951, with a running time of just under an hour, the picture garnered surprisingly good reviews for the bottom bill of a double feature. On December

12, 1951, Variety remarked, "Juve idol makes OK impression in full length pic bow." They also revealed that the show should please fans, and lead to sequels.

With the release of Mole Men on Warner's Home Video in 1987 (Laser Disc 1999), one can examine the differences between the feature and the two-parter in more detail.

The feature film plays more like 50s sci-fi than the TV two-parter, which is paced more like a serial. Besides the additional scenes, the musical score contributes to the slower pace of the feature. None of the Mutel library (more commonly known as the Capitol Cue library) music from the TV show is in the feature. Instead, composer Darrel Calker's themes provide an eerie reality to the proceedings.

Superman and the Mole Men was re-released in 1957. While the show was in production for six seasons, two other features were in the production offing. In 1954 a script called *Superman and The Ghost of Mystery Mountain* was to be produced, but never materialized. Researchers have speculated that Ghost may have been an alternative show, had the 1953 show Panic in the Sky gone over budget (it did).

The same is true for *Superman and the Secret Planet* in 1957. No explanation was given as to why this project never reached the light of day.

Superman and the Mole Men introduced George Reeves to a character that he could not escape, even in death.

CAST: George Reeves, Phyllis Coates, Jeff Corey, Walter Reed, J. Farrell MacDonald, Stanley Andrews, Ray Walker, Hal K. Dawson, Frank Reicher, Beverly Washburn, Stephen Carr, Paul Burns, Margia Dean, Byron Foulger, Irene Martin, John Phillips, John Baer, Adrienne Marden, Billy Curtis, Jack Banbury, Jerry Marvin, Tony Baris.

A LIPPERT RELEASE; Produced by Robert Maxwell, Barney A. Sarecky; Directed by Lee Sholem; Original Screenplay: Richard Fielding (Robert Maxwell); Cameraman: Clark Ramsey; Film Editor: Al Joseph, A.C.E.; Music: Darrel Calker; Art Director: Ernest Fegte; Assistant Director: Arthur Hammond; Sound Cutter: Bud Hayes, A.S.C.; Sound Engineer: Harry Smith; Wardrobe: Izzy Berne; Make-Up: Harry Thomas; Dialogue Director: Stephen Carr; Script Clerk: Mary Chaffee; Property Master: George Bahr; Special Effects: Ray Mercer, A.S.C.
Original Theatrical Release: December 4, 1951. Running Time 58 minutes.

BUGLES IN THE AFTERNOON
Love Triangles in the Evening

Bugles in the Afternoon is a "Cavalry vs. Indians" flick. It begins with a brief flashback to the day that Colonel Kern Shafter (Ray Milland) was dishonorably discharged for having attacked a fellow officer with a saber. Shafter

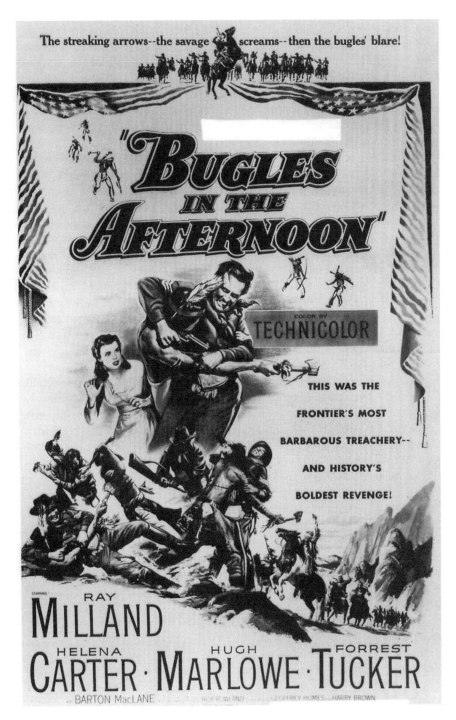

The one-sheet for *BUGLES IN THE AFTERNOON*.

and Captain Garnett (Hugh Marlowe) had been locked into an ongoing brawl over their pursuit of the same woman. Unhappy with civilian life, Shafter joins a regiment in the Dakota Territory and is appointed to the rank of Sergeant. As luck would have it, Garnett is in command there, and the two men are soon at each other's throats. Even more remarkable, the two of them again fall for the same woman, this time a demure young thing named Josephine (Helena Carter, who in *Invaders From Mars* (1953) is every baby boomer boy's wet dream).

Lt. Smith (George Reeves) enters the picture when it's time for Garnett to confront the Sioux Indians, who have apparently slaughtered some prospectors. Garnett (who now outranks his old adversary) selects Shafter for the mission, hoping he'll get killed in the line of duty. Shafter, however, amazes everyone with his self-assurance as he rides through a band of hostile Indians to apprehend the killers. (These events culminate just before Custer's Last Stand.) The other significant scene with Reeves is the one where an exhausted Shafter reports to the cavalry outpost. (Another scene where George is with a young lady is hardly worth mentioning.) Lt. Smith is surprised to see that Shafter is still alive, as Garnett had reported him dead. When the lieutenant discloses that the regiment has embarked for Little Big Horn, Shafter requests permission to follow suit. Lt. Smith obliges, and orders him to accompany Osborne (Ray Montgomery) in delivering an important message to the Major.

The war is on. Amid all the bloodshed, Shafter and Garnett finally release their hostilities in a life-threatening fight. Garnett, who resorts to dirty fighting, is killed by an Indian just as he's about to strike Shafter with a large rock. After surviving this private skirmish, as well as the big battle, Shafter ends up in a military hospital bed. He receives a letter announcing that the President has fully restored his rank of Captain. Thus, Shafter wins kudos from the War Department and the affections of Josephine.

Despite the old fashioned "love triangle" formula (which was outdated even in 1952), Bugles has much to offer in the way of great location settings and explosive action. It is interesting to note that the producer of the film, William Cagney, was the brother of screen legend James Cagney. Be on the lookout for future Superman villain Ray Montgomery and Hugh Beaumont (Beaver's dad on Leave It To Beaver as well as the Adventures of Superman co-star in "The Big Squeeze), in uncredited bit roles.

DISTRIBUTED BY WARNER BROS. PICTURES; A William Cagney Production; Directed by Roy Rowland; Color by Technicolor; Screenplay by Geoffrey Homes and Harry Brown, from a novel by Henry Maycox; Director of Photography: Wilfred M. Cline, A.S.C.; Art Director: Edward Carrere; Film Editor: Thomas Reilly, A.C.E.; Sound by C. A. Riggs; Set Decoration: Lyle B. Reifsnider; Wardrobe by Leah Rhodes; Technical Advisor: Col. C.B. Benton; Make Up Artist: Gordon Bau; Technicolor consultant: Mitchell Kovalesky; Assistant Director: William Kissel; Special Effects by Ralph Webb; Musical Direction: Ray Heindorf; Music by Dimitri Tiomkin. Original Theatrical Release: December 28, 1951. Running time: 85 minutes.

RANCHO NOTORIOUS
A Rapist on a Secret Ranch!

Mention the name Fritz Lang and most film buffs will recall the director's silent sci-fi classic *Metropolis* (1926), or his later film noire thrillers such as *Man Hunt* (1941) and *The Woman in the Window* (1944). Although the western genre wasn't typical Lang territory, the director did tackle such projects as *The Return of Frank James* (1940) and *Western Union* (1941), both produced by 20th Century-Fox. With *Rancho Notorious*, Lang was back in the saddle with this offbeat tale of "hate, murder, and revenge," as explained in the lyrics to the film's recurrent theme song. Marlene Dietrich stars as the aging, but still captivating, rancher who harbors a gang of outlaws in exchange for a percentage of their loot. George has a supporting role as a lecherous desperado who has sought refuge at the hidden ranch.

The story begins in a small town in Wyoming during the 1870s. Vern Haskell (Arthur Kennedy) is an easy-going cowboy engaged to a young woman named Beth (Gloria Henry) who presides over the general store. One day, after presenting Beth with an elegant brooch, Vern rides away not realizing that he's just seen his fiancee for the last time. When he returns, the sheriff and several townsfolk are standing over Beth's corpse. The town doctor makes it clear that Beth had been raped, stating that "she wasn't spared anything." The presence of blood on the victim's fingernails further exemplifies the savageness of the attack.

Vern embarks on a journey to learn the identity of Beth's killer. Through a series of inquiries, he learns about a ranch called Chuck-A-Luck, the likely hiding spot of the unknown assailant. In order to find the place, Vern seeks out Altar Keane (Dietrich), the woman whose name is linked to the mysterious locale. He soon discovers that the key to Chuck-A-Luck is a rancorous character named Frenchy Fairmont (Mel Ferrer) who is also Keane's lover. Knowing that Frenchy is in jail, Vern gets himself arrested, then ingratiates himself by formulating an escape. Believing that Vern is a fellow outlaw, Frenchy leads the way to the secluded Chuck-A-Luck ranch.

Frenchy finally brings Vern and Altar face to face, acknowledging that if it weren't for this new acquaintance he'd be "hanging from the end of a rope!" Altar agrees to let Vern stay at the ranch, provided that he abides by her rules. No fighting, no questions asked, and lots of hard work. She introduces the new arrival to the other nefarious inhabitants of the ranch, some of whom are downright quirky. "Preacher" (Frank Ferguson), for example, is a villain who carries a Bible with him wherever he goes. Then, there's the devilishly handsome Wilson (George Reeves). "Look at that smile," says Altar in her rich baritone voice. "He spends most of his time chasing the ladies. No girl is safe when he's around!" Noticing the deep scratches on Wilson's leering face, Vern is immediately reminded of Beth's blood-stained fingernails. Wilson says his wounds were inflicted by a bobcat. Vern, however, remains suspicious and scowls at Wilson whenever he sees him.

Marlene Dietrich, John Raven, Frank Ferguson (seated, background), George, and Jack Elam (seated, foreground) in a scene from *Rancho Notorious*.

A party is held one evening where Altar, draped in a sexy black gown, sings "Get Away Young Man." Vern is stunned when he sees Altar wearing the brooch he had given Beth just before her death. Seconds later, the authorities burst onto the property, searching for Frenchy and two other robbers. Vern protects Altar, and the ranch, by concocting an impromptu cover up. After the lawmen depart, Vern seizes the opportunity to ask Altar about the brooch. She reacts angrily, restating the house rule that "no questions are to be asked." Amid all this tension, Vern and Altar must grapple with the fact that they've fallen for each other. This unforeseen complication arouses the anger of Frenchy, who now regards Vern as a bona fide rival.

During an unsuccessful bank robbery in a distant town, Frenchy sustains a near-fatal wound. With Frenchy incapacitated, one of the other residents must ride back to Chuck-A-Luck in order to pay Altar her ten percent share. The men begin to scoff at this notion, voicing displeasure over what they perceive as Altar's persistent greediness. Wilson's refusal to make the delivery is not attributable to monetary issues; he's simply too preoccupied with a gorgeous female who is eagerly awaiting his attention. When cards are drawn to select a designee, Vern cheats so he can be the one to make the return trip.

Back at Chuck-A-Luck, Vern and Altar finally embrace. Unable to repress his emotions any longer, Vern again questions Altar about the brooch. Altar, now in a more responsive mood, reveals that the brooch was a gift from Kinch (Lloyd Gough), one of the Chuck-A-Luck regulars. Vern goes into a tirade, and discloses the true reason for his presence at the ranch. He eventually confronts Kinch in the saloon, and challenges him to a draw. Kinch, however, is a coward and stalls long enough to be saved by the sheriff. Although the killer is carted away by the law, he is rescued by the Chuck-A-Luck gang just as he's about to be jailed.

When Frenchy returns to Chuck-A-Luck, Altar declares her intention to relinquish the ranch. Suddenly, the outlaws descend upon the place, seething with anger over Altar's disclosure about Kinch, and her ongoing demands. Frenchy tries to appease the men (even if only temporarily) by offering them ownership of the property, but this ploy does not work. When Vern shows up to even the odds, the climactic gun battle erupts. Wilson, positioned outside, fires at Frenchy through an open window. Altar tries to shield Frenchy from the bullets and is shot in the process. Although a few of the scoundrels manage to flee, Wilson and Kinch are not among them. Vern and Frenchy survive the attack, but Altar dies a quiet death. The last scene depicts Vern and Frenchy riding away from Chuck-A-Luck, a place tainted by "hate, murder, and revenge."

An interesting cast, with William Frawley out on loan from I Love Lucy, Gloria Henry (the future mom of Dennis the Menace), Frank Ferguson, and Dan Seymour (one of Warner Brothers most beloved gangsters, who co-starred with George a year earlier on Superman in "The Stolen Costume").

CAST: Marlene Dietrich, Arthur Kennedy, Mel Ferrer, Gloria Henry, William Frawley, Lis Ferrady, John Raven, Jack Elam, George Reeves, Frank Ferguson, Francis McDonald, Dan Seymour, John Kellogg, Rodric Redwing.

AN RKO RADIO PICTURE; Produced by Howard Welsch; Directed by Fritz Lang; Screenplay by Daniel Taradash; Original story by Silvia Richards; Color by Technicolor; Technicolor consultant: Richard Mueller; Director of Photography: Hal Mohr, A.S.C.; Production Supervisor: Ben Hersh; Editorial Supervisor: Otto Ludwig, A.C.E.; Assistant Director: Emmett Emerson; Set Decorator: Robert Priestly; Sound: Hugh McDowell and Mac Dalgleish; Production Designer: Wiard Ihnen; Make-Up Artist: Frank Westmore; Wardrobe: Joe King; Hairstylist for Miss Dietrich: Nelliemarie Manley; Miss Dietrich's Wardrobe designed by Don Loper; Music: Emil Newman; Songs, "Legend of Chuck-A-Luck," "Gypsy Davey," "Get Away Young Man"—Music and Lyrics by Ken Darby; Ballad "Legend of Chuck-A-Luck" Sung by William Lee. Original theatrical release: March 6, 1952. Running time: 89 minutes.

THE BLUE GARDENIA
A Thespian Watches His Career Slip Away

How could George Reeves not be frustrated by his marginal contribution in *From Here To Eternity*, which garnered multiple Academy Award nominations and won eight Oscars?! Just as his career was on the upswing, the influence of the planet Krypton began what is commonly referred to by tabloid journalists as 'The Superman Curse.' George Reeves, like all of us, was carried away by the winds of fate.

The Blue Gardenia is a highly entertaining example of Reeves noire. While Reeves did not have the high caliber role he had in 20th Century-Fox's *Man At Large*, Reeves' essay of Captain Sam Haynes (hard-boiled copper) proves beyond any doubt that George could have played any detective role shy of Charlie Chan, and turned in a four-star performance!

Harry Prebble (Raymond Burr) is an artist who is nearly as successful with the opposite sex as he is with a paintbrush. He is a popular fixture at a Los Angeles telephone company, where he can easily recruit models among the many curvaceous switchboard operators. When the burly artist renders a quick sketch of Crystal Carpenter (Ann Southern), he is wily enough to jot down her telephone number. He does this when Crystal supplies the number to Casey Mayo (Richard Conte), a renowned columnist for the Los Angeles Chronicle.

Crystal shares an apartment with two other young women: Norah Larkin (Anne Baxter) and Sally Ellis (Jeff Donnell), who also work as telephone operators. On the evening of her birthday, Norah opens a letter from her boyfriend, stationed in Korea, who writes that he has found someone new and will not be marching home when his tour of duty is over. While crying tears aplenty, the telephone rings. Prebble is on the line, with the drawing and phone number in hand, still in pursuit of the unobtainable Crystal. Norah goes along with Prebble's well-polished discourse, but doesn't actually identify herself. Acting on impulse, she shows up for a date at a Polynesian restaurant called The Blue Gardenia. Though he was expecting Crystal, the artist isn't the least bit disappointed when lovely Norah appears instead. Norah apologizes for her duplicity. "I want to forget the events of earlier this evening," she sobs. "The evening begins as of right now," says Prebble, who buys the dejected woman a blue gardenia and indulges her with rounds of a potent drink. (During this sequence, Nat King Cole sings the romantic "Blue Gardenia," which serves as the film's theme song.)

With Norah completely drunk, Prebble invites her back to his apartment with the assurance that others will be present for a late night party. With no one but Norah in his darkened living room, Prebble plays a phonograph record of Blue Gardenia and begins to make sexual advances. When his inebriated guest realizes what is happening, she puts up a struggle which culminates in her smashing a mirror and striking the lecherous artist with a fireplace poker. Norah blacks out. After waking up in a disoriented state, she

In *THE BLUE GARDENIA*, George was given his best chance for a movie career comeback—but Superman got in the way. Richard Conte, George, and veteran character actor Larry Blake (who guest starred in the Superman adventures *The Secret of Superman* and *Jet Ace*).

flees into the rainy night, leaving behind a blood-stained handkerchief, her shoes, and a tattered blue gardenia.

The next day, the newspapers are filled with the lurid account of the murder. At the crime scene, an investigation is led by a steely-eyed veteran, Captain Sam Haynes (George Reeves), who seems to derive pleasure from scoffing at everyone. Looking for a scoop, Casey shows up while Haynes is grilling Prebble's former cleaning woman—played by the acerbic Almira Sessions, who appeared in a 1951 Superman episode entitled "A Night of Terror." Haynes and Casey piece all the clues together and deduce that the killer is a blonde female who wore a black dress with a blue gardenia, and fits into a size five-and-a-half shoe. Before long, everyone in LA is chattering about the murderess, now appropriately nicknamed "The Blue Gardenia."

In an attempt to expedite the investigation, Casey utilizes an unconventional strategy: a published letter to the killer, offering a top-notch legal defense, among other benefits, in exchange for her exclusive story. Several eccentrics call the newspaper, claiming to be the mysterious assailant, but Casey simply shrugs them off. Captain Haynes also delights in phoning the reporter, chiding him for resorting to such an elaborate tactic. "By the way," he says sarcastically," Has the little lady turned herself in to you yet? If she

Richard Conte, Anne Baxter, Ann Sothern, and George in a lobby card scene from *THE BLUE GARDENIA*. COURTESY OF JERRY MEZEROW.

does, please be sure to give her our number. We'll be happy to hear from her." That same evening, Norah makes a late-night visit to Casey's office. After introducing herself as "friend" of the Blue Gardenia, the two of them get acquainted over hamburgers at an all-night diner. Norah promises to deliver the wanted woman, but first needs to be reassured that the newspaper's deal is legitimate. In the meantime, Crystal has noticed Norah's increased jitters, and the fact that her roommate is no longer in possession of her expensive black dress and suede pumps. After returning home, Norah breaks down and tells Crystal the whole story.

The next evening, Crystal shows up at the diner for a midnight meeting with Casey. The reporter says that he suspected her all along, as she had posed for Prebble and inadvertently given him her phone number. Crystal quietly points to Norah, seated in the next booth, who finally confesses that she is the woman that the police have been tracking. At this point, Casey is embarrassed to admit that his paper won't be able to honor any of its promises. Horrified, Norah heads straight for the door where she is immediately nabbed by Haynes. With her worse fear confirmed, Norah concludes that she has been victimized by Casey. The reporter, however, can't quite figure out how Haynes knew exactly where and when to apprehend Norah, as he hadn't disclosed his previous meeting with her. Haynes exposes the snitch when he laconically thanks the diner attendant for keeping his ears open. Casey tried to dissuade Haynes from making an arrest, but the captain remains unmoved and quickly points out the penalties for aiding and abetting a criminal.

After Norah is booked and fingerprinted, Casey stumbles upon a significant discrepancy. The police officers concluded that Prebble must have played a recording of "Blue Gardenia" just before his death. Yet, that wasn't the album that was found on the turntable on the morning of the investigation. This new mystery is the catalyst for a probe by Casey and Haynes, who revisit the crime scene to trace the origin of the replaced album. When they begin questioning the manager (Larry Blake) at the Melrose Music Shop, a scream is heard from the stockroom where a young woman has slit her wrists in an attempt to avoid arrest. The woman is Rose Miller (Ruth Storey), a nondescript clerk who had sold the record to Prebble. She is also his ex-lover.

A flashback reveals that Rose was present in the Prebble home sometime after Norah smashed the mirror and passed out on the sofa. It was actually Rose who struck the artist with the poker, in a fit of anger over finding him with another woman. Captain Haynes listens intently as the true killer concludes her confession from a hospital room, in the presence of Casey and a much-relieved Norah. The attending physician at the patient's bedside is none other than Robert Shayne, who played Inspector Henderson on the Adventures of Superman.

After being acquitted, Norah is flanked by her roommates as she happily faces the reporters who have gathered outside the courthouse. In the last moments of the film, a flirtatious Crystal again offers Casey her telephone number, the very thing that started the whole conundrum.

A standout whodunit!

CAST: Anne Baxter, Richard Conte, Ann Southern, Raymond Burr, Jeff Donnell, Richard Erdman, George Reeves, Ruth Storey, Ray Walker, Nat King Cole introducing "Blue Gardenia" by Bob Russell and Lester Lee, Almira Sessions and Robert Shayne (unbilled).

A WARNER BROTHERS RELEASE; A Blue Gardenia Production; Produced by Alex Gottlieb; Directed by Fritz Lang; Screenplay by Charles Hoffman; Story by Vera Caspary; Director of Photography: Nicholas Masuraca, A.S.C.; Musical score: Rauol Kraushaar; "Blue Gardenia" arranged by Nelson Riddle; Production Supervisor: Maurie Suess; Film Editor: Edward Mann, A.S.E.; Art Director: Emmett Emerson; Script Supervisor: Don Mcdougall; Make-up: Gene Hibbs, James Barker; Ladies' Wardrobe: Maria Donovan; Mens' Wardrobe: Izzy Berne; Special Effects: Willis Cook; Sound by Ben Winkler. Original theatrical release: March 26, 1953. Running time: 90 minutes.

FROM HERE TO ETERNITY

Exploding Hearts, and Harbors of Pearl!

This could have been Reeves' second *So Proudly We Hail*. Unfortunately, Reeves either didn't have as much screen time as we are led to believe, or his role as Stark was severely abbreviated. What could have been a shining moment for George is spoiled.

It's 1941 and the location is Schofield Barracks, Hawaii, where Private Robert E. Lee Prewitt (Montgomery Clift) has been transferred at his own insistence. Prewitt is proud of his aptitude for bugling, but not of his prowess as a boxer, as he once accidentally blinded a man. His refusal to compete in an upcoming exhibition creates much antipathy with his officers, who delight in assigning him to the worse tasks imaginable. Despite his deep-rooted diffidence, the young bugler manages to befriend Sergeant Milton Warden (Burt Lancaster) and a gregarious drudge named Private Maggio (Frank Sinatra, in a non-singing role).

Captain Dana Holmes (Philip Ober) shirks most of his responsibilities upon Warden. As a result, Warden gets to spend much time around the captain's young wife, Karen (Deborah Kerr). Karen and Warden are initially hostile toward each other, but the mounting sexual tension between them is relentless, and they soon begin an affair.

Warden casually bumps into a buddy, Sergeant Maylon Stark (George Reeves), who discloses that Karen is a woman who has been around. Stark is certain of this because he is, in fact, one of Karen's erstwhile lovers. Undaunted, Warden and Karen continue to see each other. In the film's

George and Burt Lancaster in *FROM HERE TO ETERNITY*.

most memorable sequence, the couple run off to an isolated stretch of beach where the crashing waves pound their bodies, which are pressed tightly together, as they kiss. While nestled in each other's arms, Karen explains that her "past" is solely attributable to her marriage to a drunken and philandering husband. She urges Warden to apply for a promotion, which will allow them to remain in proximity until her divorce becomes final.

Prewitt's life has also ripened. He wins the affections of a deceivingly sweet young woman named Alma (Donna Reed) who works at a club frequented by all the guys (including Sergeant Stark). At the New Congress Club, Maggio makes an enemy of a bigoted stockade sergeant (Ernest Borgnine) who later beats him to death. Angered beyond measure, Prewitt confronts his friend's killer in an alley where a deadly struggle ensues. Although Prewitt manages to overpower and kill the assailant, he sustains life-threatening wounds in the process. Fearful of prosecution, Prewitt takes refuge in Alma's apartment. In the meantime, Karen and Warden's relationship suffers a blow when she learns that he hasn't applied for the promotion as promised. This, and the fact that the captain will not consent to a divorce, brings an end to their torrid affair.

Shortly thereafter, Sergeant Stark checks in with Warden during breakfast one Sunday morning. Seconds later, all hell breaks loose as the Japanese attack Pearl Harbor. (Stark, who can be spotted intermittently throughout the film, is seen here for the last time, firing a machine gun during the climactic battle footage.) When news of the attack reaches Prewitt, he decides to return to his unit, despite the objections of Alma, who is still nursing him back to stability. Stumbling about in his civvies, Prewitt is ordered to halt. Headstrong as ever, he ignores the order and is shot and killed on the spot. Trying to conceal his remorse, Warden stands over the body and comments that Prewitt's suffering was unwarranted. The boxing matches, which the young soldier had resisted so fervently, have just been cancelled.

In the finale, Karen and Alma leave the island with the sad realization that they have lost the men in their lives forever. As their vessel sails away from the harbor, both women toss their leis into the ocean, hoping for a brighter future.

Fifty-one years later, actor/author/librettist Jack Larson shared his memories with us of the *From Here To Eternity* premiere at the Pantages Theater in Hollywood. "Monty Clift was a great friend of mine. I was what he called his 'sounding board' on the script for *From Here To Eternity*. He was staying at the Hollywood Roosevelt Hotel. When I'd finish work on Superman I would go to the hotel, and we would work on the script. He would go over the script, we would discuss his lines, and he would change things. I had nothing to do with his line changes, but he tried them out on me. He liked to do dialogue out loud. I worked with him all through the preparation stages. They went off to Hawaii to begin shooting the film. I knew that George had a part in it, but I didn't know what the part was. We had finished shooting Superman. I knew that he and Toni Mannix had gone off to Hawaii to shoot George's parts in the film. When the filming concluded, Monty went back to his home in New York. There was going to be a big sneak preview in Los Angeles, and Monty

George and Toni Mannix (right) enjoy a musical interlude at a relaxing party around the time of filming for *From Here To Eternity*. PHOTO COURTESY OF LOU KOZA.

had not seen the film. He asked me if I would go to the preview at the RKO Pantages, and look for certain things, to be very acute, and remember them accurately, because he wanted to ask me a lot of questions. George played Stark, and I went to see the preview. The Superman show had been on the air by that time. When George came on the screen, every executive from Columbia, including Harry Cohen and Buddy Adler—the vice president of production, was there. When George came on the screen, somebody in the balcony shouted out "Superman!" And then a lot of people in the audience started yelling "Superman!" It had an effect on me because I thought this was bad, but it was probably also as bad for me as an actor as it was for George. I watched the rest of the film, walked directly across the street to a bar—I remember it had pool tables. I phoned Monty from an old fashioned telephone booth at the back of the bar. He asked me a plethora of questions. He wanted to know about Burt Lancaster, and himself, things about Donna Reed—he was very worried about Donna Reed's performance. It got down to him asking which shots they used, and what got cut. These were all very technical questions that were in Monty's mind. I was able to answer them. I thought Monty's scene blowing the bugle was outstanding, after Frank Sinatra's character Maggio dies. I told him how moving it was, and that he had turned in a stellar performance.

Later on, Monty and Frank Sinatra went to see *From Here To Eternity* at the Capital Theater in New York. He called me after they saw the picture, and he said he didn't like himself in the picture, he wasn't crazy about the film, but Sinatra was wonderful. I told him that he delivered a great performance, and we had an argument on the phone about it, where he kept repeating, 'I thought I could trust you.' Finally Monty said, 'Maybe it's just me, but I hated it.'"

Reeves' cinematic future would grow no brighter than this. What a shame such a highly talented actor never made it to a higher level of notoriety. But such is justice in the Hollywood jungle.

CAST: Burt Lancaster, Montgomery Clift, Deborah Kerr, Donna Reed, Frank Sinatra, Philip Ober, Mickey Shaughnessy, Harry Ballaver, Ernest Borgnine, Jack Warden, John Dennis, Merle Travis, Tim Ryan, Arthur Keegan, Barbara Morrison, George Reeves, and Claude Akins (unbilled).

A COLUMBIA PICTURE; Produced by Buddy Adler; Directed by Fred Zinnemann; Screenplay by Daniel T. Taradash; Based upon the play by James Jones; Gowns by Jean Louis; Musical Direction: Morris Stoloff; Background music by George Duning; Song "Re-Enlistment Blues" by James Jones, Fred Karger, Robert Wells; Director of Photography: Burnett Guffey, A.S.C.; Art Director: Earl Bellamy; Technical Advisor: Brig. General Kendall J. Fielder, Retired; Makeup by Clay Campbell; Hair Styles by Helen Hunt; Sound Engineer: Lodge Cunningham; Orchestrations: Arthur Morton. Original theatrical release: September 1, 1953. Running time: 118 minutes.

FOREVER FEMALE
The Blink of a Broadway Footlight!

The bright lights of Times Square glitter on the screen as Harry Phillips (Paul Douglas) imparts the opening narration. Harry explains that he is nervously awaiting critical reaction to his latest production, *No Laughing Matter*, which has just opened on Broadway. The star of the new show is the legendary Beatrice Page (Ginger Rogers), who is also Harry's ex-wife. Though Bea is past her prime, the critics concur that she was "radiant," while the play itself was "terrible!" After the performance, Bea makes a splashy entrance at Sardi's. She is escorted by a conservative looking chap sporting a crew cut and Clark Kent-style glasses. His name is George Courtland IV (George Reeves). Amid warm applause, Bea, George, and Harry are seated at one of the best tables in the place. Standing nearby is Stanley Krown (William Olden), an aspiring playwright who has just seen the show. While surveying the faces at the star's table, Stanley asks his agent, Eddie Woods (James Gleason), about the guy who's holding the menu. Eddie says that the man is Bea's ex-hubby. Then, Eddie identifies the "crew cut" (George) as Bea's boyfriend—"This seasons', that is!"

Eddie strolls over to Bea's table and sits down. Harry introduces George as "what's his name." Moments later, when Stanley joins the group, neither Harry nor Eddie can recall George's name, even though they heard it only seconds ago. "It's a perfectly simple name," says George. "For a perfectly simple fellow," adds Harry. Bea smooths things over by asking Stanley what he thought of her performance. Stanley says she was "charming—half the time," in addition to being "condescending" and lacking in humility. "If I was still your husband, I'd ask him to step outside," Harry tells Bea. "But, as it is now, it's up to Mr. Courtland." George solemnly says, "Now you remember my name!" Although justifiably insulted, Bea likes the play that Stanley has written and wants to star in it.

The story, titled "The Unhappy Holiday," is one of those mother-daughter "relationship" yarns. The main problem is Bea's age. She can barely convince people that she's 29, and she wants to play the role of the daughter who is only 19! Bea wants the script rewritten to make the character older. Aside from this snag, she has some competition in the way of Sally Carver (Pat Crowley), a young TV commercial actress also known as Peggy Pruitt (she changes her name throughout the picture). This perky wannabe falls head over heels for Stanley and follows him everywhere, urging him to keep the original story intact so she can play the ingenue. Bea, however, also has designs on the young playwright and keeps pushing for the rewrite. Stanley goads Sally into retyping the play, which has been altered to

George (far right) watches as Ginger Rogers enchants Jesse White in a scene from *FOREVER FEMALE*. Paul Douglas is seated at the left.

On the set of *Forever Female*. George (right) seated next to Ginger Rogers as she refreshes her lipstick. Courtesy of the Academy of Motion Picture Arts and Sciences.

accommodate the aging star. Interestingly, there are no more scenes featuring George, but there are several references to him. Harry, who has his share of financial problems, has gotten into the habit of forging George's signature on the dinner tabs at Sardi's!

When "The Unhappy Holiday" opens in Washington, with Bea portraying the daughter, it flops. Disenchanted, Stanley wants to throw in the towel and stick to his day job at the vegetable market. But Bea encourages him to hang in there while she is on holiday in Europe. Before leaving, Bea and Stanley announce their engagement to the press. Harry, who is still carrying a torch for his former wife, is understandably upset by this occurrence. After Bea leaves town, Stanley and Harry learn that the show is being presented by a regional company outside of New York. When the two of them check it out, they discover that Sally (or Peggy) is playing the lead in the first version of the show, using her "real" name, Clara Mootz. Stanley realizes that the girl was right all along, as the concept works brilliantly with a 19-year-old as the main attraction.

During the drive back to Manhattan, Harry convinces Stanley that he should meet his future mother-in-law. The home they visit is actually occupied by Bea, not her mother. She had never intended to go to Europe, but merely wanted a two-month rest from dieting, massaging, hair-dying, and the other "little tortures" that are inflicted on actresses. At this point, Bea tells Stanley that she isn't in love with him and that he should get on with his life. In the friendliest possible way, Harry tells the young man to "beat it." With Stanley gone, Bea confesses that she was responsible for the production, hoping that the show and the girl would both fail. Now she's forced to admit, rather tearfully, that both were "wonderful." Harry suggests that she swallow her pride and take on the more suitable role of the mother.

Eventually, "The Unhappy Holiday" becomes the biggest hit of the season, with Clara Mootz emerging as Broadway's hottest sensation. Now it's Clara's turn to make a big splashy entrance at Sardi's, which she does, with a beaming Stanley on her arm. In a moment of nostalgic bliss, Bea and Harry peek through the window to observe the young couple. While climbing into a taxi, the two veterans talk about their plans to remarry. Bea jokingly suggests that this might be Harry's way of dealing with the enormous amount of back alimony he owed her.

Another disappointing outing for George, and not a memorable picture in any of these fine actors' resumes. Watch for TV's favorite pitchman Jesse White, King Donovan from *Invasion of the Body Snatchers*, Vic Perrin from *Rocky Jones, Space Ranger* and the control voice from The Outer Limits, and Marion Ross, future super-mom on Happy Days.

CAST: Ginger Rogers, William Holden, Paul Douglas, James Gleason, Jesse White, Marjorie Rambeau, George Reeves, King Donovan, Vic Perrin, Russell Gaige, Marion Ross, Richard Shannon, Pat Crowley.

A PARAMOUNT PICTURE; Produced by Pat Duggan; Directed by Irving Rapper; Written by Julius J. Epstein and Phillip G. Epstein; Suggested by J.M. Barrie's play "Rosalind;" Director of Photography: Harry Stradling, A.S.C.; Art Direction: Hal Pereira and Joseph MacMillan Johnson; Special Photographic Effects: Gordon Jennings, A.S.C.; Process Photography: Farciot Edouart, A.S.C.; Set Decoration: Sam Comer and Ross Dowd; Editorial Advisor: Doane Harrison; Costumes: Edith Head; Edited by Archie Marshek. A.S.E.; Assistant Director: John Coonan; Make-Up Supervision: Wally Westmore; Sound Recording by Harry Lindgren and John Cope; Music Score: Victor Young. Original theatrical release: December 1, 1953. Running time: 93 minutes.

STAMP DAY FOR SUPERMAN
Economic Lessons in a Metropolis Grammar School

Although *Stamp Day for Superman* contains the standard opening from the second season of the TV series, the film was never syndicated with the other 104 episodes. It was originally intended for presentation in schools as a public service program. Over the years, clips from this episode have turned up in various documentaries and videos pertaining to George Reeves and/or Superman. It made its debut with film collectors on the bootleg market in the mid-1970s as a public domain 16mm short.

It is evening in Metropolis. Clark Kent (George Reeves) is escorting Lois Lane (Noel Neill) home from work. As they stroll down the street, the reporters stop to admire some puppies in a store window. Suddenly, they hear a burglar alarm emanating from the Metropolis Jewelry Store. Lois immediately heads for an all-night drug store where she can phone the police. Kent, on the other hand, ducks into a dark alley and emerges as Superman. The Man of Steel gains entrance to the crime scene by bending the bars on a rear window. He confronts a young man who reveals that his "partner" fled as soon as the alarm went off. Superman can't believe this young offender didn't run away also. The startled burglar attributes his actions to financial pressures. He says his life might have turned out better if he had learned to save and manage money. Knowing he can't run from the police forever, the young man promises to turn himself in. Superman lends a sympathetic ear, and leaves the premises just as the police sirens become audible. Afterwards, Lois says she got a good look at the other robber when she bumped into him as he charged down the alley.

In the office the next morning, Jimmy Olsen (Jack Larson) proudly shows Kent a portable typewriter he managed to purchase from the interest accrued on his savings bonds. The two of them are soon joined by Lois, who comments on her eyewitness story of the jewel robbery. Kent asks Jimmy if his alma mater has a stamp day program, as he'd like to write a feature story about kids helping Uncle Sam by buying bonds. Before the two men leave for the school, Lois borrows Jimmy's typewriter.

At the public school, a boy asks Kent if Superman might make an appearance there. While Kent can't promise anything, he is confident the request can be fulfilled. In the meantime, Lois receives a call from a character named Blinky (Billy Nelson), who says he's the man she bumped into last night. He won't surrender to the police, but will give himself up to Lois. Sensing a scoop, she agrees to meet Blinky at a selected location.

Kent and Jimmy chat with the principal, Mr. Garwood (Tris Coffin), about the stamp day program. During their meeting, Kent begins to worry when he realizes Lois hasn't shown up at the school as planned. He phones his editor, Perry White (John Hamilton), who hasn't the slightest idea where Lois can be found. Suspecting trouble, Kent dashes back to the Daily Planet Building.

Blinky has Lois tied to a chair. "The things I can walk into with my eyes wide open," she says with a whine in her voice. Because Lois is a witness,

George wears the uniform proudly in a 1953 publicity photo used to promote the *Adventures of Superman*.

Blinky intends to do away with her. But Blinky isn't the brightest bulb in the universe, and makes the mistake of expressing interest in the typewriter Lois has brought along. Taking advantage of this opportunity, she gives the thug a quick typing lesson. Using various key strokes, Lois "draws" a face, then folds the paper into an airplane which she sails out the window. Amazingly, someone finds the paper in the street and brings it to Perry White. The editor shows it to Kent, who immediately notices a hidden address in the typed drawing. Wasting no time, Kent races down that familiar corridor which leads to the storeroom. A second later, Superman leaps through the window, soars through the city, and crashes through a wall just in time to rescue Lois. After restraining Blinky with a metal floor lamp, Superman flies back to the school.

With the stamp booth as a backdrop, Superman warmly addresses a group of students who are enthralled by his presence. The Man of Steel stresses the importance of saving money, and encourages the kids to participate in stamp day. He assures the youngsters that the stamps will enable them to purchase bonds, just as their parents do through the payroll savings plan at work. "And so, boys and girls," he concludes, "Be super citizens and have a super future by saving regularly with United States savings stamps at school." Superman waves good-bye as he makes an undramatic exit through a door.

Back at the office, Jimmy tells Lois that Blinky has been sentenced to prison while the young accomplice (referred to as Jess) was placed on probation. To make the ending even happier, Kent presents his co-workers with stamp albums. Lois notices that Kent is holding an extra book. "Who's that for?" she asks. A close-up reveals that Superman is the intended recipient. "Oh, just for a friend of mine," says Kent with his wink and world-famous smile.

George strikes a pose in a publicity photo for *Stamp Day for Superman*.

Donating their services for this U.S. Treasury short were two familiar faces in the Superman guest star roster, Tristram Coffin and Billy Nelson.

Veteran character actor Tris Coffin was no stranger to the Saturday Matinee Serial crowd. Co-starring as the heavy in most of his serial appearances, Coffin worked in Republic's *Dick Tracy's G-Men* (1939), *Mysterious Doctor Satan* (1940), *Spy Smasher* (1942), *Perils of Nyoka* (1942), *Jesse James Rides Again* (1947), *Federal Agents vs. The Underworld Inc.* (1949), *Radar Patrol vs. Spy King* (1949), and starring as Jeff King in the classic *King of the Rocketmen* (1949). He was in one serial at Universal, *Sky Raiders* (1941), and for Columbia he appeared in *Bruce Gentry—Daredevil of the Skies* (1949), and *Pirates of the High Seas* (1950). In 1951, Coffin guest starred in two Superman episodes, "Case of the Talkative Dummy" and "Mystery of the Broken Statues." He returned to the Superman set in 1954 for "Clark Kent Outlaw," and in 1956 for the show "Whatever Goes Up." He starred in his own television series, *26 Men*, co-starring Kelo Henderson in the 1950s, and had an off track role in the low budget programmer *Ma Barker's Killer Brood* (1959). Coffin's other features include *The Corpse Vanishes* (Monogram 1942), *The Shanghai Chest* (1948), *The Invisible Informer* (1946), *Destroyer* (1943), *A Star Is Born* (1954), *The Night The World Exploded* (1957), and *The Crawling Hand* (1963).

He was even busier on television, co-starring in such shows as 77 Sunset Strip, Bronco, Sugarfoot, The Real McCoys, The Alaskans, The Lone Ranger, I Love Lucy, Cisco Kid, The Adventures of Wild Bill Hickock, My Little Margie, Climax, Judge Roy Bean, Lux Video Theatre, The Time Tunnel, and Gomer Pyle, U.S.M.C.

Coffin was the nephew of American journalist Tris Coffin. He was born in 1909 and died in 1990 in Santa Monica, California.

His co-star Billy Nelson had a long career playing bit and small roles from the mid 30s to the late 50s. Some of his more notable films were *Calling All Crooks* (1938), *Wildcat* (1942), *I Live On Danger* (1942), *False Faces* (1943), *When Strangers Marry* (1944), *The Kid From Brooklyn* (1946), *The Undercover Man* (1949), *His Kind of Woman* (1951), *The Pride of St. Louis* (1952), *The Seven Little Foys* (1955), *Somebody Up There Likes Me* (1956), and the court-room classic *12 Angry Men* (1957). Superman producer Whitney Ellsworth always put Nelson's acting talents to good use by giving him solid character roles with an accent on comedy. Nelson was born July 19, 1903 and passed away on June 12, 1979, in Los Angeles, California, and was a favorite *Adventures of Superman* guest star.

CAST: George Reeves, Noel Neill, Jack Larson, John Hamilton, Billy Nelson, Tris Coffin.

PRESENTED BY THE UNITED STATES TREASURY DEPARTMENT; Directed by Thomas Carr; Written by David Chantler. Closing credit title: "This motion picture was donated to the United States Treasury Department as a public service by Superman, Inc."

SUPERMAN FLIES AGAIN

Stratospheric Zombies, Clever Canines, and Odd Clowns

The man of steel flies through three adventures taken from the second season of Superman: "Jet Ace," "The Dog Who Knew Superman," and "The
Clown Who Cried."

The adventure begins with Superman (George Reeves) rescuing a pilot
who has fallen unconscious during the test flight of a new jet fighter. The
"Jet Ace" is Chris White (Lane Bradford), nephew of Daily Planet editor
Perry White (John Hamilton). Overworked and fatigued, Chris is persuaded
to take a much-needed rest in the solitude of his uncle's cabin. There, Chris
completes a top-secret flight report which he hides in the barrel of a shot-
gun. Though he doesn't realize it, Chris is about to be abducted by two
spies, Nate (Ric Roman) and Frenchy (Richard Reeves). Later, when Perry
learns that his nephew is missing, he sends Clark Kent and Jimmy Olsen
(Jack Larson) up to the cabin to investigate. Though the reporters do not
find Chris, they do catch a glimpse of the kidnappers searching for the
report. After failing to locate the document, the thugs speed down the highway arrogantly—until their vehicle is brought to an abrupt halt by a caped
figure. While holding the doors tightly shut from his position atop the car,
Superman asks: "What did you do with Captain White?" Nate and Frenchy
admit that they were hired to abduct Chris, under direct orders from Steve
Martin (Larry Blake).

Martin, a disgruntled reporter for a rival newspaper, drags Chris back
to the cabin and ties him up. When Chris refuses to turn over the report,
Martin sets the place ablaze. Eventually, Perry learns that his nephew was
recently seen at the cabin, at which point Kent quietly sneaks away in order
to switch to Superman. The hero saves both Chris and the document from
the flames. Afterward, Kent sets a trap by having Perry inform the authorities that Chris perished in the fire. When another test flight is conducted,
Martin and other members of the press gather at the office of General
Summers (Selmer Jackson) to witness the event. Martin is mildly stunned
to see Chris enter the room. A fight erupts and Chris beats the daylights out
of Martin. Lois Lane (Noel Neill) watches in amusement as the two men
thrash it out. When Lois criticizes Kent for not pitching in, he comments,
"Let the boy have some fun!" After the brawl, Chris remarks he could have
used some help from Superman. Kent observes, "Chris, you put on a pretty
good Superman performance all by yourself!"

During his next outing, Kent's attention is focused on the crowd gathered around a rustic well where a little dog has apparently fallen in. And so
begins the lighthearted saga of Corky—"The Dog Who Knew Superman."
Corky's neurotic owner, Joyce (Dona Drake), blames the accident on her
boyfriend, Hank (Ben Welden), a small-time hoodlum. Like a "human drill"
Superman bores through the earth, then appears at the top of the well with
the unharmed pooch in his arm.

The "human drill" effect is a variation of a Lydecker Brothers flying dummy gag. In Darkest Africa (the first Republic serial, released in 1936), the Lydeckers introduced the flying dummy for the villainous "Batmen of Joba" characters. They were utilized in such cliffhanger classics as *Adventures of Captain Marvel* (Republic 1941), *King of the Rocketmen* (Republic 1949), *Radar Men From the Moon* (Republic 1952), *Zombies of the Stratosphere* (Republic 1952), and the twelve featurette television shows (1953, syndicated 1954) *Commando Cody, Sky Marshall of the Universe.* Republic didn't use the human drill aspect of the effect, but the Adventures of Superman did twice more in the color years ("Dagger Island"—1955, and "Divide and Conquer"—1957). Alert viewers will be able to see the wires in "The Dog Who Knew Superman."

Before the crowd disperses, Corky retrieves a glove that had been dropped on the ground by Kent, just before making the switch to you-know-who. Later, Hank recognizes this piece of apparel as a link between Superman and his secret identity. If he can identify the owner of the glove, he'll be in a position to blackmail the superhero into submission—or so he believes.

Corky clearly knows who the glove belongs to. But the mutt runs away from Hank and ventures across town, straight to the desk of Clark Kent, where he displays loads of canine affection for his rescuer. (The most amusing aspect of this encounter is Kent's ability to communicate with the ani-

British lobby card.

British lobby card.

mal on a nearly human-to-human level!) When Corky is subsequently placed under Jimmy Olsen's charge, Hank has the cub reporter kidnapped in order to gain access to the dog.

After much chaos, Corky does lead the half-witted hoodlum toward the person he's been seeking. But Hank is dismayed to find himself standing before Superman himself, rather than the "secret identity" figure he was expecting to encounter. As a result, Hank is arrested for kidnapping Jimmy.

Kent is now faced with the unpleasant task of saying good-bye to Corky. He tells the pooch that Superman's true identity is a secret that must be kept just between them. "So be a pal and go on home, much as I'll hate to lose you," he says softly. Whimpering pathetically, Corky takes one last look at his hero before straying out of the office. Lois then walks in. "What's the matter, Clark?" she asks. "You look as though you've lost your best friend." With an ineffable sadness, Kent responds, "Maybe I have, Lois. Maybe I have."

It is a tribute to the talents of George, director Tommy Carr, and Corky that this scene, dripping with sentimentality, holds up more than 50 years after it was filmed.

There's also a touch of pathos in "The Clown Who Cried," a tale of stolen identity wedged between the rigors of circus life and the excitement of live television. Rollo the Clown (William Wayne) is a kind-hearted soul who will soon be performing on a charity telethon that is expected to raise a half-million dollars. Shortly before the broadcast, Rollo is confronted by his former partner, a clown known as "Crackers" (Peter Brocco), who is now down on his luck and in need of money. After learning of Rollo's involvement with the telethon, Crackers clobbers his fellow thespian on the head, ties him up, and impersonates him on the show. Since the telethon is sponsored by the Daily Planet, Clark Kent handles the emceeing while Lois, Jimmy, and Perry tackle the telephone pledges.

With Crackers hiding behind Rollo's trademark make-up and costume, no one has reason to suspect that the man on stage is an imposter and a criminal. But at one point during the telecast, the clown pulls a gun on Kent and Lois, demanding that they fork over the proceeds they've collected. After Crackers absconds with the cash, Kent places an urgent call to Inspector Henderson (Robert Shayne), who saw the stunt on TV and thought it was all part of the act. By this time, Rollo has managed to free himself and meets up with Crackers in a dark alley. The two clowns get into a nasty struggle which escalates to the rooftop of a building. Since the two figures are virtually indistinguishable, the police don't know which man is their target. One clown pushes the other over the edge, but both topple off the building just as Superman arrives on the scene. Superman catches one clown, while the other hits the ground. Seriously injured, Crackers asks Superman how he knew which man to save. "The kind of man you are is what gave you away," says Superman. "I can't imagine Rollo pushing anyone off a roof, not even you." This scene is augmented by a dynamic musi-

British lobby card.

One-sheet from the 20th Century-Fox compilation feature *SUPERMAN FLIES AGAIN*.

British lobby card.

cal score composed by Miklos Rozsa. The real Rollo is brought to the studio and closes the show with his slapstick routines.

The Adventures of Superman always had the best of the B-movie bad guys. Lane Bradford, who plays Perry White's nephew Chris White, comes from an acting family. His father, John Merton, a veteran character man (1901-1959) began his film career in 1934 with *Sons of the Desert* and concluded with the 1956 production of *The Ten Commandments*. His forté was playing villains with credits in both Republic and Columbia serials. He worked with George on *The Adventures of Sir Galahad* (as Ulric), and was a featured heavy in such serials as *The Lone Ranger, Dick Tracy Returns*, and *Zorro's Fighting Legion*.

Lane was born in 1923, and made his film debut in 1946. He starred as the head zombie in Republic's third and final Rocketman serial, *Zombies of the Stratosphere* (Republic 1952). He co-starred with Noel Neill and Superman guest star Keith Richards in Republic's twelve chapter cliffhanger, *James Brothers of Missouri* (Republic 1950). He can be seen on reruns of Bonanza as one of the Virginia City bullies, in more than a few episodes.

Retiring from films in 1968, his dream was to own his own boat. He accomplished this, but sadly died on June 7, 1973 from a cerebral hemorrhage in Honolulu, Hawaii. Lane played in the color shows "Test of a Warrior," and "The Phantom Ring."

First season favorite Richard Reeves was back on set as the baddie 'Frenchy' in "Jet Ace." Reeves was born Richard Jourdan Reeves on August

10, 1912 in New York City. His first film appearance was in 1943 in *This Is The Army*, and his last role was in the low budget Chesse classic, *Billy the Kid vs. Dracula* in 1966. He appeared in numerous television shows such as I Love Lucy.

Reeves was back for the color episode "The Big Freeze," making his second appearance on the Adventures of Superman. He passed away March 17, 1967.

Playing the antagonist Steve Martin is unsung character actor Larry Blake. Blake's career spans five decades, with ninety feature films, and one hundred and two small screen guest spots. His debut on the Superman show in 1951's eerie "The Secret of Superman," features Peter Brocco as the evil Doctor Ort. Blake's superb portrayal of Ort's henchman Raush has made "Secret" a favorite of Superman fans the world over.

Blake was born on April 24, 1914 in Brooklyn, New York, and passed away on May 25, 1982. He is the father of Lon Chaney Sr. expert and author Michael F. Blake, and a familiar face to 50s sci-fi fans, appearing in such favorites as *Creature With the Atom Brain* (1955), *The Werewolf* (1956), *Earth vs. the Flying Saucers* (1956), *Beginning of the End* (1957), and in Universal's bio-pic *Man of a Thousand Faces* (1957), the story of Lon Chaney Sr. Blake has a small part with George, as the record store clerk in Fritz Lang's 1953 production *The Blue Gardenia* (Warner Brothers).

"The Dog Who Knew Superman" features Ben Welden (who had more guest shots on Superman than any other day player) and his sidekick from "The Machine Who Could Plot Crimes" Billy Nelson. Welden specialized in gangster parts from his days at Warner Brothers. With Superman, his gangsters were generally played for laughs. He was in *Tear Gas Squad* with George for Warners in 1940. Other titles in his resumé include *The Big Sleep* (1946), *Prison Nurse* (1938), *Crime Ring* (1938), *Smashing the Rackets* (1938), and *Bullet Scars* (1942). He was born in Toledo, Ohio on June 12, 1901, and died October 17, 1997 at the Motion Picture Home in Woodland Hills, California.

"The Clown Who Cried" is a television show within a television show. Guest actor Peter Brocco, who had already cut quite a sinister figure as the truth serum dispensing Doctor Ort in "The Secret of Superman," was back as the kind clown in this Jekyll and Hyde/under the big top/telethon adventure of Superman.

Brocco appeared in one hundred seventeen films, and one hundred eighteen television shows in his seven decade career. A native of Reading, Pennsylvania, Brocco was born on January 16, 1902, and passed on December 20, 1992 in Hollywood. He worked up until a year before his death in such films as *Other People's Money* (1991), *War of the Roses* (1989), *Throw Momma From the Train* (1987). His first film part was in 1932's *Devil in the Deep*.

He made his television debut on November 17, 1952, on "Dangerous Assignment," starring Brian Donlevy, which was originally a radio show. His other Superman guest spot was as 'The Spectre' in the 1955 color show "The Phantom Ring."

CAST: George Reeves, Noel Neill, Jack Larson, John Hamilton, Robert Shayne, Lane Bradford, Selmer Jackson, Richard Reeves, Jim Hayward, Larry Blake, Mauritz Hugo, Sam Balter, Bud Wolfe, Ric Roman, Ben Welden, Billy Nelson, Dona Drake, John Daly, Lester Dorr, William Wayne, Peter Brocco, Mickey Simpson, Harry Mendoza, George Douglas, Charles Williams, Richard D. Crockett, Richard Lewis, and Harvey Parry.

A TWENTIETH CENTURY-FOX RELEASE; Produced by Whitney Ellsworth; Directed by Thomas Carr and George Blair; Screenplay by David Chantler; Director of Photography: Harold Stine, A.S.C.; Production Manager: Clem Beauchamp; Production Coordinator: David S. Garver; Film Editor: Harry Gerstad; Assistant Directors: Jack R. Berne, Robert Justman, Ivan Volkman; Special Effects: Thol Simonson; Photographic Effects: Jack R. Glass; Story Editor: Mort Weisinger; Sound Engineer: Jen L. Speak; Re-recording: Ryder Sound Services, Inc. Original Theatrical Release: 1954.

SUPERMAN IN EXILE

Toxic Hero, Fugazi Reeves, and a Precocious Parakeet!

This excellent feature is compiled from three TV episodes: "Superman in Exile," "The Face and the Voice," and "The Whistling Bird."

The City of Metropolis is on the brink of disaster due to a nuclear pile at Project X. Responding to an urgent bulletin, Superman (George Reeves) painstakingly switches the rods in the reactor, thus preventing a catastrophe. But exposure to the atomic monstrosity has charged his body with an incredible level of radioactivity, a fate sadly confirmed by the nearest Geiger counter. He glows in the dark (a very impressive Jack R. Glass optical effect) and can cause house plants to shrivel just by waving his hands over them. As a result, we find "Superman in Exile" in a cabin high atop Blue Peak Mountain. This spells trouble for Clark Kent, whose prolonged absence from work has caused Lois Lane (Noel Neill) and Jimmy Olsen (Jack Larson) to suspect that their old pal may actually be Krypton's sole survivor! As Professor Adams (Joe Forte) frantically searches for a cure, word of Superman's condition sends shockwaves around the world.

A foreign agent known as Ferdinand (Leon Askin) has been bragging about some jewels that his country will be exhibiting in Metropolis. With Superman out of the way, Ferdinand has no difficulty convincing two hoods, Regan (Phil Van Zandt) and Skinny (John Harmon), to hijack the plane transporting the gems. On the pretense of granting an exclusive story, the threesome manage to trick Lois into joining them. That night, the reporter finds herself a prisoner on the tiny aircraft piloted by Skinny. At the same time, a mammoth thunderstorm approaches the mountain region where Superman has exiled himself. Recalling Professor Adams' theory that an enormous shock might counteract the radioactive charge, Superman propels himself directly into the storm. Bolts of lightning strike him mercilessly as he soars through the clouds. It is the fifth strike that finally eradicates the deadly "glow" from his body.

Now that he can intercept the plane without contaminating it, Superman gives the passengers a rough ride by tugging at the tail of the aircraft. Fearing a sudden crash, Skinny brings the plane down at the nearest airfield, where the sheriff is on hand to make the appropriate arrests.

This episode contains some of the most breathtaking work of photographic effects man, Jack R. Glass. His work on the second season has

Print ad for *SUPERMAN IN EXILE.*

Hayden Rorke of "I Dream of Jeannie" fame analyzes George.

brought a reality to the show that holds up today. The dynamic day and night flying shots (with Si Simonson's mechanicals) of the 1953 season rank with the best of 50s Sci-Fi flix. Glass also worked on "Rocky Jones, Space Ranger."

It has often been said that George's favorite Superman episode was "The Face and the Voice." It's quite obvious that he is enjoying every minute of this rare opportunity to perform beyond the parameters of his Clark Kent/Superman duality. The story begins with a big-time hood named Fairchild (Carlton Young), offering a hoodlum $25,000 to have his face surgically altered to resemble Superman. Despite his dis-dem-doze crudeness, "Boulder" (Reeves, with gray hair and gangster duds) already bears a slight resemblance to Superman. But with plastic surgery, extensive voice lessons, and a crash course in refinement, he becomes a dead-ringer for the caped hero.

With his new face and voice, Boulder is ready to begin the "career" that Fairchild has masterminded. Outfitted in a duplicate Superman costume, he walks into a grocery store and calmly asks for all the money in the cash register. Obviously stunned, but totally compliant, the proprietor turns over the money. After all, Superman must have a good reason for doing such a thing. Even more puzzling is the fact that "Superman" has donated the stolen money (an insignificant sum) to charity. This and similar stunts cause everyone to conclude that Superman has finally lost his marbles. Even Clark Kent worries that his alter-ego may need professional help, and pays a visit to his pal Tom (Hayden Rorke), who happens to be a psychiatrist. (Rorke would go on to portray another psychiatrist, some twelve years later, on the popular sitcom "I Dream of Jeannie").

The inevitable showdown between Boulder and Superman occurs when Fairchild attempts to heist a shipment of gold bullion. Superman tracks down the truck from which Boulder and Fairchild are removing two million dollars worth of gold bricks. At this point, Fairchild's greed overtakes him and he attempts to get rid of Boulder, not realizing he is confronting the real Man of Steel. Fairchild falls and is knocked unconscious. Boulder attempts to make a run for it, but doesn't get very far, thanks to Superman. The closing scene is set at Mercy General Hospital, where Boulder has been placed under arrest by Inspector Henderson (Robert Shayne), with Clark and Jimmy acting as witnesses. Boulder requests that his former face be restored. "I should-da known," he grumbles. "It takes more than a face and a voice! There's only one real Superman!"

"The Whistling Bird" is a lesser-known, but perfectly enjoyable Superman adventure. Professor Oscar Quinn (Sterling Holloway) has always wanted to invent something great for humanity. And so he has—a new and stronger glue, available in multiple flavors, to be used on postage stamps! But the stuff turns out to be one of the most powerful (and highly volatile) explosives ever con-

Toni Carroll, Joseph Vitale, Jack Larson, and Allene Roberts.

cocted. To make matters worse, a secret ingredient of the formula is known only to Schyler, the professor's pet parakeet. When Oscar attempts a second experiment (his first one wrecked the lab) the Whistling Bird seems to have "forgotten" the key element. That's because the real Schyler has been bird-napped by enemy agents, and the current occupant of the cage is an imposter!

The spies hold Oscar, his niece Nancy (Allene Roberts), and Jimmy at gunpoint. Naturally, they have forced the professor to produce another batch of the explosive. Superman, as usual, arrives in the nick of time to save the day. First, he rescues the threesome from a water-filled cubicle, then smothers the impending explosion by drinking the formula. When Superman tracks down the spies, he is once again faced with drinking another beaker of the nasty-tasting stuff. "Oh, no. Not again!" he moans. "You're not worth saving," he warns the offenders. "But run for your lives, this may explode at any minute." It does. Superman saves the spies from the explosion, but not the law.

The wrap-up scene in Clark Kent's office is short and sweet. Safely back in his cage, Schyler demonstrates his perceptiveness by cooing, "Oooh, Superman! Oooh Superman!" Lois becomes incredulous. "Professor, until now I thought Schyler was a pretty smart bird," she remarks. "But when he starts to call Clark Superman . . . ?" Suddenly, the bird renders a perfectly executed wolf-whistle. "He just whistled at you, Lois," says Kent. "What do

Jack Larson, Allene Roberts, George, and Sterling Holloway.

Sterling Holloway's voice makes it difficult for George to keep a straight face.

you think of his mind now?" Lois gives her best "Gee-what-can-I-say?" smile as the picture fades.

Like the old Universal Pictures logo "A Good Cast is Worth Repeating" so are the Adventures of Superman players. The villains in "Superman in Exile" are top drawer. Leon Askin's energetic portrayal of Ferdinand, the felonious foreign agent, is straight off the pages of a DC Comic, full of hyper-campiness.

Askin, who began his film and television career in the late 40s, was born in Vienna, Austria on September 18, 1907. His first movie work was on *Hotel New Hampshire* (1948), as an accent coach. Askin can be seen in *The Road to Bali* (1952), *The Robe* (1953), *Knock on Wood* (1954), *Valley of the Kings* (1954), *Son of Sinbad* (1955), *Spy Chasers* with the Bowery Boys (1955). He had an extensive career in German films, including the Doctor Mabuse film series, as well as *Sherlock Holmes and the Deadly Necklace* (1962). In the late

60s he appeared in such shows as *What Did You Do in the War, Daddy?* (1966), *Perils of Pauline* (1967), *The Maltese Bippy* (1969). He was a cast member from 1965-71 on "Hogan's Heroes." As of this writing (May 2004), his last film credit was 2001, and he co-starred in the 1954 season show "King for a Day," (another Jack Larson tour de force, taken directly from a Jimmy Olsen comic book story). In September of 2005 he will be ninety-eight years old. He guest starred on such popular television shows as Disneyland, Outer Limits, Honey West, I Spy, My Favorite Martian, Bob Hope Presents, The Hardy Boys/Nancy Drew Myteries, Happy Days, Three's Company, and Diff'rent Strokes.

Askins' co-star Phil Van Zandt from "Exile" and 1954's "King for a Day" wasn't so lucky. He was found dead on February 16, 1958, of an over-dose of barbituates. Lack of work was cited as the motive. Van Zandt was born on October 4, 1904, in Amsterdam, Holland, and appeared in one hundred eighty-seven films. Highlights of his cinematic career include *Citizen Kane* (1941), *City of Missing Girls* (1941), *All Through the Night* (1942), *Sherlock Holmes and the Secret Weapon* (1942), *Adventures of the Flying Cadets* (1943), *Tarzan Triumphs* (1943), *Tarzan's Desert Mystery* (1943), *The Hitler Gang* (1944), *House of Frankenstein* (1944), *A Thousand and One Nights* (1945), *Monsieur Beaucaire* (1946), *The Big Clock* (1948), *The Shanghai Chest* (1948), *Cyrano de Bergerac* (1950), *The Desert Fox* (1951), *The Ghost Chasers* (1951), *Viva Zapata* (1952), *The Big Combo* (1955), *To Catch a Thief* (1955), *Around the World in Eighty Days* (1956), *Man of a Thousand Faces* (1957), and his last film, *Fifi Blows Her Top* (1958).

His television work was sparse, to say the least. His first appearance on Superman was as gangster Nick Malone in the episode "Crime Wave" from the 1951 season. He can also be seen in such television favorites as The Adventures of Wild Bill Hickok, Fury, Rin Tin Tin, Our Miss Brooks, to name a few.

"The Face and the Voice" is a natural progression of a story from 1942, written by Jay Morton, for the Superman Fleischer cartoon "Showdown." If ever there was a showcase for George's acting talents on the Adventures of Superman—this is it! Playing Boulder is diametrically opposed to Clark Kent and Superman, and this gives George a chance to flex his acting chops for the Baby Boom audience. His Leo Gorcey interpretation of Boulder is priceless!

The head villain, Fairchild, whose brainchild was a gangster 'Superman' is superbly essayed by veteran actor Carlton Young. Young came to the Superman set well prepared for this kind of material, having worked in such genre serials as *Dick Tracy* (1937), *Fighting Devil Dogs* (1938), *Buck Rodgers* (1939), *The Lone Ranger Rides Again* (1939), *Zorro's Fighting Legion* (1939), *Adventures of Red Ryder* (1940), *The Adventures of Captain Marvel* (1941).

He appeared with comedy teams Abbott & Costello, and the East Side Kids (*Buck Privates*, *Keep 'Em Flying*, and *Pride of the Bowery*) in 1941, and ten years later he worked on Robert Wise's sci-fi classic *Day the Earth Stood*

Still (1951). Young put in an appearance with an all-star cast (Robert Mitchum, Vincent Price, and Jane Russell) in the film noir thriller *His Kind of Woman* (1951), and finished out his acting career with roles in the Western favorites *The Man Who Shot Liberty Valance* (1962), and *Cheyenne Autumn* (1964). He was born in 1907, and succumbed to the ravages of cancer on July 11, 1971, in Hollywood.

Young's henchman was played by a veteran of some three hundred fifty-five films, and fifty-four television guest spots (including three Adventures of Superman shows, the aforementioned "Flight to the North," and "Blackmail"). George Chandler served as the president of Screen Actors Guild from 1960 to 1963. He was born on June 30, 1898, and passed on June 10, 1985. His best remembered role was that of Uncle Petrie on the Baby Boomer fave Lassie. George has a hilarious scene with character man Percy Helton, in which Helton is his frustrated voice coach. Helton's first celluloid work was in 1916, and his last was *Butch Cassidy and the Sundance Kid* (1969). He has featured roles in *Funny Girl* (1968), *The Sons of Katie Elder* (1965) and *Hush, Hush, Sweet Charlotte* (1965). Helton was born in New York in 1894, and died in Hollywood on September 11, 1971.

Parakeets, sex sirens, flavored postage stamp glue, all lead to a wacky episode with another dose of indigestion of the imagination. The kindly, yet slightly nutty, Uncle Oscar Quinn makes his second appearance ("The Machine Who Could Plot Crimes" being the first) in the 1953 season show "The Whistling Bird." It's hard to tell who is the more feather-brained in this episode, the bird or his human counterparts.

Sterling Holloway was perfect casting for Uncle Oscar, with his high-pitched eccentric delivery. Born in Cedartown, Georgia, on January 4, 1905 (a day and nine years before George), he expired on November 22, 1992 from cardiac arrest. His forté was voice-overs in the latter part of his career. The Cheerios Bee and Winnie the Pooh were two of his best remembered voices. He was featured in one hundred motion pictures, and was a guest star on many television shows.

His niece, Nancy, was played by three-time Superman co-star Allene Roberts ("Haunted Lighthouse," Monkey Mystery," and "Whistling Bird"). Born in Birmingham, Alabama on September 1, 1928, her cinema career was short (11 films), starting in 1947 with Edward G. Robinson in the creepy film *The Red House*. 1949 saw her in *Knock on Any Door* with Humphrey Bogart, and in 1951 she co-starred with real life tough guy Lawrence Tierney in *The Hoodlum*. Her television career was a wee bit longer at fifteen guest shots, including Dragnet, The Public Defender, Four Star Playhouse, and The Schlitz Playhouse of Stars. As of this writing, we presume she is still alive.

The femme fatale seductress of the piece (Dorothy Manners) is played by Toni Carroll, who has an even shorter career than Miss Roberts. She has four film credits, "Superman in Exile" being one of them. Other than the Adventures of Superman, her TV work consists of two appearances on Science Fiction Theater in 1955.

It would be interesting to view these theatrical features (with the custom filmed 60-second transitions pieces) in their original 35-millimeter format, projected on a large screen, if any of them still exist (doubtful).

CAST: George Reeves, Noel Neill, Jack Larson, John Hamilton, Robert Shayne, Leon Askin, Joe Forte, Robert S. Carson, Phil Van Zandt, John Harmon, Don Dillaway, Gregg Barton, Sam Balter, Hayden Rorke, I. Stanford Jolley, George Chandler, Percy Helton, Carlton Young, William Newell, Nolan Leary, Sterling Holloway, Joseph Vitale, Otto Waldis, Toni Carroll, Allene Roberts, Marshall Reed, and Jerry Hausner.

A TWENTIETH CENTURY-FOX RELEASE; Produced by Whitney Ellsworth; Directed by Thomas Carr and George Blair; Screenplay by Jackson Gillis; Director of Photography: Harold Stine, A.S.C.; Production Manager: Clem Beauchamp; Production Coordinator: David S. Garber; Film Editor: Harry Gerstad; Assistant Directors: Jack R. Berne, Robert Justman, Ivan Volkman; Special Effects: Thol Simonson; Photographic Effects: Jack R. Glass; Story Editor: Mort Weisinger; Sound Engineer: Jean L. Speak; Re-recording: Tyder Sound Services, Inc. Original Theatrical Release: 1954.

SUPERMAN AND SCOTLAND YARD
English Spirits, the Folgers Lady in Lingerie, and a Menace From the Stars!

This Fox compilation feature is derived from three episodes of the Adventures of Superman, all filmed in 1953. The segments are, respectively, "A Ghost for Scotland Yard," "The Lady in Black," and "Panic in the Sky."

Clark Kent (George Reeves) and Jimmy Olsen (Jack Larson) are in London. A sidewalk newsvendor (Clyde Cook), who is amply supplied with Superman comics, enlightens Jimmy about the legendary Brockhurst, a deceased magician who hated everyone, especially his manager, Sir Arthur McCray (Colin Campbell). A master illusionist, Brockhurst always said he would return from the grave five years after his death. With five years having elapsed, the press is filled with lurid predictions about "A Ghost for Scotland Yard." From the Daily Planet offices in Metropolis, Lois Lane (Noel Neill) telephones Clark and informs him that their boss, an old friend of Sir Arthur's, wants an exclusive story about the Brockhurst case. Later that night, as Sir Arthur drives on a treacherous stretch of road, he is shocked by a gigantic apparition of Brockhurst (Leonard Mudie) in the moonlit clouds. Sir Arthur faints at the wheel, but Superman intercepts the vehicle and brings it to a screeching halt.

While conducting a little nocturnal sleuthing, Superman finds a strip of motion picture film at the site where the "ghost" nearly caused Sir Arthur's

Newspaper ad for
*SUPERMAN AND
SCOTLAND YARD*.

demise. In the meantime, Jimmy is about to become the next target of the mad magician who is, of course, very much alive and on the loose. At the carriage house on the McCredy estate, Jimmy encounters the raving Brockhurst, who admits to having killed a man in the course of perfecting his "return from the grave" trick. Inspector Farrington (Patrick Aherne, a real life friend to George and Toni Mannix), tries to intervene but Brockhurst has a gun aimed at the cub reporter's back. Brockhurst is so insane that he is willing to die for real and attempts to blow the place up (just like today's terrorists). Superman, however, swiftly intercepts the bomb

Lobby card for the feature film release (*note the title of* Superman in Scotland Yard).

and throws it through the roof just before it detonates. With their work completed, Clark and Jimmy embark for the States. On their way to the airport, the newsvendor gives them some great material to read on the plane—the latest issue of "Superman" magazine. No one notices the irony.

Back in Metropolis, Jimmy is spending the night at the apartment of a vacationing friend. Spooked by the mystery novel he has been reading, the cub reporter begins seeing strange things and hearing odd noises. In need of reassurance, he phones Clark Kent, who is working late at the office. Kent concludes that Jimmy is suffering from "indigestion of the imagination," and tells him to go to sleep. Later that night, after Jimmy sustains a bump on his head, Superman checks the place out, but doesn't detect anything sinister.

The next day, Jimmy encounters oddballs, including a mysterious "Lady in Black" (Virginia Christine) whose face is hidden behind a gauze-thin veil. Jimmy is perplexed when she tosses a package of currency at him, the first of several inexplicable events. Eventually, Jimmy comes to the conclusion that a neighbor, Mr. Frank (Frank Ferguson), has been murdered. Once again, Jimmy causes Superman to investigate the premises, this time with a policeman. And once again, Superman finds nothing out of the ordinary. The next time Jimmy calls for help, Kent uses his super-hearing to decipher the background chatter on the phone line. Superman races over to the apartment building where Mr. Frank and his wife (the veiled woman), are trafficking in stolen paintings. After roughing up the male members of the ring, Superman goes rather easy on Mrs. Frank. With his super-breath, he exposes her identity by simply blowing the veil off her face.

Jimmy decides to discard the mystery novel he had been reading, appropriately entitled "The Lady in Black!"

There's an asteroid streaking toward Metropolis. At an observatory, Superman informs Professor Roberts (Jonathan Hale) that he may be able to knock the thing off its course. Roberts, however, warns that this "Panic in the Sky" may contain unknown elements from cosmic space, such as Kryptonite, which may prove lethal. Nevertheless, Superman assumes the risk.

In one of the most dramatic and expensive sequences ever devised for the series, the Man of Steel crashes into the celestial body with spectacular vigor. A massive explosion (achieved via animation) indicates that the immediate danger is over. Superman makes it back to earth in one piece, but his shaky landing indicates that something is wrong. He hitches a ride with a lady farmer back to Metropolis, and back in his apartment, Clark Kent is

George and Noel Neill study the telescope that reveals a great danger to planet earth.

baffled by the Superman costumes hidden in his closet. The unthinkable has actually happened: Superman has lost his memory.

Weakened by the ordeal he has endured, Kent passes out in the shower and crashes through the glass partition. Jimmy is stunned to find his mentor lying unconscious, yet completely devoid of any wounds or bruises. When Kent awakens in bed, he is totally disoriented and does not recognize his closest friends—Jimmy, Lois, and Perry White (John Hamilton). Naturally, the blow to Kent's head is the suspected cause of his amnesia. The next day, Clark returns to work, hoping that the familiar surroundings will restore his memory. To everyone's disappointment, the idea is a failure. But there is a bigger problem to ponder: No one has seen Superman since his collision in space.

George and Noel Neill at the observatory.

Professor Roberts shows up at the Daily Planet to report that Superman merely "sidetracked" the asteroid instead of destroying it. As a result, numerous disasters (earthquakes, tidal waves) are occurring around the globe due to the imbalance in the solar system. The asteroid must be obliterated, but there are no missiles that can venture that far into space. The professor orders Lois to find Superman—immediately!

While contemplating in his apartment, a frustrated Kent (wearing the costume and his specs) smashes a wooden piece of furniture with his fist. A small feat, but significant enough to stimulate something in his brain. With his memory now intact, Kent exclaims: "Professor Roberts! The observatory!" A few frames later, Professor Roberts and the Daily Planet brigade are relieved to see Krypton's favorite son. The professor arms Superman with an atomic device which must be flown out to the asteroid. After landing on his target, Superman detonates the bomb which destroys the celestial menace forever.

Back at the office, Clark Kent types up the story of Superman's near-catastrophic encounter. Feeling like his old self, and a bit mischievous, Kent tells Lois that he now knows Superman's secret identity. "Well, come on . . . who?" snaps Lois. With a beseeching smile, Kent responds, "Oh, just knock me on the head some time and you'll find out!"

One of the strongest of the five feature packages, "Ghost for Scotland Yard" and "Panic in the Sky" bookend the mystery "Lady in Black," which is a wonderful showcase for Jack Larson's acting talents. "Ghost" is the company's second foray into the spirit world (if you don't count the first season's "Mystery in Wax"). All the ghosts in Superman's world are fugazis, but it's still great fun to watch them scare the "Jeepers" out of Jimmy Olsen.

Leonard Mudie is stellar as the evil Brockhurst. Born Leonard Mudie Cheetham, on April 11, 1884, in England. Mudie entered films in 1921 and died three days after his 81st birthday in 1965. He was a guest star of the 1951 episode "Drums of Death." Patrick Aherne, who plays Inspector Farrington, was Brian Aherne's brother, and had a 32-year film career before succumbing to cancer on September 30, 1970.

"Lady in Black" features John Doucette from the first season's "Birthday Letter," Reeves' frequent screenmate Frank Ferguson, and the scintillating Virginia Christine, who portrayed Princess Ananka in Universal Studio's last serious Mummy flick *The Mummy's Curse* (Universal 1945).

"Panic in the Sky" features veteran character actor Jonathan Hale, who had a pivotal role in the 1951 Superman show "The Evil Three." Nine years after leaving the silver screen he was found dead (February 28, 1966), of a self-inflicted gunshot. According to Quinlan's "Character Stars," Mr. Hale was recently widowed.

As an episode of the Superman television series, "Panic" is the show's zenith, and in 1954 it was adapted for comics as "The Menace from the Stars."

Cast: George Reeves, Noel Neill, Jack Larson, John Hamilton, Robert Shayne, Leonard Mudie, Colin Campbell, Norma Varden, Patrick Aherne, Evelyn Halpern, Clyde Cook, Frank Ferguson, Virginia Christine, Mike Ragan, John Doucette, Rudolph Anders, Jonathan Hale, Jane Frazee, Clark Howat, Thomas Moore.

A TWENTIETH CENTURY-FOX RELEASE; Produced by Whitney Ellsworth; Directed by Thomas Carr and George Blair; Screenplay by Jackson Gillis; Director of Photography: Harold Stine, A.S.C.; Film Editor: Harry Gerstad; Special Effects: Sol Simonson; Story Editor: Mort Weisinger; Assistant Directors: Jack R. Berne, Robert Justman, and Ivan Volkman; Sound Engineer: Jean L. Speak. Theatrical Release: 1954.

SUPERMAN'S PERIL

Pirates in the Bay, Jimmy Bogart, and a Synthetic Green Rock

This Fox feature is constructed from three Superman television episodes: "The Golden Vulture," "Semi-Private Eye," and "The Defeat of Superman."

It begins when Jimmy Olsen (Jack Larson) finds a message-in-a-bottle launched from the S.S. Golden Vulture, a salvage ship currently anchored off the coast. Though the writing on the note has been obliterated by sea-water, Lois Lane (Noel Neill) learns that the Vulture has been in the Caribbean, "dragging for sunken treasure." Sensing a possible story, she and Jimmy decide to check out the ship. After meeting Captain McBain (Peter Whitney), a pirate wannabe, the two reporters soon realize they're in the presence of a bonafide lunatic. Scurvy (Vic Perrin), the mate who placed the message in the bottle, tries to warn Jimmy of impending danger by slipping him a note. McBain catches this, flies into a rage and detains his two "guests." With his fellow reporters missing, Clark Kent (George Reeves) embarks on an investigation that begins on the docks and culminates on the Vulture. It is on the ship that Kent learns how the captain is operating a "fence" in which jewelry is stolen, then altered to resemble "Spanish treasure from the Caribbean." The reconditioned items are then sold to museums as the real thing.

Kent is apprehended by McBain's henchmen. With his hands tied behind him, Kent is blindfolded and made to walk the plank, a spectacle witnessed by a grief-stricken Lois and Jimmy. Seconds after Kent has plunged into the sea, Superman makes a spectacular landing on deck. In one of the most dynamic fight scenes of the series, Superman takes on the rowdy crew, and immobilizes them in a matter of seconds. The final showdown is initiated by McBain, whose last act of defiance is thrusting a sword into Superman's chest (to no avail, of course).

Lois and Jimmy beg Superman to rescue Kent. Lois tells the action ace she'll never forgive him if Kent drowns. Realizing he can't assume both identities simultaneously, Superman makes a plausible statement in antici-pation of his exit, and the re-emergence of his alter-ego. "All right, I'm going," he warns. "But I'm finished here and I won't be back." Superman then dives into the ocean and vanishes. A few seconds later, Kent resurfaces in the same spot. This is too much of a coincidence for Lois, who once again surmises what is painfully obvious: Clark Kent is Superman. To sidetrack her thought process, Kent takes hold of Lois's hand, then "accidentally" yanks her into the cold water!

Suspicions about Superman's secret identity are the catalyst for "Semi-Private Eye." This time, Lois is determined to bring home proof that her colleague is the Man of Steel. So she engages a private investigator, Homer Garrity (Elisha Cook, Jr.) to follow Kent and report on his activities. Since Garrity has just completed a high-profile blackmail case (which nearly cost him his life), he accepts the assignment.

The fun begins when Lois and Garrity get kidnapped by two hoods: Cappy (Richard Benedict) and Noodles (Douglas Henderson). From here on, the show belongs to Jimmy. After rattling off some Bogart-like dialogue, the reporter-turned-sleuth sets out to rescue his pals, decked out in a sinister trench coat and fedora. After receiving a tip from a pool hall attendant, Jimmy encounters a thug named Fingers (Paul Fix), whom he follows to a cheap apartment with hopes of procuring a "confession." However, the only thing Jimmy manages to do is handcuff himself to a bed frame. Fingers pulls the phone out of the wall, and walks out of the apartment laughing.

Murray Alper (left) wants to know why George is snooping around with questions regarding the *Golden Vulture*.

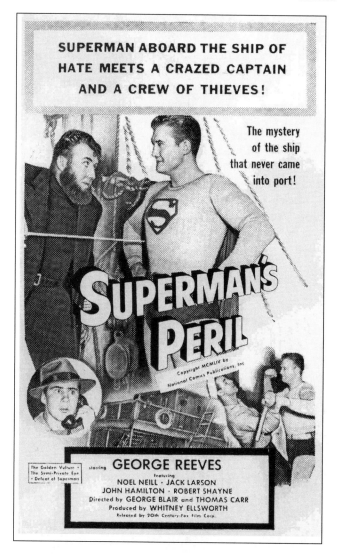

SUPERMAN ABOARD THE SHIP OF
HATE MEETS A CRAZED CAPTAIN
AND A CREW OF THIEVES!

The mystery
of the ship
that never came
into port!

SUPERMAN'S
PERIL

*Copyright MCMLIV by
National Comics Publications, Inc*

The Golden Vulture ·
The Semi-Private Eye
· Defeat of Superman

starring **GEORGE REEVES**
featuring
NOEL NEILL · JACK LARSON
JOHN HAMILTON · ROBERT SHAYNE
Directed by GEORGE BLAIR and THOMAS CARR
Produced by WHITNEY ELLSWORTH
Released by 20th Century-Fox Film Corp.

Newspaper ad for
SUPERMAN'S PERIL.

In the meantime, Cappy tries to get Garrity to turn over some incrimi-nating evidence in the blackmail case. Lois urges him not to cooperate. When Fingers arrives at the hideout, still amused about the crazy kid play-ing detective, Lois and Garrity are relegated to the cellar. Meanwhile, as Kent is scrutinizing the detective's office, he uncovers a wire recording that reveals what happened to Lois and Garrity. By this time, Jimmy, having freed himself from the bed frame, shows up at the hideout pretending to be armed. But a trap door in the floor opens up, and Jimmy is instantly reunited with Lois and Garrity—in the cellar! Because Garrity won't turn over the evidence, Cappy and Noodles fill the cellar with gas.

At the pool hall, Superman's sudden appearance startles the attendant, who nervously tosses two billiard balls at the hero in self-defense. Superman catches the billiards and crushes them like eggshells. He encounters no resistance in obtaining Cappy's address, and arrives in time to inhale the gas that has permeated the cellar. Cappy and Noodles, who have been safely positioned behind a steel door, make a move to escape. But Jimmy and Garrity employ some quick judo flips, and the two hoods wind up on their backsides. After carrying Lois out of the room, Superman asks how she got involved with Garrity in the first place. As Jimmy is about to disclose Lois's intentions, she quickly interrupts him. Jimmy then asks Garrity if he has a spare set of keys. Once again, Detective Olsen has handcuffed himself, this time to a chair.

The final third of the film is derived from "The Defeat of Superman." After learning that Superman is vulnerable to Kryptonite, a thug named "Happy" King (Peter Mamakos) decides to settle the score by procuring a chunk of the deadly metal. To accomplish this, King and his associate Ruffles (Sid Tomack) team up with an elderly scientist named Meldini (Maurice Cass). King manages to lure Jimmy and Lois to a remote location and lock them in the basement. What the two reporters don't know is that King has commissioned Meldini to manufacture some "synthetic" Kryptonite. Then, when Superman attempts to rescue his pals, he falls directly into the trap that King has methodically devised.

British lobby card.

George does a little deck cleaning aboard the *Golden Vulture*

Shortly after Superman barges into the basement, a small block of metal drops down from a wall duct. The superhero is immediately affected and collapses. Jimmy makes several attempts to get the Kryptonite out of the room, but fails. By this time, King and his accomplices have taken to the highway. With Superman's condition growing steadily worse, Lois becomes almost hysterical. "He can hardly breathe!" she cries. Superman musters up enough strength to utter a few words: "Lead pipe! Sink!" Realizing that lead can act as a shield, Jimmy disconnects the pipe from a sink and places the metal inside. No longer exposed to the lethal rays, Superman is instantly "cured."

Because Kryptonite is the only thing that can kill him, Superman hurls the pipe into the air, making it disappear into the night. King and his cohorts, still speeding down the highway, notice the mysterious object streaking across the sky. Ruffles loses control of the vehicle, causing it to careen off the road. The next Daily Planet headline declares: "Happy King Dead in Crash." In a rare twist, Superman did not rescue Jimmy and Lois. They rescued him!

The Adventures of Superman show often dealt with holdovers in time. Knights of the Round Table, Indians and cowboys, voodoo priests, and of course pirates (well, in this case a single pirate). "The Golden Vulture" (long a fan favorite) gives guest star Peter Whitney a tour de force role as the Lone Buccaneer Captain McBain. Whitney began his cinema career in 1941. He worked in pictures until 1970, appearing in *Whistling in Dixie* (1942), *Action in the North Atlantic* (1943), *Mr. Skeffington* (1944), *The Brute Man* (1946), *Gorilla at Large* in 3-D (1954), *Wonderful World of the Brothers Grimm* (1962), and *In the Heat of the Night* (1967). His portrayal of McBain is on the edge of madness; abusing his first mate, crowing pirate songs at the top of his voice, and flashing his treasure at anyone with an eye for a doubloon. Whitney was born in Long Branch, New Jersey in 1916 and passed away in Santa Barbara, California on March 30, 1972.

His long-suffering First Mate was played by veteran Vic Perrin. Ten years after his voyage on the Golden Vulture, Perrin would become the control voice of The Outer Limits. Born in Menomonee, Wisconsin on the 26th of April, 1916 and died Independence Day 1989. His uncredited debut was in 1947's *Magic Town*. He had parts in *Forever Female* (1953), *The Twonky* (1953), was the narrator of *Spartacus* (1960), and played Dr. Hart in *Black Tuesday* (1954). Perrin worked on 102 television shows (as a recurring character on several) such as Dragnet, Gunsmoke, Studio 57, Frontier, Soldier of Fortune, Rawhide, The Rebel, Rocky Jones Space Ranger, and a host of others including the voice of Nomad, a captured satellite in a Star Trek episode. He was perfect as Scurvy the sailor sending messages in bottles.

Gangsters and comedy is what's in store in "Semi-Private Eye." This show is one of the best examples of Jack Larson's superb comedic timing. His real life friend Elisha Cook, Jr. co-stars with Jack as Homer Garrity.

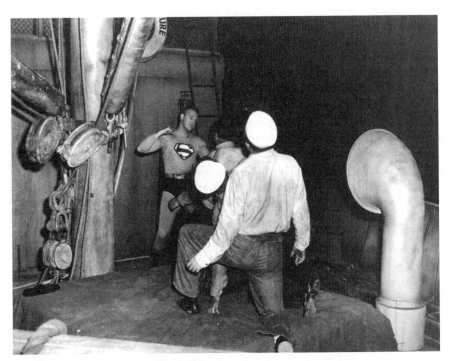

More deck cleaning as the fight continues.

Cook was born the day after Christmas 1903, in San Francisco. His first credit is *Her Unborn Child* (1930), with roles in *Sergeant York* (1941), *Stranger on the Third Floor* (1940), *Man at Large* (as the hotel clerk) (1941), *The Maltese Falcon* (1941), *Ball of Fire* (1941), *A Haunting We Will Go* (1942), *Dillinger* (1945), *The Big Sleep* (1946), *Shane* (1953), *Voodoo Island* with Boris Karloff (1957), *House on Haunted Hill* (1950), *The Haunted Palace* (1963), *Rosemary's Baby* (1968), *Blackula* (1972), *Tom Horn* (1980), and a plethora of others. He passed away in Big Pine, California on May 18, 1995.

Richard Benedict, who played Baby Face Stevens in the first season episode "Night of Terror" was an actor, writer, and director, who was born on January 8, 1920. His first film as an actor was *Winged Victory* (1944). He was in *O.S.S.* (1946), *Backlash* (1947), *Post Office Investigator* (1949), *Angels in Disguise* (1949), his first with the Bowery Boys. Other Bowery Boys films are *Let's Go Navy* (1951), *Jalopy* (1953), *Spychasers* (1955), and *Monkey On My Back, The Barney Ross Story* (1957). He co-stars in the science fiction films *Beginning of the End* (1957); and the prototype for the Alien series, *It, Terror From Beyond Space* (1958) as a TV director. He worked on such TV faves as Hawaiian Eye, Combat, The Fugitive, I Spy, Get Smart, The Invaders, Mannix, Night Gallery, Charlie's Angels, The Rookies, and The Hardy Boys Mysteries. Benedict died in Studio City, California of a heart attack on April 25, 1984.

"Semi-Private Eye" sports one of Jimmy Olsen's classic examples of good intentions, bad outcome, as evidenced by his hilarious bumbling encounter with actor Paul Fix. The scene with Fix and Larson is classic comedy noir.

Paul Fix's first screen appearance was in *The Perfect Clown* in 1925. He appeared in such classics as 1932's *Scarface*, and the Lionel Atwill vehicle *The Sphinx* (1933). With sixty years of credits, career highlights include *The Westerner* (1934), *Reckless* (1935), *Valley of Wanted Men* (1935), *Charlie Chan at the Race Track* (1936), *After the Thin Man* (1936), *The Buccaneer* (1938), *Mr. Moto's Gamble* (1938), *The Saint in New York* (1938), *Black Friday* (1940), *Dr. Cyclops* (1940), *The Ghost Breakers* (1940), and *Alias Boston Blackie* (1942). His last film was *Wanda Nevada* (1979), ending a two hundred thirty-nine film marathon, which included three screen scenario credits and ninety-seven TV guest shots. Small screen fans remember Paul for his sympathetic sheriff in The Rifleman. Fix was born in Dobb Ferry, New York on March 13, 1901 and died October 14, 1983 in Los Angeles.

"The Defeat of Superman" has to be one of the top three all-time Superman episodes. Finally, we get a birds-eye view of how TV's Man of Steel accomplishes those spectacular landings. One of the most awe-inspiring optical shots from the 1953 season, this along with all the flying work made the Baby Boomers believe there really was a Superman!

Enhancing this show is a trio of villains aptly headed by veteran actor Peter Mamakos as Happy J. King, the verbose mobster. Mamakos appeared in *A Mask for Lucretia* (1949), *Between Midnight and Dawn* (1950), *Tarzan and the Slave Girl* (1950), the Bowery Boys vehicle *Let's Go Navy* (1951), *The Searchers* (1956), *The Ten Commandments* (1956), *Spook Chasers* (1957), *Looking for Danger* (1957), *Sabu and the Magic Ring* (1957), *Ship of Fools*

Publicity photo aboard the *Golden Vulture*.

(1965), *For Pete's Sake* (1974) and *The Man with Bogart's Face* (1980). Like fellow Superman guest star Paul Fix, Peter has a screen writing credit for an original story that was used on the popular TV series Checkmate.

His support work on 1950s TV shows was more fruitful, with frequent featured parts on The Lone Ranger, Adventures of Kit Carson, Terry and the Pirates, The Cisco Kid, Adventures of Fu Manchu, Broken Arrow, Adventures of Jim Bowie, Zorro, Gunsmoke, Bronco, Richard Diamond Private Detective, Mr. Lucky, Wyatt Earp, Rawhide, Bourbon Street Beat, Wagon Train, and a host of others. His last TV assignment was 1990s mini series Lucky Chances. Peter was born December 14, 1918 and as of this writing is still alive.

Happy King's henchman is aptly played by actor Sid Tomack. Tomack's film career begins in 1944 with *A WAVE, a WAC, and a Marine*, where he played himself. Two years later he appeared as Irikie Bowers in the 1946 production of *The Thrill of Brazil*. He can be glimpsed in such films as *Framed* (1947), *Blondie's Holiday* (1947), *I Love Trouble* (1948), *The Babe Ruth Story* (1948), *Knock on Any Door* (1949), *Crime Doctors Diary* (1949), *Sorrowful Jones* (1949), *House of Strangers* (1949), *Alias Nick Beal* (1949), *The Lemon Drop Kid* (1951), *The Kettles in the Ozarks* (1956), *Too Much Too*

Soon—where he plays twins (1958), *Space Children* (1958), *The Wackiest Ship in the Army* (1960), and his last role was in *Sail a Crooked Ship* (1961). Born in Brooklyn on September 8, 1907 he passed away in Palm Springs, California on November 12, 1962.

For the mad scientist who synthesizes Kryptonite, producer Whitney Ellsworth cast "Rocky Jones, Space Ranger" co-star Maurice Cass. Born October 12, 1884 in Vilna, Lithuania, Cass's first celluloid appearance was for Dr. Lee DeForrest in an experimental sound-on-film picture in 1923. This film ran at the Rivoli theater in New York. He was a playwright and stage player, with film credits in such shows as *Wife vs. Secretary* (1930), *The Big Broadcast of 1937* (1936), *Charlie Chan at the Opera* (1936), *Give Us This Night* (1936), *This is My Affair* (1937), *The Firefly* (1937), *The Lone Wolf in Paris* (1938), *Mr. Smith Goes to Washington* (1939), *Federal Operator 99* (1945), *Wonder Man* (1945), *The Notorious Lone Wolf* (1946), *Cat Man of Paris* (1946), *Spook Busters* with the Bowery Boys (1946), *Sorrowful Jones* (1949), *We're Not Married* (1952), and his last film, the short *So You Want to Be a Musician* (1952). From 1952 until his death he was Professor Newton on "Rocky Jones, Space Ranger." He died June 8, 1954 in Hollywood at the age of 70.

With "The Defeat of Superman" we are given a more human view of the Man of Steel, helped on by a riveting performance from Noel Neill, in the basement scene where she pleads with Jimmy to dispose of the Kryptonite.

CAST: George Reeves, Noel Neill, Jack Larson, John Hamilton, Robert Shayne, Peter Whitney, Vic Perrin, Robert Rice, Murray Alper, Wes Hudman, Saul M. Gorss, Carl H. Saxe, Dan Turner, William J. Vincent, Elisha Cook, Jr., Paul Fix, Douglas Henderson, Richard Benedict, Alfred Linder, Maurice Cass, Peter Mamakos, Sid Tomack.

A TWENTIETH CENTURY-FOX RELEASE; Produced by Whitney Ellsworth; Directed by Thomas Carr and George Blair; Screenplay by Davis Chantler and Jackson Gillis; Director of Photography: Harold Stine, A.S.C.; Film Editor: Harry Gerstad; Special Effects: Sol Simonson; Story Editor: Mort Weisinger; Assistant Directors: Jack R. Berne, Robert Justman and Ivan Volkman; Sound Engineer: Jean L. Speak. Theatrical Release: 1954.

SUPERMAN AND THE JUNGLE DEVIL
Leftover Mind Machines, Blonde Apes, and a Double Exposure

Like the other four Fox compilation features, *Superman and the Jungle Devil* is comprised of three black and white episodes from TV's Adventures of Superman. The segments, filmed in 1953, are "The Machine That Could Plot Crimes," "Jungle Devil," and "Shot in the Dark."

Al Kikume takes a spear to George in this scene from *SUPERMAN AND THE JUNGLE DEVIL*. Note the stains of perspiration around George's underarm from filming exteriors on an interior set with little if any air conditioning.

To facilitate the feature film format, one-minute wrap-arounds were shot to link the episodes together. A more comprehensive explanation can be found in the Tenth Anniversary Edition of "Superman On Television," written and compiled by Michael Bifulco (published in 1998).

While this trio is not the strongest entry in the series of features, the shows will interest most Superman fans who appreciated the Man of Steel's exploits in the 1950s.

It begins with Larry McCoy (Billy Nelson), a fallen hoodlum, awakening to the disturbing clatter of a machine. He traces the noise to his neighbor Oscar (Sterling Holloway), a bespectacled inventor who has developed a "mechanical mind" called Mr. Kelso. "There's no machine in the entire world like Mr. Kelso," says Oscar. Dispensing its answers on streams of tickertape paper, the machine can easily tackle any problem, particularly those involving time and distance. After a brief demonstration, McCoy tricks Oscar into getting the machine to calculate a foolproof plan for robbing a bank.

The next day, McCoy and his dim-witted partner, Nosey (Ben Welden), pull a successful robbery at the Metropolis First National Bank. The heist, which transpired during business hours, baffles Inspector Henderson (Robert Shayne) and two star reporters for the Daily Planet: Clark Kent

(George Reeves) and Lois Lane (Noel Neill). While sitting in his office recounting the latest headlines, Kent detects the sound of an alarm. Seconds later, Superman soars over to the Metropolis S&L, and catches Nosey red-handed. The "Man of Steel" confiscates the satchel Nosey is holding, but finds nothing except an old shirt. The crooks have outsmarted Superman—or so it seems. When Oscar finally gets wind of what's going on, McCoy assaults him and takes over control of the machine.

Lois then finds a note, addressed to Clark Kent, indicating that someone is threatening to disclose Superman's secret identity. She follows Kent to a desolate alley located behind several factories. When Lois is abducted, Kent attempts to rescue her, but both reporters ultimately wind up as captives in McCoy's getaway truck. Lois rides in the front seat with Nosey; Kent occupies the back of the vehicle with McCoy. Since he's going to get rid of these "nosey" reporters anyway, McCoy has no qualms about revealing details of the next robbery—and what is about to happen to Oscar. After hearing all he needs to know, Kent knocks McCoy out. Not wasting a sec-

Al Kikume (left) watches as Leon Lontoc shakes hands with George in a scene from *SUPERMAN AND THE JUNGLE DEVIL*.

Print ad for
*SUPERMAN
AND THE
JUNGLE DEVIL*.

ond, the reporter switches to Superman and saves Oscar from a stick of dynamite—just in time.

Superman flies to the scene of the impending crime. Hovering in mid-air, the action hero smiles approvingly as he witnesses the police taking Nosey into custody. Something has obviously gone wrong. Knowing that the crooks were up to no good, the mechanical brain deliberately miscalculated the robbery, thereby preventing another crime. Back at Oscar's laboratory, Lois asks Clark how he acquired so much knowledge about Superman. Kent shrugs off her inquisitiveness. Even Oscar is curious. "Who is Superman?"

The one-eyed
Tiki god from
JUNGLE DEVIL.

he asks the clattering machine. Mr. Kelso dispenses an answer: "Wouldn't you like to know!"

Far away from the streets of Metropolis, Dr. Harper, (Damian O'Flynn) and his wife Gloria (Doris Singleton) are being held prisoner on the island of Zinaya. The Harpers are explorers who ran afoul of the natives. Apparently, Gloria committed a heinous offense when she removed a diamond eye from the head of a sacred idol. Though she only intended to admire the jewel, Gloria accidentally dropped it in some quicksand after being startled by the natives. As a result, the Harpers and their guide (Nacho Galindo), are prevented from leaving the island—until the diamond is retrieved and returned to its rightful place. "It's gone," says Dr. Harper, "and with it, we've lost our last chance of making friends with these people."

Clark Kent has been assigned to locate the Harpers. He explains to cub-reporter Jimmy Olsen (Jack Larson) that the husband and wife team are on the island to procure a "rare drug of terrific medical value." Though Kent intends to handle this assignment alone, Lois manages to get herself included. Even Jimmy horns in on the act, and turns up as a stowaway on the tiny plane headed for the remote locale. The arrival of the reporters angers the natives, who demand that one of these "white men" be sacrificed. Kent suggests that everyone select a pebble for a pith helmet; the person who draws the one and only black pebble is the one to be sacrificed. While gathering the pebbles, Kent picks up a piece of coal, knowing that it will be of great use later on. Using his X-ray vision to deliberately select the black pebble, Kent makes himself the sacrificial lamb.

As Kent is about to be burned at the stake, the natives dance around him. A puff of smoke temporarily clouds everyone's view, allowing Kent to turn into Superman. Suddenly, the so-called jungle devil, which is nothing more than a feeble looking gorilla, appears out of nowhere. It's hard to believe that this is the menacing creature everyone is afraid of. Nevertheless, the natives run for their lives. Superman does a few seconds worth of battle with the beast, then knocks it on its behind, saving the chief in the process. Because the natives attribute the expulsion of the jungle devil to Kent, the reporter is quickly reunited with his friends. "I'm afraid that jungle devil was just some poor gorilla that escaped from the circus," Kent explains. "Took to the woods; he wasn't much of a problem."

Remembering the coal he had picked up, Kent places his hand in the quicksand and uses his super-strength to pressure the black lump into a

Doris Singleton and Damian O'Flynn examine the Tiki god with the diamond eye in *SUPERMAN AND THE JUNGLE DEVIL.*

diamond. After pretending to "find" a diamond in the quicksand, Kent replaces the missing eye on the idol. The natives are ecstatic over the restoration and bid a friendly good-bye to the white men.

Back in Metropolis, Clark Kent has a big problem waiting for him. A teenage photographer named Alan (Billy Gray of Father Knows Best fame), has snapped a picture of Kent taking off his shirt, partially revealing the famous Superman insignia. Does this "Shot in the Dark" prove that Clark Kent and Superman are one and the same person? Not according to the fast-thinking reporter, who says Alan snapped separate photos of Superman and Kent, in the exact location, but forgot to wind his camera. Thus, the finished product is nothing more than a double exposure. With this lame explanation, the suspicions of Alan's mother and Jimmy Olsen are temporarily arrested.

Alan also snapped another interesting subject—a man, with a bunch of tulips, standing next to a theater advertisement. This man desperately wants the picture and has offered to pay Alan a thousand dollars. But Alan won't sell it. As a result, the boy's home is burglarized. The thief does steal a picture from Alan's darkroom—the one of Kent/Superman!

At his office in the Daily Planet building, Kent studies the picture of the strange man with the tulips. He remains cool when Burt Burnside (John Eldredge), the man in the snapshot, shows up with a gun. As Burt is about to get the photo out of Kent's hands, Jimmy grabs it and darts out of the office. A chase ensues, and Jimmy escapes via the Valley Express subway

Doris Singleton, Damian O'Flynn, and George discuss the diamond that belongs in the eye of the Tiki god in *Superman and the Jungle Devil*.

Leon Lontoc (left), a veteran native character actor, has a hold on George in a scene from *SUPERMAN AND THE JUNGLE DEVIL*.

line. Burt is so desperate to get the photo that he'll even sabotage public transportation. Two of his thugs arrange to have the Valley Express crash into another train. Superman, however, breaks the electrical connection that would have caused the collision.

Kent and Jimmy learn that Burt was reported dead a few years earlier; his demise resulted in a huge insurance payoff. The reporters also learn why Burt is so desperate to get the photo of himself standing outside the theater. The snapshot proves he was alive when the play—"Molly and Me"—opened in Metropolis a short time ago. Burt is still breathing, of course, but someone else isn't. As Inspector Henderson points out, "That other body was no department store dummy!" So Kent sets a trap by concocting a story to the effect that the photo has been entered in a contest. The crooks now attempt to intercept the photo before it can be delivered through the mail. They shoot the driver of the mail truck, not realizing it is Superman in disguise. However, all Burt gets for his trouble are bags filled with torn strips of newspaper.

Superman bursts into the gang's hideout. Burt threatens to disclose Superman's identity, unless he's willing to make a deal. Burt will relinquish

The blonde gorilla confronts native witch doctor Leon Lontoc and George on the set of
SUPERMAN AND THE JUNGLE DEVIL. Note the stage rigging in the upper right corner.

the so-called double exposed print, but only if Superman will help him escape the police. Superman doesn't make deals, and discreetly uses his X-ray vision to burn the photo that might jeopardize his secret. Inspector Henderson and his men close in on Burt, who attempts to demonstrate, once and for all, that Clark Kent is Superman. Pulling out a revolver, Burt fires a shot directly into Kent's chest. But the reporter is not harmed; he attributes his survival to the "lucky silver dollar," tucked in his breast pocket, which obstructed the bullet! "Imagine you being Superman!" laughs Henderson. Jimmy adds a left-handed compliment: "Don't worry, Mr. Kent. We think you're all right just like you are!" Not saying a word, Kent smiles at the camera.

This trio of shows has an abundance of George's friends featured in co-starring roles. "Jungle Devil" features two amigos, Damian O'Flynn and James Seay.

O'Flynn appeared with George (unbilled) in *So Proudly We Hail* as military physician. The next year, he was Colonel Ross in *Winged Victory*, along with Reeves and Molemen co-star Walter Reed. Reed and O'Flynn were questioned after George's death about money that the cops thought was stashed in George's house. The story was a couple years old, and the police were up another blind alley!

O'Flynn was born on January 29, 1907, and died on August 8, 1982. He entered films in 1937, and was often a bit player. His film career concluded in 1963. His television appearances are more noteworthy. Beginning in 1943, he can be seen as a supporting player in such small screen favorites as The Jack Benny Program, Richard Diamond, Private Detective, Rawhide, Bourbon Street Beat, 77 Sunset Strip, The Gale Storm Show, Wagon Train, Adventures of Wild Bill Hickock, Maverick, Burns & Allen, December Bride, the Adam West–Batman series, and a host of other shows.

Also along for the monkeyshines of "Jungle Devil" was George's good friend and future pallbearer, James Seay. Seay was a journeyman actor, with 106 movie credits, and 90 television guest spots in his 20-year career. Besides his appearances on Superman, Seay was a supporting player on Cowboy G-Men, Hopalong Cassidy, The Millionaire, Science Fiction Theater, Cisco Kid, Circus Boy, Four Star Playhouse, Tales of Wells Fargo, M Squad, Cheyenne, Perry Mason, Man From U.N.C.L.E., The Fugitive, and others too numerous to mention in this volume.

His movie exploits are no less voluminous, with parts in *The Green Hornet Strikes Again, Face Behind the Mask, They Died With Their Boots On, The Asphalt Jungle, When Worlds Collide, The Day the Earth Stood Still, War of the Worlds, Beginning of the End*, and *The Amazing Colossal Man*.

Seay was born on September 30, 1914, and passed away in Capistrano Beach, California, on October 10, 1992. He sometimes worked under the moniker James Lawry.

Holding the bananas and vines is Doris Singleton, best known as Caroline Appleby on the perennial TV favorite I Love Lucy. She portrays Gloria Harper, Dr. Harper's bungling yet remorseful wife.

Her television career spans four decades, with appearances on My Three Sons, Alfred Hitchcock Presents, Richard Diamond, Private Eye, Perry Mason, Trackdown, Gunsmoke, Checkmate, Twilight Zone, Dick Van Dyke, All In the Family, Love American Style, Here's Lucy, The Monsters, and Dynasty. Her last appearance was in the TV movie Deadly Messages in 1985.

"A Shot in the Dark" comes from much earlier in the 1953 season, and offers standout performances from guests Billy Gray, John Eldridge, and Frank Richards from the first season's episode "Night of Terror."

CAST: George Reeves, Noel Neill, Jack Larson, John Hamilton, Robert Shayne, Sterling Holloway, Billy Nelson, Ben Weldon, Stan Jarman, Sherry Moerland, Sam Balter, Russel Custer, Doris Singleton, Damian O'Flynn, Nacho Calindo, James Seay, Al Kikume, Leon Lontoc, Steve Calvert, Vera Marshe, Billy Gray, John Eldridge, Frank Richards, Alan Lee.

A TWENTIETH CENTURY-FOX RELEASE; Produced by Whitney Ellsworth; Directed by Tommy Carr and George Blair; Screenplay by Roy Hamilton, Peter Dixon, and David Chantler; Director of Photography: Harold Stine, A.S.C.; Film Editor: Harry Gerstad; Special Effects: Sol Simonson; Story Editor: Mort Weisinger; Assistant Directors: Jack R. Berne, Robert Justman and Ivan Volkman; Sound Engineer: Jean L. Speak. Theatrical Release: 1954.

WESTWARD HO THE WAGONS!

Last Cinemascope Frames in a Technicolor Round-Up

While this Disney flick hardly rates as a classic, it is still entertaining enough to keep the little ones planted in front of the screen. Filmed in splendid Technicolor and Cinemascope, the visuals are undeniably stunning, especially the night footage. Though George has an important supporting role as the wagon master, his screen time is remarkably sparse. Some enthusiasts will have difficulty adjusting to his scruffy, gray-haired look. The make-up department didn't have to dye George's locks (he was prematurely gray) but they did apply an abundance of whiskers to ensure that his character appeared fatherly (or grandfatherly, perhaps) and completely dissimilar to Superman. While it was relatively easy to disguise George's face, there wasn't much that could be done about his voice, which resonates on the soundtrack like a familiar chord.

Authoritative, yet persuasively friendly, Captain James Stephens (George Reeves) leads a wagon train bound for Oregon. John "Doe" Grayson (Fess Parker) is the level-headed practitioner who entertains the kids with stories and songs. All goes well until the inevitable first sign of trouble—the realization that a thousand dollars worth of horses have been swiped by the hostile Pawnee Indians. Young Danny Thompson (David Stollery) proves his bravery by retrieving his horse, Chieftain, along with the other horses, almost single-handedly. But Danny isn't so lucky during his next encounter with the Pawnees, while he and the other kids are gathering firewood. He is abducted, held captive and made to witness a threatening war dance. During the preparatory ritual, Danny manages to escape his captors, only to experience subsequent terrors when the Pawnees initiate the actual war. The attack forces the pioneers to relinquish their personal possessions (books, furniture and mementos) in order to lighten the wagons for a hasty retreat. Knowing that the Pawnees value livestock more than scalps, the horses are let go in order to avoid bloodshed.

The wagon train arrives at Fort Laramie, where a trading post is operated by the amiable, but non-committal, Bissonette (Sebastian Cabot). At the post, the Chief of the Sioux Indians becomes taken with Myra Thompson (Karen Pendleton), Danny's little sister. The chief wants to adopt the child because she represents, in his mind, "good medicine" (good luck). With an eye toward the future, the chief views Myra as the perfect match for his son, Little Thunder (Anthony Numkena). With Bissonette acting as a mediator, the Indians sit down for a pow-wow with Captain Stephens, offering the guarantee of "safe passage" in exchange for the child. Stephens unapologetically explains that Myra does not have a father, only a brother and an adult sister, Laura (Kathleen Crowley), who would never agree to such a proposal. Clearly offended by the captain's negative response, the Indians walk away from the meeting in stony silence.

Everyone begins to worry that an attack by the "friendly" Sioux Indians is imminent. However, all attention is shifted when Little Thunder falls off a horse and lapses into a coma. Though the pioneers had nothing to do with the accident, the tension between the two camps is almost palpable. John believes he can square things with the Indians by rendering treatment to Little Thunder. He is warned, however, that if the boy should die, the entire wagon train will be considered "bad medicine," something tantamount to a death sentence.

Upon examination, John realizes that Little Thunder sustained a broken clavicle, and the resultant bone splinters have punctured his neck. The boy's condition is further complicated by internal bleeding and swelling. Nevertheless, John begins his task by waving a feather over the patient, with just enough panache to convince the onlookers that the proper "spirits" are being invoked. Then, by utilizing a knife, he manages to relieve the pressure in the neck. Seconds later, Little Thunder opens his eyes. His parents break into tearful smiles, and John breathes a sigh of relief.

George and actor Franchot Tone in the Hollywood Hills in July, 1956, around the time of filming for *WESTWARD HO THE WAGONS!*

It's time for the wagon train to move on. Grateful for the miracle that has been performed, the chief wishes all a safe journey and presents Myra with a special gift. Danny and Little Thunder, once opponents, are now united in friendship.

George's strong work in *Westward Ho the Wagons!* is further proof that with proper management and a stable agent, he could have had a budding career as a middle aged character player, like his friends and Superman co-stars Tristram Coffin, Terry Frost, Frank Fergeson, Dabbs Greer, Phillips Tead, Jack Littlefield, Ben Welden, Herb Vigran, and a host of others.

Fess Parker was a kid television star in his own right, and Jeff York played his antagonist Mike Fink in the highly successful Disney television series, Davey Crockett.

In a "truth is stranger than fiction" scenario, Iron Eyes Cody, who was known for decades for his Native American roles ("Many Stars" the medicine man in *Westward Ho the Wagons!*) was discovered to be a Sicilian after his death in 1999.

Westward Ho the Wagons! would mark the end of George's career as a motion picture actor. It is widely known that he was eagerly looking forward to directing movies, rather than appearing in them, after completing the last round of Superman episodes he intended to film in the fall of 1959. Tragically, his unexpected death on June 16, 1959, deprived us of the TV episodes, the possibility of any Reeves-directed features, and of Reeves himself.

CAST: Fess Parker, Kathleen Crowley, Jeff York, David Stollery, Sebastian Cabot, George Reeves, Doreen Tracey, Barbara Woodell, John War Eagle, Cubby O'Brien, Tommy Cole, Leslie Bradley, Morgan Woodward, Iron Eyes Cody, Anthony Numkema, Karen Pendleton, Jane Liddel, Jon Locke.

A WALT DISNEY PRODUCTION; Produced by Bill Walsh; Directed by William Beaudine; Screenplay by Tom Blackburn; Based on a novel by Mary Jane Carr; Filmed in Cinemascope; Color by Technicolor; Photographed by Charles P. Boyle, A.S.C.; Art Director: Mary Aubrey Davis; Edited by: Cotton Warburton, A.C.E.; Second Unit Director: Yakima Canutt; Special Process: Ub Iwerks, A.S.C.; Sound Supervision: Robert O. Cook; Sound Recording: Dean Thomas; Unit Manager: Ben Chapman; Assistant Director: William Beaudine, Jr.; Matte Artist: Peter Ellenshaw; Set Decoration: Emile Kulr, Bertram Granger; Costumes: Chuck Keehne, Gertrude Case; Make-Up: David Newell; Hair Stylist: Lois Murray; Music by George Bruns; Orchestration: Edward Plumb; Songs by George Bruns, Tom Blackburn, Stan Jones, Paul Smith, Gil George. Original theatrical release: September 20, 1956. Running time: 90 minutes.

EPILOGUE

A Tear, A Memory, And Hope

George Reeves kept his private life private, his public life humble, and his head about him until the last six months of his life. He was many things to many, and to millions of people, in a bygone age. The Nifty Fifties, a happy time with a face of sadness. A paranoid time, which sometimes lacked a conscience. To George Reeves fans, the time of their lives, but we at this point ask ourselves why. Why has George Reeves stuck in our minds? Why has all this meant so much? Especially as the generation that popularized Superman is dying in droves.

The only possible answer is George Reeves, for six fleeting years, to our hearts and minds was Superman. He wasn't allowed to be George Reeves. How would you readers feel if you couldn't be you? We only have our imaginations to understand what George Reeves had to deal with, selling his soul and likeness to a comic book franchise. None of us will ever walk a mile in this man's shoes; none of us will solve this mytery. Many have tried; all have failed. "Superman Curse" some have said. Yes, there is a curse on those who would improperly use George Reeves. This has been proven time and time again. Whether it be Bio-pics, or cheap tabloid bull, somehow there is a karmic rightness that follows this man. It can't be explained, but to people who care, it is real.

With "Behind The Crimson Cape," we hope to have given you the full picture of George Reeves' life and career as an actor. For further exploration of George's death and life, Lou Koza's two CD-Rom set *Saving George Reeves* is highly recommended.

George Reeves was a class act, not only as an actor, but as a human being. It's been forty-six years of memorializing, and forty-five years of life on planet Earth; and the mere mention of his name prompts a wide variety of responses. Was he murdered? Did he commit suicide? The conspiracy theories are plentiful and widespread, but after four and a half decades, no one has solved the crime! No one has come close.

Hollywood revisionists only add fuel and confusion to a dying fire, embellishing the facts of his life. They attempt to play God. They fail.

What is left are his films, the Superman television shows, a handful of rare television appearances. The Internet and eBay still buzz with George information. Jim Nolt's *The Adventures Continue* is one of the most popular web sites. Metropolis, Illinois is home to Jim Hambrick's "Super Museum," the world's largest collection of Superman memorabilia and George Reeves artifacts.

"Truth, Justice, and the American Way" adorns bookshelves country wide. Larry Ward's biography of the First Lady of Metropolis is a treasure trove of Noel Neill's memories and her fabulous collection of photographs of her in the Golden Age of Hollywood.

In Grand Rapids, Michigan, Michael Bifulco continues to fill orders for *Superman on Television* and *Speeding Bullet*, as does Cult Movies magazine in Hollywood, California.

And somewhere in the eternal night, a video screen is flickering, and the face of our hero glows from four and a half decades gone. A moment frozen in time; and then the eternal wink, and nod.

Only then did we know that our world would be safe, and our sleep would be secure—thanks to a man named *George*.

PHOTO GALLERY
George Reeves and Friends

The State Fair Tour of 1957 (left to right) Don Hollington, Freddie Hernandez, Natividad Vacio, Noel Neill, and Gene LaBell in Albuquerque, NM, on August 17.

Natividad, Don, and Freddie on stage in Asheville, NC, on August 26, 1957.

George's friend and fellow actor, Natividad Vacio, was also a school teacher and often invited George into his classroom to entertain his kids.

Jack Larson, Noel Neill, and George on the set of the *Beware the Wrecker* episode.

George, Tyler McDuff, Jack, Noel, and John Hamilton enjoy some birthday cake on the set of *The Boy Who Hated Superman*.

Natividad, George, Don, and Freddie on the outdoor stage at the Colorado State Fair in Pueblo on August 20, 1957 . . .

. . . and the band plays on . . .

. . . until Noel joins in with George and the band.

George and Noel on stage in North Carolina. According to Larry Ward's biography of Noel Neill, "Truth, Justice and the American Way," there were only three people in the audience at this performance—a boy and his parents.

George with Noel after her costume change. No doubt it was a hot night in North Carolina with Noel in that outfit—no matter how many people were in the house!

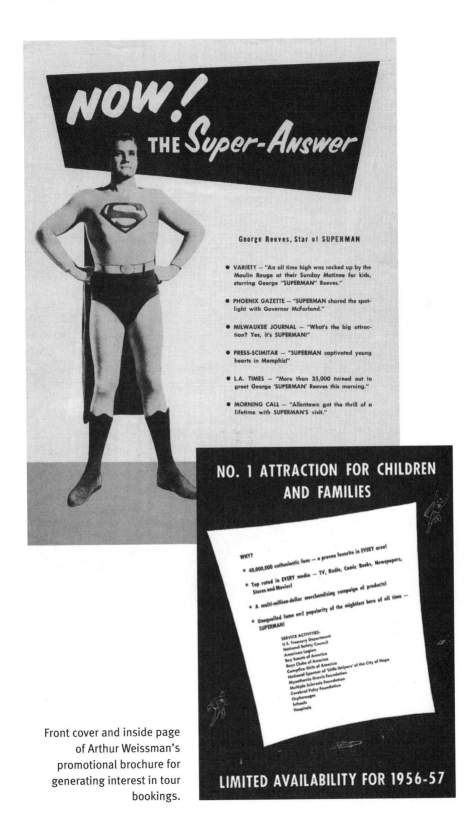

Front cover and inside page of Arthur Weissman's promotional brochure for generating interest in tour bookings.

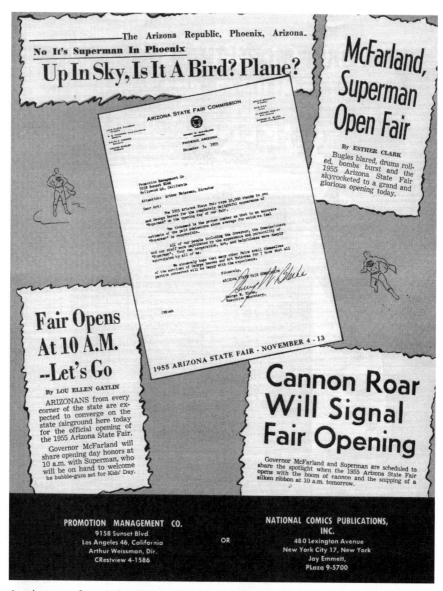

Another page from Arthur Weissman's brochure promoting interest in George's personal appearnce tour.

Opposite page: Noel joins George and the band (Don Hollington, Freddie Hernandez, and Natividad Vacio) on stage at the Colorado State Fair.

George and Noel sing and dance with the band.

Noel Neill and Natividad Vacio dazzle the crowd with a Mexican folk dance.

George and Noel admiring a new Chrysler Imperial.

Gene LaBell and a local clown have a few words while George sets up the following act at center stage.

After a costume change, George alerts the crowd of a *Mr. Kryptonite* sighting.

Mr. Kryptonite (Gene LaBell) arrives on the scene and boasts to the crowd of his superiority to *Superman*. Let the contest begin . . .

309

George and Gene perform another knockout finish to a popular stage show.

George, Noel, and Gene LaBell pose with an unkown performer for a souvenir picture.

Noel Neill, Whitney Ellsworth's mother, and George on the set of *Dagger Island*.

Ted Hecht and Noel Neill
in costume from the set of
The Tomb of Zaharan.

Another one of those Si Simonson walls that allowed George to make a spectacular entrance in a scene from the *Brainy Burro* episode that he directed. Note that Carmelita looks a wee bit guilty.

Carmelita, starring as the Brainy Burro, takes her cues from George, the director of the episode.

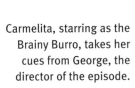

Queta Vacio, George, and Natividad Vacio on the set of *The Brainy Burro.*

Edward LeVeque, Carmelita, and George on the set of *The Brainy Burro.*

Noel Neill in "South of the Border" wardrobe on the set of *The Brainy Burro* with Carmelita.

Noel in a publicity photo with Carmelita.

George comes to the
rescue of Jack Larson
on the set of
The Perils of Superman.

Jack Larson hanging
around between scenes
on the set of
The Perils of Superman.

318

A dashing portrait of Robert Shayne as Wm. J. Henderson of the Metropolis Police Department.

George and Noel in a posed publicity photo from *The Wedding of Superman*.

A revealing takeoff as George leaps skyward over the cameraman.

George and Judy Ann Nugent from *Around the World with Superman*.

320

George and Judy Ann Nugent on the flying bar modified to carry passengers high over Metropolis and points of interest as we go *Around the World with Superman*.

James Craven is about to take a punch for creating the *Riddle of the Chinese Jade* as Phyllis Coates stands by holding the title trophy.

George and Danny Thomas at the premier of *THE EGYPTIAN*.

George lifts Ed Hinton off the ground in a gag photo from *The Phantom Ring*.

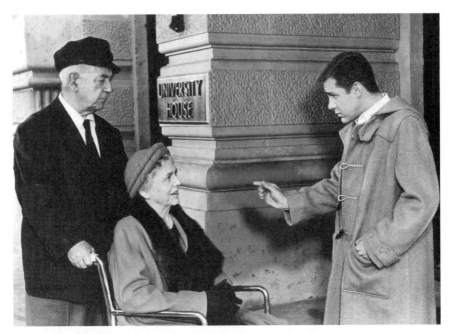

Cecil Kellaway, Ethel Barrymore, and Jack Larsen in a scene from
JOHNNY TROUBLE (1957) filmed at Warner Bros.

Stuart Whitman and
Jack Larson in a scene
from *JOHNNY TROUBLE*.

Title lobby card for
SMART POLITICS
featuring
Gene Krupa
and Noel Neill,
from Monogram's
"Teen Agers" series.

Noel (right) in a
scene from
SMART POLITICS.

Noel featured in
another film from
the "Teen Agers"
series entitled
CAMPUS SLEUTH.

June Presisser, Freddie Stewart, and Noel Neill in a publicity photo for *Campus Sleuth*.

Noel Neill and Sterling Holloway (Uncle Oscar) in a scene from the Columbia short *Man or Mouse* (1948).

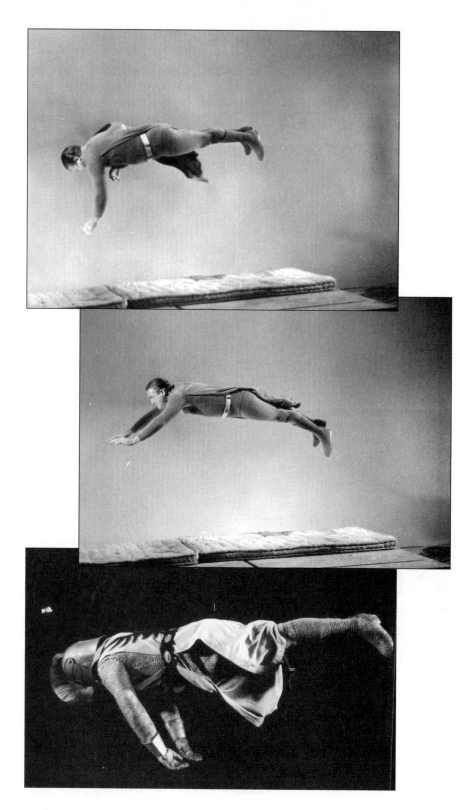

Above and on previous page: George doing his time on the flying bar.

Rare photo with Frank Scannell, George, and an unidentified person on the set of *The Man with the Lead Mask.*

George enjoys the California sun at the home of a friend in Apple Valley.
PHOTO COURTESY OF LOU KOZA

George and Jack on the set of *The Man in the Lead Mask*.

George attends to customers at Hess' Department Store in Allentown, PA.

Lita Baron seems to have grown a beard as she dances with George (with whom she appeared in *JUNGLE JIM*) at the "Hollywood Circus Ball" according to a feature article in *People Today*, May 1955.

Toni Mannix, George, and a friend enjoy the evening at the "Hollywood Circus Ball" in 1955.

A publicity photo from the color years. Wonder why George is smirking?

BIBLIOGRAPHY

SUPERMAN SERIAL TO CEREAL. Big Apple Books, 1976, Gary Grossman

SUPERMAN ON TELEVISION. Bifulco Books, 1988 and 1998 editions, Michael Bifulco

SPEEDING BULLET - THE MAN, THE MYTH, THE MYSTERY. Cult Movies #14, Jan Alan Henderson

SPEEDING BULLET - THE LIVE AND BIZARRE DEATH OF GEORGE REEVES. Michael Bifulco Books, 1999, Jan Alan Henderson

TRUTH, JUSTICE, AND THE AMERICAN WAY - THE LIFE AND TIMES OF NOEL NEILL, THE ORIGINAL LOIS LANE. Nicholas Lawrence Books, 2003, Larry Thomas Ward

SPAWN OF SKULL ISLAND. Luminary Press, 2002, George E. Turner & Orville Goldner, Expanded and Revised by Michael H. Price & Douglas Turner

FORGOTTEN HORRORS - THE DEFINITIVE EDITION. Midnight Marquee Press, 1999, by George E. Turner & Michael H. Price

FORGOTTEN HORRORS 2 - BEYOND THE HORROR BAN. Midnight Marquee Press, 2001, by Michael H. Price & George Turner

FORGOTTEN HORRORS 3 - DR. TURNER'S HOUSE OF HORRORS. Luminary Press, 2003, by Michael H. Price & John Wooley with George E. Turner

HUMAN MONSTERS - THE DEFINITIVE EDITION. Luminary Press, 2004, by Michael H. Price with George E. Turner

WHO WAS WHO ON SCREEN. R. R. Bowker Co., 1984, by Evelyn Mack Truitt

SUPERMAN IN THE FIFTIES. D.C. Comics Press, 2002

TO BE CONTINUED. Labor of Love Press, 2000, by Ken Weiss

QUINLAN'S CHARACTER STARS. Reynolds & Hearn, 2004, by David Quinlan

THE FILM ENCYCLOPEDIA. HarperPerennial, 1994, by Ephraim Katz

INDEX

The numbers in bold-italic indicate pages with a photograph.